Women in Classical Islamic Law

Women in Classical Islamic Law

A Survey of the Sources

By

Susan A. Spectorsky

BRILL

LEIDEN • BOSTON
2012

Cover illustration: from al-Harīrī's *Maqāmāt* (maqāma9): Abū Zayd & his wife standing before the *qāḍī*. Bibliothèque nationale de France, MSO Arabe 6094, f 27v.

This book is printed on acid-free paper.

This paperback was originally published in hardback under ISBN 978 90 04 17435 1 as volume 5 in the series *Themes in Islamic Studies*

Library of Congress Cataloging-in-Publication Data

Spectorsky, Susan A. (Susan Ann)
Women in classical Islamic law : a survey of the sources / by Susan A. Spectorsky.
p. cm. -- (Themes in Islamic studies ; v. 5)
Includes bibliographical references and index.
ISBN 978-90-04-17435-1 (hardback : alk. paper) 1. Women--Legal status, laws, etc. (Islamic law) 2. Women--History--Sources. I. Title. II. Series.

KBP526.3.S64 2010
297.082--dc22

2009035416

ISBN 978 90 04 21151 3 (paperback)
ISBN 978 90 04 17435 1 (hardback)

PRINTED IN THE NETHERLANDS

In Memory of
Joe

CONTENTS

Preface ix

Introduction 1

1. Women in the Qur'ān 21
2. Marriage in the Formative Period 61
3. Divorce in the Formative Period 105
4. From the Formative to the Classical Periods 143
5. Women's Lives 179

Conclusion 203

Works Cited 207

Index of Qur'ān Verses 213
Index of Names 215
Subject Index 219

PREFACE

Given the many ways the author of a book on the history of women in classical Islamic law can approach such a topic, it is important to establish at the outset what this study does and does not do. In particular, it is not a social history, a study of how real women lived in a particular time or place. Instead, I would like to emphasize the subtitle, *A survey of the sources*. In 1976, in *An Introduction to Islamic Law*, Schacht wrote, "The details of the growth of doctrine within each school, though amply documented by the existing works, still remain a subject for scholarly investigation." Since then a tremendous amount of work has been done in studies of particular scholars or particular topics. But the fact remains that libraries are filled with primary sources whose length and difficulty are daunting for the beginning student of Islamic law.

What I have tried to do in the chapters that follow is survey what some pre-modern jurists have said about women in order to provide a framework for those who wish to delve further into the legal aspects of women's lives. I have chosen a number of jurists and texts for their importance within each school and for their accessibility. Specialists will know that by limiting my survey to Sunni scholars I have left out many equally important scholars and texts. Also, they will know that by concentrating especially on marriage and divorce I have left aside a number of important aspects of women's lives. They will be correct on both counts, but the limits of an introductory survey are always to some extent arbitrary, and the topics I have chosen here reflect both the main emphases of the source texts and the kinds of questions I have been asked over the years both by students and colleagues.

Contemporary debate about the role of women in Islam—like contemporary debate about the role of women in any context—tends to take place between two extreme views. The first, the more "conservative" view, is that at some time in the past women lived in accordance with their proper roles in the social, religious and political order. The advocates of this view urge that women return to this particular ideal time. The other, the more "liberal" view, is that at a certain time—again in the past—men denied women full participation in the rights and benefits they themselves enjoyed. The advocates of this view embrace calls for change to correct perceptions of and behavior toward women. This study will not contribute directly to either the "conservative" or "liberal" side of the debate about the rôle of women in Islam, but will offer some historical information which I hope those engaged in the debate as well as those who simply want to know what it is about will find useful.

Any specific book about early Islam must mention terms, concepts, and historical data of general significance; for these I frequently refer to the *Encyclopaedia of Islam*, which is readily available. Unless otherwise noted, all references to *The Encyclopaedia of Islam* are to the second edition. In general, I have followed the system of transliteration used there except that I have used *j* for *dj* and *q* for *ḳ*. I have not changed the spelling of words common in English usage, such as Baghdad, Mecca or Sunni. Both Muslim (A.H.) and Common Era (C.E.) dates are given in parentheses after the names of prominent early jurists and *ḥadīth* transmitters.

I would like to thank two editors formerly at Brill, Olaf Köndgen who initially gave me the opportunity to work on this project and Trudy Kamperveen who was a patient and kind editor throughout my many delays. This year at Brill, Kathy van Vliet has been an extremely helpful editor. Among my colleagues, I owe special thanks to Remke Kruk and David Powers who read earlier drafts of parts of the manuscript and made encouraging and valuable suggestions. My friend Margaret Black has been a careful and precise copy editor. I could not do my work without the help and support of my husband Joel. Mistakes that remain are my responsibility.

INTRODUCTION

What should a woman do? One immediate—and virtually universal—answer is that she should marry. Therefore it is not surprising that a book about women in classical Islamic law will mainly be about women marrying. A woman may do things outside her home, but the basis of the law—the verses in the Qurʾān that set out rules and regulations for her life—indicates clearly that her wifely role is her primary one. The emphasis in the Qurʾān is reflected in legal texts, where most of the material devoted to regulating women's lives is found in the chapters on marriage and divorce. Other chapters, those on ritual purity, prayer, witnessing, or *ḥadd* punishments for example, certainly include material specifically about women, but for the most part they are devoted to Muslims in general, or to Muslim men.

A girl or a woman is given in marriage to a suitable groom for an appropriate marriage portion.[1] Her marriage contract is concluded for her by her guardian in the presence of two witnesses. If she is still a minor, she is betrothed, but lives at home until she comes of age. Once she has reached puberty, she takes up residence in her husband's house. At any time a husband is free to divorce his wife. After a divorce the woman waits an *ʿidda*, a period of time either of three months or three menstrual periods, after which she is free to remarry. Before her *ʿidda* ends, her husband can return to her, but he can do this only twice. A third divorce is final, and a couple may remarry only on the basis of a new contract. A man may also repudiate his wife by swearing an oath that separates the couple or by accusing his wife of adultery in order to deny paternity of a child she bears. In some circumstances a wife may initiate a divorce that her husband grants her in return for a monetary

[1] "Marriage portion" is the expression I will use for the Arabic words *mahr* or *ṣadāq*, which refer to a payment by the groom to the bride. There is no consistent English expression for this transaction. Dowry or dower refers to payment by a bride's father to the groom, although it is sometimes used in texts on Muslim marriages to refer to the marriage portion. Other expressions used are "bridal gift" and "bridewealth." For the "marriage portion," see *EI*, s.v. "Mahr."

compensation. These regulations have been outlined in a number of modern books that use a variety of evidence to try to reconstruct the lives of pre-modern Muslim women, but these books do not prepare a reader for the complexities of the thinking of pre-modern jurists on issues that affect women, or clarify what they agree and disagree on.[2]

What I hope to accomplish in this volume is something between an introduction and a specialized monograph on Islamic law as it relates to women. For the person who has already read a modern survey but who is not yet ready to read pre-modern *fiqh* works, I have selected a number of texts from the formative and classical periods of Islamic law to describe and discuss what they say about women. I have left out female slaves, both as wives and concubines, and also Jewish and Christian women who are discussed in legal texts as wives of Muslim men, concentrating instead on free Muslim women both because they were the major concern of classical jurists and because they are of greatest interest to modern readers.[3] I have further limited the scope of this work by concentrating on jurists of the four surviving Sunni schools of law, the Ḥanafī, Mālikī, Shāfiʿī, and Ḥanbalī, although I will mention the opinions of other jurists for comparison and contrast.

"Islamic law" is a translation for both *sharīʿa* and *fiqh*. To be more precise, *sharīʿa* "constitutes an entire way of life. It embraces right ways of worshipping God, of interacting with fellow human beings, of conducting one's personal life, even of thinking and believing."[4] *Fiqh*, on the other hand, is "the discipline concerned with the articulation of actual rules of law."[5] A specialist in *fiqh* is a *faqīh* or a jurist. *Fiqh* may further be divided into *uṣūl al-fiqh*, the "roots of law," or legal theory, which is the study of the methodology for arriving at legal rulings, and *furūʿ al-fiqh*, the "branches of law," or substantive law, which is a discussion of the rulings themselves.[6] In this work I describe what the jurists say these rulings are rather than how they can be justified, although

[2] For example, see John L. Esposito and Natana J. DeLong-Bas, *Women in Muslim Family Law*; Esposito, *Islam the Straight Path*; Frederick M. Denny, *An Introduction to Islam*.

[3] For an excellent study of interfaith marriage in early Islam, see Yohanan Friedmann, *Tolerance and Coercion in Islam*, Chapter 5. For a study of slavery in early Islam, see Jonathan E. Brockopp, *Early Mālikī Law*, Chapters 3 and 4.

[4] Weiss, *The Spirit of Islamic Law*, 17–18.

[5] Ibid., xi.

[6] See *EI*, s.v. "Sharīʿa," especially 3. "Sharīʿa in Muslim literature" and 4. "Sharīʿa and fiqh."

obviously *uṣūl* and *furūʿ* cannot be entirely separated, and this is largely a matter of emphasis. However, when I use the word "law," I mean *furūʿ*, and when I use the word "jurist," I mean a specialist in legal rulings rather than one in theory or jurisprudence.

The formative period of Islamic law is generally agreed to include the first three centuries of Islam, the 7th through 9th centuries C.E. There was development after the first three hundred years, but the major topics and problems of law had already been established.[7] The jurists of these first three centuries were engaged in the process of formulating a combination of specific rules and general principles that would be construed by subsequent generations of scholars into the substantive material of classical Islamic law as it was taught in the different schools of law (*madhhab*s). Because of the importance of the founders for defining and elaborating the basic questions of Islamic law, I will devote the most space to describing their views. However, it is important to remember that "formative" does not end abruptly at the turn of the 4th/10th century, and transition from formative to classical continued well into that subsequent century.

The classical period is harder to delimit. Although there is general agreement that classical jurists built upon the work of the founders, earlier surveys of the development of Islamic law have limited this period to the 4th through 6th centuries of Islam (10th through 12th centuries C.E.) and concluded that thereafter, in the post-classical period, Muslim jurists merely commented upon earlier creative work. According to this time frame, the periods I concentrate on are thus the formative and classical. However, recent studies have shown that Muslim jurists continued to build creatively upon the work of their predecessors, and the classical period can also be said to extend into early modern times.[8]

---

[7] For confirmation of this view, see Chafiq Chehata, *Etudes de Droit Musulman*, 17. Chehata points out that the works attributed to the founders of the Sunni law schools come at the end of a period of development rather than the beginning of one. See also Vesey-Fitzgerald in Khadduri and Liebesny, *Law in the Middle East*, v. 1, "Nature and Sources of the Sharīʿa," 92; Crone, *Roman, Provincial and Islamic Law*, Chapter 2.

[8] See Chehata, *Etudes de Droit Musulman*, 17–18; and Schacht, *Introduction to Islamic Law*, Chapter 10, for the earlier view; see, for example, Calder for the latter: "In spite of an insistence (not just Western) on the terminology of decline, the great achievements of Islamic jurisprudence are probably spread fairly evenly from the mid fourth/tenth century to the thirteenth/nineteenth centuries." Norman Calder, "Law," Chapter 57 in *A History of Islamic Philosophy*, eds. S. H. Nasr and O. Leaman (part II), 986.

Plan of the Book

Chapter 1, on the Qur'ān, provides an overview of the verses particularly relevant to the legal position of women. Then, in a chapter on the marriage contract and one on divorce, I discuss the different problems jurists debated in the formative period. In chapter 4, I select particular issues discussed in the previous two chapters to explore how several classical authors dealt with them. I base my discussion on texts from the 4th/10th–6th/12th centuries, adhering to the traditional time frame for the "classical" period, and then in Chapter 5 use texts from both the formative and classical periods to describe some aspects of women's lives that receive less attention from jurists than the marriage contract and divorce. Chapter 5 is followed by a brief concluding discussion. In the rest of this introduction, I will provide an overview of the historical development of Islamic legal interpretation and of the basic concepts necessary to understand discussions of Islamic law.

Muḥammad, His Companions, and the Successors

According to Muslim tradition, the Prophet Muḥammad began to receive the revelations of the Qur'ān in about 610 C.E. and continued to do so until his death in 632.[9] Sometimes he received revelations directly related to contemporary events and was able to guide the growing community of Muslims on the basis of them. At other times his leadership was based on his prophetic authority and his role as the first and best Muslim. He led by word and deed, and his model behavior, called *sunna*, was emulated by his family and his close associates, the Companions.[10] During his lifetime he was available to explain and interpret the Qur'ān, both as lawgiver and adjudicator. But the Qur'ān is not a code of laws, and it does not set out a theory of law as a guiding framework for further legal development. Thus after his death the Qur'ān, along with what people remembered of his *sunna*, needed to be understood in the changing context of the expanding Muslim empire.

---

[9] For the pre-Islamic calendar in Arabia, see *EI*, s.v. "Tārīkh," section iv, and for the Muslim calendar, section iii. The first Hijra year started in July of 622.

[10] For the Prophet's Companions, see *EI*, s.v. "Ṣaḥāba"; *EQ*, s.v. "Companions of the Prophet."

During the first century of Islam, as the Arab-Muslim armies conquered large portions of the Near East, many of the Prophet's Companions settled in the cities of these newly conquered areas. Not all of them, certainly, but a number of them provided legal guidance to their fellow Muslims and to the rapidly increasing number of new converts. They established, at first informally, groups of like-minded scholars who discussed how to understand the Qurʾān and the Prophet's *sunna* in order to decide on the most Muslim way to proceed in a given situation or to resolve a disputed question. Some of these Companions were governors, others were appointed as *qāḍī*s, others were distinguished only by having known the Prophet. The first four caliphs, Abū Bakr (r. 11–13/632–34), ʿUmar (r. 13–23/634–44), ʿUthmān (r. 23–35/644–56), and ʿAlī (r. 35–40/656–61) are among the Companions who often appear in legal literature. Other prominent Companions include ʿAbd Allāh b. ʿAbbās (d. 68/687–88),[11] who is known as one of the foremost Qurʾān scholars among the Companions; ʿAbd Allāh b. ʿUmar (d. 73/693),[12] a son of the Caliph ʿUmar, who was particularly famed for his knowledge of legal questions, and Anas b. Mālik (d. 91–3/709–11), the Prophet's servant, who is a source of many traditions about the practice of the Prophet's family.[13]

The scholarly activities of the Companions were carried on by their children and grandchildren, the Successors. In Mecca and Medina and in the garrison cities of the Umayyad empire, such as Kufa and Basra in Iraq and Fusṭāṭ in Egypt, Successors gathered to discuss how best to interpret and carry out the dictates of the Qurʾān. Like the Companions, but in much greater number, some were governors, others *qāḍī*s, and yet others were private scholars whose reputations for learning attracted fellow scholars and students to their study sessions, usually held in mosques, sometimes in their homes. Some of the Successors disseminated the legal opinions they had received from the Companions, both orally and in writing, to one another, to their students, and to the leadership of the larger Muslim world of the later Umayyad and the ʿAbbāsid periods.[14] These were Islam's early jurists (*fuquhāʾ*, sing., *faqīh*).[15] In addition, stories circulated about the life of the Prophet

---

[11] For his life, see *EI*, s.v. "ʿAbd Allāh b. al-ʿAbbās."
[12] See *EI*, s.v. "ʿAbd Allāh b. ʿUmar."
[13] See *EI*, s.v. "Anas b. Mālik."
[14] For the Successors, see *EI*, s.v. "Tābiʿūn."
[15] See *EI*, s.v. "Fiqh."

and the early community that showed by example what actions might be appropriate in various situations in order to live in accordance with the *sunna*. The word *sunna* during this period meant both the Prophet's model behavior and that of the early community during the period when it was led by the first four caliphs. Some Successors collected these stories, and they became Islam's early traditionists, or *ḥadīth* scholars. In the formative period these activities were not necessarily separate, and the same person often both collected traditions and gave legal opinions that were sometimes based on traditions and sometimes not.

Under the Umayyads (41–132/661–750), the caliphs continued to play an active role in legal discussions and decisions. However, opposition to the nature of their rule, both from Shīʿī partisans and from those who believed their interest in power outweighed their interest in governing in accordance with the Qurʾān and *sunna*, created tension between the caliphs and the scholars, leading many of the latter to eschew government appointments and patronage. This tension increased under Abbasid rule. Caliphs and governors always appointed *qāḍī*s, and in the classical period often supported institutions of religious learning, but the scholars evolved as a self-sustaining group, largely independent of the government.[16]

I have referred to the Companions and Successors as scholars. They constitute the early *ulamā*ʾ (singular, *ʿālim*, scholar, learned person), who saw it as their task to take the lead in understanding how the lives of all believers could be lived in accordance with the will of God.[17] To this end the jurists among them—followed by their students and their students' students—worked to develop a set of rules and regulations based on an effort to understand His will as it had been revealed to the Prophet in the Qurʾān. These rules and regulations are what we find discussed in detail in the works of the founders of the Sunni *madhhab*s, as well as in the earliest surviving collections of traditions. We also know of the existence of notebooks, compiled by Companions and Successors, but the written record of their activity is found only in later texts, the first of which date from the 2nd/8th and 3rd/9th centuries.

[16] For a description of the relations between the religious scholars and Umayyad and Abbasid rulers, see Hodgson, *The Venture of Islam*, 1:241–79 ("The Islamic Opposition, 692–750") and 315–58 ("The Sharʿī Islamic Vision, *c.* 750–945").

[17] See *EI*, s.v. "ʿUlamāʾ."

These include the earliest surviving collections of traditions and the works of the founders of the Sunni schools of law. A third category is composed of Qurʾān commentary, which I will describe in the next chapter.

The Tradition Collections

Ḥadīth is the term for the traditions of Islam that are narratives about the Prophet's life and the lives of those around him.[18] All the information we have about this period has come down to us in the form of traditions. They document the *sunna*. *Ḥadīth* is usually translated as Tradition when it refers to the whole body of material or to the process of studying it (as in *ʿilm al-ḥadīth*, the discipline of studying Traditions). An individual tradition is also a *ḥadīth*. The plural is *aḥādīth*, but it is read more easily in an English work like this one as "traditions" or *ḥadīths*. An individual *ḥadīth* consists of a text, a *matn*, containing information about something the Prophet did, said, or affirmed by his silence. Sometimes the *matn* contains information about a member of the Prophet's family or a Companion or Successor. The *matn* is preceded by an *isnād*, a chain of authoritative transmitters, beginning with the most recent, that gives credibility to the information in the *matn*. In an *isnād* the person relating the *matn* of the tradition should have heard it from a reliable transmitter who in turn heard it from another, most likely slightly older, transmitter, and so on, back to the person who is the subject of the *matn* or who first related it. An *isnād* that ends with "on the authority of the Prophet" means that the *matn* reports an action, saying, or affirmation made by the Prophet himself. One that ends on the authority of a Companion or Successor relates something the Prophet or a fellow Companion or Successor approved of, or said, or did.[19]

A *ḥadīth* collection is either a *musnad* or a *musannaf*. In a *musnad*, the traditions are arranged according to the names of the earliest transmitter in the *isnād*, usually a Companion, but sometimes a Successor. Occasionally a scholar of the next generation or two will be the first transmitter and also occasionally an Umayyad caliph. Perhaps the most famous *Musnad* was compiled by Ibn Ḥanbal (d. 241/855). In a

---

[18] See *EI*, s.v. "Ḥadīth."
[19] For *isnād* criticism, see *EI*, s.vv. "Ḥadīth"; "al-Djarḥ wa'l-Taʿdīl."

muṣannaf, traditions are arranged according to subject matter; perhaps the most famous of these is the *Ṣaḥīḥ* compiled by Bukhārī (d. 256/870). For women's issues, the Prophet's wives often figure in traditions, either as part of the *matn*, or as the earliest transmitter of an *isnād*. This is especially true of ʿĀʾisha, usually described as the Prophet's favorite wife.[20] For Sunni Muslims, six *muṣannaf*s became the standard reference works for traditions on the authority of the Prophet; they embody his *sunna* and offer guidance in all aspects of a Muslim's life. Known as the Six Books, these were compiled over the course of the 3rd/9th century.[21] They are organized in chapters, starting with those on *ʿibādāt*,[22] or matters of ritual and worship (e.g., purity, prayer, fasting, alms, pilgrimage), and followed by those on *muʿāmalāt*, or relations among human beings (e.g., buying and selling, marriage and divorce, inheritance, warfare, torts)[23] that constitute the rules for conducting life in an Islamic society. Although the contents of each collection are similar, and there is much overlap, they are not identical.

Two other collections of *muṣannaf*s, one compiled by ʿAbd al-Razzāq (d. 211/827) and one by Ibn Abī Shayba (d. 235/849), mirror discussions in *fiqh* texts of the formative period and contain many more Companion and Successor traditions than the Six Books. That is, in addition to recording information from and about the Prophet, the *matn*s also record information from and about the Companions and Successors. Modern scholars are only beginning to integrate these collections into their research.[24] I make extensive use of them in Chapters 2 and 3. Many of the traditions found in these collections are also in the Six Books, sometimes with ʿAbd al-Razzāq and Ibn Abī Shayba in the *isnād*.

[20] See *EI*, s.v. "ʿĀʾisha bt. Abī Bakr."

[21] The Six Books are by Bukhārī (d. 256/870), Muslim b. al-Ḥajjāj (d. 261/875), Ibn Māja (d. 273/887), Abū Dāwūd (d. 275/888), Tirmidhī (d. 279/892), and Nasāʾī (d. 303/915). There are articles on each of these men in *EI*. The collections by Bukhārī and Muslim are considered more authoritative than the other four. The best guide in English to the contents of these collections remains that of A. J. Wensinck, *A Handbook of Early Muhammadan Tradition*.

[22] See *EI*, s.v. "ʿIbādāt."

[23] See *EI*, s.v. "Muʿāmalāt."

[24] For these men, see *EI*, s.vv. "al-Ṣanʿānī, ʿAbd al-Razzāq b. Hammām"; "Ibn Abī Shayba." For a fuller description of ʿAbd al-Razzāq's life and work, see Motzki, *The Origins of Islamic Jurisprudence*, 54–74, and for Ibn Abī Shayba, see Lucas, "Where are the Legal *Ḥadīth*? A Study of the *Muṣannaf* of Ibn Abī Shayba."

Studying *ḥadīth*s and evaluating their transmission history is a major field of research, both in traditional Islamic scholarship and in modern Western scholarship, and therefore it is important at the outset to make clear exactly how I plan to use *ḥadīth*s in the chapters that follow. I am particularly concerned to differentiate between the *matn*, the text of a tradition, and its *isnād*, or chain of transmitters. I assume that the *matn*s found in the collections of traditions I refer to contain information that was part of the scholarly understanding of the past, regardless of whether they are preceded by a "reliable" chain of transmitters. I think these traditions are evidence from and about the first two centuries of Islam, and I am not concerned with whether, at that time, they were remembered, misremembered, or even fabricated.[25] I will use the material in the actual *matn* and not examine the isnād unless the jurist makes reference to particular authorities in the *isnād* to prove a point. However, since it is impossible to read the works of any Muslim jurist of the formative or classical period without encountering many Companions and Successors either as transmitters in *isnād*s or as subjects of *matn*s, I use many of their names in the traditions I quote, and an index of names identifies the ones most widely encountered.[26]

Founders

The founders of the Sunni schools of law are Abū Ḥanīfa (d. 150/767), Mālik b. Anas (d. 179/795), Shāfiʿī (d. 204/820), and Aḥmad b. Ḥanbal (d. 241/855). They are more properly referred to as eponymous founders, for they did not in any way claim to be establishing schools; rather, subsequent generations of students recorded their teaching and built on their works, thereby turning them retrospectively into the founders of the four Sunni *madhhab*s. The texts recording their teachings, compiled either by them or their students, are the foundational *fiqh* texts

[25] For two scholars who precede me in treating traditions this way, see Musallam, *Sex and Society in Islam*, 15, where the author says: "Arguments about the origins of *ḥadīth* have diverted attention from their true historical value: regardless of whether these traditions can be traced back to the Prophet or not, they *are* authentic documents of the first two Islamic centuries"; see also Burton, *An Introduction to the Ḥadīth*, xxiii where he points out that the attribution of a *ḥadīth*, its *isnād*, does not have a bearing on the date of the actual content of the *matn*.

[26] For discussion of biographical dictionaries of traditionists, see *EI*, s.v. "Ṭabaḳāt."

for the development of the body of literature associated with each school.[27] I will describe these briefly here and more fully in subsedquent chapters.

Abū Ḥanīfa is the earliest of the founders and the one about whom the least is known.[28] He lived in Kufa and, as a young man, studied with the Successor Ḥammād b. Abī Sulaymān (d. 120/738), who had himself studied with the slightly older Successor, Ibrāhīm al-Nakhaʿī (d. 96/715), at one time *qāḍī* of Kufa.[29] Ibrāhīm al-Nakhaʿī had transmitted traditions from the Companion Ibn Masʿūd (d. 32/652–3)[30] and from the Prophet's wife ʿĀʾisha, as well as from the Prophet's servant, Anas b. Mālik. Although Abū Ḥanīfa is the eponymous founder of the Ḥanafī school, there are no extant *fiqh* works attributed to him. We learn of his legal opinions through the works of his two main students Abū Yūsuf (d. 182/789) and especially Shaybānī (d. 189/805).[31] Abū Yūsuf lived in Kufa until appointed *qāḍī* in Baghdad by the caliph Hārūn al-Rashīd (r. 180–93/796–809). In addition to studying with Abū Ḥanīfa, Abū Yūsuf also spent some time in Medina studying with Mālik b. Anas. Shaybānī studied briefly with Abū Ḥanīfa before his death and then became a student of Abū Yūsuf's. Like Abū Yūsuf, he also studied with Mālik in Medina and, again like Abū Yūsuf, he was a *qāḍī* in Baghdad during the caliphate of Hārūn al-Rashīd.

Mālik b. Anas spent virtually his entire life in Medina and became widely known as an esteemed teacher of *fiqh* and transmitter of traditions. He studied with a number of Successors, including Nāfiʾ (d. 117/735) the *mawlā* (freedman) of ʿAbd Allāh b. ʿUmar and Ibn Shihāb al-Zuhrī (d. 124/742).[32] Mālik never became a *qāḍī*, but his standing was such that when he lent the weight of his reputation to a revolt against the caliph in 145/762, many residents of Medina were persuaded to join it. Mālik himself did not take part, but when the revolt was suppressed, the governor of Medina had him flogged. This incident did not affect his scholarly prestige. In 160/777 the caliph

[27] For a useful series of articles on *madhhab* development, see Bearman, et al., eds., *The Islamic School of Law*. For the historical development of the schools, see Melchert, *The Formation of the Sunni Schools of Law, 9th–10th Centuries C.E.* See also *EI*, s.v. "Madhhab."

[28] See *EI*, s.v. "Abū Ḥanīfa, al-Nuʿmān b. Thābit."

[29] See *EI*, s.v. "al-Nakhaʿī, Ibrāhīm."

[30] See *EI*, s.v. "Ibn Masʿūd."

[31] See *EI*, s.vv. "Abū Yūsuf Yaʿḳūb b. Ibrāhīm"; "Shaybānī, ʿAbd Allāh Muḥammad b. al-Ḥasan."

[32] See *EI*, s.vv. "Mālik b. Anas"; "Nāfiʿ"; "Zuhrī, Ibn Shihāb."

al-Mahdī (r. 159–69/775–85) consulted him about enlarging the Kaʿba, and in 179/796 (shortly before Mālik died), the caliph Harūn al-Rashīd was on a pilgrimage and visited him. Mālik's *Muwaṭṭaʾ* (*The Well-paved Path*) is a general outline of the legal doctrines of Medina. Mālik uses traditions from the Prophet, the Companions, the Successors, and other early jurists to support his doctrines, but he also merely states them without mentioning traditions; sometimes he quotes a tradition and disagrees with it. The overriding authority for Mālik is the continuous practice of Medina, the home of the Prophet, and he often says decisively, "This is our practice here."[33]

Shāfiʿī (d. 204/820) grew up in Mecca and then as a young man of about twenty years of age went to study with Mālik in Medina until the latter's death. During this period Shāfiʿī also spent some time in the Yemen, where in 174/790 he appears to have supported a Shīʿī revolt led by Yaḥyā b. ʿAbd Allāh (d. 187/803),[34] and also in Iraq, where he had some contact with Shaybānī. It is not known how much time he spent in either place. For the last six years of his life, he lived and taught in Egypt.[35] Shāfiʿī was the first jurist expressly to set out a theory for legal reasoning. At its core were his identification of the *sunna* with the contents of formal traditions on the authority of the Prophet, rather than more generally with the contents of traditions on the authority of the Companions and Successors, and his insistence that doctrines be based on the Qurʾān and the *sunna*, rather than on the reasoning (*raʾy*, see below) of individual jurists. Shāfiʿī's *Risāla* (*Epistle*) is the work in which he sets out his legal methodology.[36] Shāfiʿī records his *fiqh* in his *Kitāb al-umm* (*The Source Book*), in which he discusses all the issues found in the works of Shaybānī and Mālik, but in much greater detail and with more attention to method.

Ibn Ḥanbal (d. 241/855) lived most of his life in Baghdad, but traveled extensively in order to collect traditions.[37] He studied with Abū Yūsuf

---

[33] For a discussion of the several extant versions of the *Muwaṭṭaʾ*, see the article on Mālik in *EI* and Goldziher, *Muslim Studies*, 2:198–226.

[34] For this revolt and his role in it, see *EI*, s.v. "Yaḥyā b. ʿAbd Allāh b. al-Ḥasan."

[35] See *EI*, s.v. "Shāfiʿī, Muḥammad b. Idrīs" for a biographical sketch based on premodern sources. For a skeptical appraisal of these sources and a discussion of Shāfiʿī's life based on clues found in his works, see Schacht, "On Shāfiʿī's Life and Personality." See Lowry, *Early Islamic Legal Theory*, 6-7 for a summary biography of Shāfiʿī and reference to a number of secondary sources.

[36] For a comprehensive analysis of this work, see Lowry, *Early Islamic Legal Theory*.

[37] See *EI*, s.v. "Ibn Ḥanbal, Muḥammad b. Aḥmad."

in Kufa and also with the traditionist ʿAbd al-Razzāq in Ṣanʿāʾ. During his lifetime he was regarded mainly as a traditionist and a theologian rather than a jurist, and he became notorious for insisting, in the face of imprisonment and torture, that the Qurʾān was the uncreated word of God, in opposition to the Muʿtazilī position that God created the Qurʾān in time.[38] However, both during his lifetime and subsequently, fellow scholars and students collected and transmitted his legal opinions, which are found in the extant collections of his *masāʾil* (responses). These consist of questions about difficult points of law or cases put to Ibn Ḥanbal by colleagues and students and the answers he gave.[39]

It is noteworthy that all these men studied either with Successors (Abū Ḥanīfa, Mālik) or with each other, or both (Abū Yūsuf, Shaybānī, Shāfiʿī, Ibn Ḥanbal). It is also noteworthy that they come at the end of a period of legal development, and the positive law described in their works had already been fully formed. They are pivotal figures who end the formative period and, since their works became the foundational texts for the Sunni *madhhab*s, initiate the classical period.

The *fiqh* texts of the individual founders, like the *muṣannaf*s, start with the chapters on *ʿibādāt* (acts of worship), which are followed by those on *muʿāmalāt* (transactions). The *muʿāmalāt* are not all organized the same way, although all cover much of the same material. In addition, different authors include chapters not found in the works of others.[40] Shāfiʿī's *Kitāb al-umm*, in particular, has several methodological sections not found in other early *fiqh* works, and *Kitāb al-umm* also includes several sections on disagreement (*ikhtilāf*, see below) among jurists on particular topics.[41]

In chapters 2 and 3, where I discuss marriage and divorce in the formative period, I base my description of the rules and regulations governing women's lives on works attributed to these men. There is

[38] See *EI*, s.vv. "Miḥna" and "Muʿtazila"; and see Melchert, *Aḥmad ibn Ḥanbal*, 8–16.

[39] I have used four of the five extant collections of Ibn Ḥanbal's *Masāʾil*. The contents of these collections overlap, but each version includes material not found in the others. See the bibliography for publication details.

[40] Schacht noted that the order of the material in *fiqh* texts goes back to the 2nd/8th century (*Introduction*, 113). However, the only study of this question remains an article by W. Heffening, "Zum Aufbau der islamischen Rechtswerke."

[41] See *EI*, s.v. "Ikhtilāf."

some controversy, however, about both attribution and dating: in his *Studies in Early Muslim Jurisprudence* (published in 1993), Norman Calder suggested that the texts attributed to Mālik and Shaybānī were actually compiled a century after their deaths on the basis of earlier teaching by these men and that Shāfiʿī's *Kitāb al-umm* was reworked and added to over the 3rd/9th century. Thus Calder refers to them as works that show organic growth over time rather than as authored texts.[42] Several scholars subsequently have questioned his dismissal of the traditional dating. They note that all early texts have a redactional history, and they use a variety of arguments to affirm that despite textual difficulties and variants, the above-mentioned jurists really were the originators of these texts, if not authors in the contemporary sense.[43] Although Calder has many useful things to say about the evolution of legal thought, I subscribe here to the traditional view and assume that the founders of the Sunni schools were responsible for the texts attributed to them and that we can use these texts to describe the state of the law as it was understood at the beginning of the classical period.

Ikhtilāf

When the Companions and Successors settled in different cities of the early Muslim empire, they considered whatever existing legal institutions and practices were in place with a view to incorporating Muslim religious beliefs and practices into all aspects of public and private life. Each of these cities had local mores, and even in the same place, scholars often knew and remembered different traditions narrating the Prophet's *sunna*. Certainly they all agreed on the broad outlines of the law, but the combination of regional variation and different traditions frequently resulted in disagreement or *ikhtilāf* about the most Muslim way to proceed in a given situation. Sometimes disagreement was between cities: the scholars of Kufa, for example, would disagree with

---

[42] Calder, *Studies in Early Muslim Jurisprudence*, Chapters 2–5. Calder makes no mention of Ibn Ḥanbal or his *Masāʾil*.

[43] See for example, two reviews of Calder's book: Burton, "Rewriting the Timetable of Early Islam"; and Muranyi, "Die frühe Rechtsliteratur zwischen Quellenanalyse und Fiktion." See also Motzki, *The Origins of Islamic Jurisprudence*, xvi. For a viewpoint that is between Calder's and those who reject his ideas outright, see Melchert, "The Meaning of *Qāla ʾl-Shāfiʿī* in Ninth Century Sources." For a refutation of Calder's later dating of Mālik's *Muwaṭṭaʾ*, see Hallaq, "On Dating Mālik's *Muwaṭṭaʾ*."

those of Medina; at other times it was local, and the Kufans or the Medinese might disagree among themselves. Discussions of these early disagreements were integrated into the teachings of the founders and the doctrines of the different *madhhabs*. As part of this process, early on in the formative period, jurists developed a set of five qualifications into which all human acts can be divided. An obligatory act is a *farḍ* or a *wājib*.[44] Performing it leads to reward, omitting it to punishment. At the other end of the scale are acts that are forbidden (*ḥarām*) and lead to punishment.[45] In between are those acts that are recommended (*mandūb* or *mustaḥabb*), neutral or indifferent (*mubāḥ*), and disapproved of (*makrūh*). These middle three categories, which provide room for nuance and interpretation, are the qualifications jurists were most concerned with evaluating.[46]

Moreover, all jurists believed that human reasoning is fallible and therefore subject to error. *Ikhtilāf* among them, in fact, distinguishes between human reasoning and infallible texts because it reflects the limitations of human understanding. As Baber Johansen puts it, human reasoning is "contingent." This notion of contingency legitimates *ikhtilāf* and the continued existence of the different *madhhabs*. "It is also indispensable for the *fiqh* as a learned discipline whose inner cohesion can only be guaranteed through the acknowledgment that while all scholars and schools of *fiqh* equally derive their norms from the revelation, no scholar's and no school's normative interpretation of the revelation can claim a privileged access to truth. All scholars and schools of *fiqh* share in the same activity: probable, but fallible interpretation of infallible texts."[47]

Legal Theory (uṣūl)

Like the Companions and Successors before them, the founder jurists based their opinions on a continuous exploration of how best to live in accordance with the Qurʾān by following the model set by the Prophet, as well as by the Companions or Successors. However, new situations

---

[44] See *EI*, s.v. "Farḍ." Jurists further distinguish a *farḍ ʿayn*, an act which all Muslims must perform (e.g., prayer) from a *farḍ kifāya*, an act that only a certain number of Muslims or a certain segment of the community must perform (e.g., *jihād*).

[45] See *EI*, s.v. "Ḥadd."

[46] For an explanation of these terms, see Kemali, *Principles of Islamic Jurisprudence*, 413–31.

[47] Baber Johansen, *Contingency in a Sacred Law*, 37.

and questions required solutions for which precedents from the *sunna* of the Prophet and the early community were not readily available. To make a decision about a new problem, a jurist gave an opinion (*raʾy*).[48] In a legal context *raʾy* means a judgment call on a particular issue. *Ijtihād*, effort, or *ijtihād al-raʾy*, is the thoroughness with which a jurist seeks to reach a correct opinion.[49] In a widely cited tradition that encapsulates this process, the Prophet asks Muʿādh b. Jabal, whom he is sending to the Yemen as *qāḍī*, how he will judge if a case is brought before him. Muʿādh replies that if he finds nothing in the Qurʾān or the *sunna*, he will not flag in the process of crafting his own opinion. The Prophet expresses satisfaction at Muʿādh's answer.[50] *Raʾy* incorporated the use of analogy (*qiyās*) by drawing a parallel between one problem and another. *Raʾy* also could be based on *istiḥsān*, literally, considering something good, but in a legal context meaning departing from strict analogy by giving weight to considerations of equity or the general interest.[51] Jurists of the 2nd/8th and 3rd/9th centuries are sometimes described as fitting into two groups, the adherents of opinion (*aṣḥāb al-raʾy*) and the adherents of tradition (*aṣḥāb al-ḥadīth*).[52] "*Aṣḥāb al-raʾy*" was a pejorative term used by the *aṣḥāb al-ḥadīth* to refer to those jurists who allowed too much room for human reasoning, rather than relying entirely on the guidance provided by the *sunna* found in traditions. As Christopher Melchert has pointed out, these two groups were ideal types, and actual jurists were somewhere in the middle.[53]

Over the course of the 2nd/8th century, the number of traditions from the Prophet as well as from Companions and Successors grew enormously, either in response to different understandings of the Qurʾān and *sunna*, or to politico-religious divisions within the Muslim community, or, as we noted above, to local conditions. Thus different traditions were available to support a variety of opinions. Shāfiʿī

[48] See *EI*, s.v. "Raʾy."

[49] See *EI*, s.v. "Idjtihād."

[50] For this tradition, see Abū Dāwūd, *Sunan*, 9:368f; Ibn Ḥanbal, *Musnad*, 5:230, 236, 242. For other instances of this tradition, see Wensinck, *A Handbook of Early Muhammadan Tradition*, s.v. "Muʿādh b. Djabal."

[51] See *EI*, s.vv. "Ḳiyās" and "Istiḥsān." In the article on *istiḥsān*, a quotation from Abū Yūsuf's *Kitāb al-kharāj* illustrates this process: Abū Yūsuf says: "'According to the *ḳiyās* this and that would be prescribed but I have decided according to my opinion' (*al-ḳiyās kāna an ... illā annī istaḥsantu*)."

[52] *EI*, s.vv. "Aṣḥāb al-raʾy" and "Aṣḥāb al-ḥadīth."

[53] See Melchert, "Traditionist-Jurisprudents and the Framing of Islamic Law," 393.

responded to the vast number of traditions in circulation by insisting that the authority of the Prophet was paramount and that of Companions and Successors only subsidiary. For Shāfiʿī, *sunna* meant *sunna* of the Prophet, discovered in traditions with sound *isnād*s that went back to him in an uninterrupted chain of transmission. In his *Risāla*, Shāfiʿī excluded *raʾy* from legal reasoning and insisted that legal questions could be settled only by *qiyās*, understood as strict analogy based on the Qurʾān, the *sunna* of the Prophet found in traditions, and consensus *(ijmāʿ)*, a retrospective agreement on the undisputed practice of the Muslim community.[54] This meant that *ḥadīth* on the authority of the Prophet came to reflect divine authority, which, while not equal to the Qurʾān, was equally authoritative as a source for *qiyās*.

Gradually all jurists were influenced by Shāfiʿī and came to base their doctrines on the Qurʾān and the *sunna* of the Prophet found in traditions with sound *isnād*s. By the end of the 4th/10th century it was generally understood that there were four theoretical bases for legal reasoning (the *uṣūl al-fiqh*): the Qurʾān and the *sunna*, the two material bases of the law, which together are referred to as *naṣṣ*,[55] consensus (*ijmāʿ*), the agreement of jurists on the practice of previous generations, and analogy (*qiyās*), drawing parallels between new cases and those already decided upon, utilizing the other three sources. But this formal structure was not yet in place in the 2nd/8th century. It evolved over the 3rd/9th century, the period in which the traditionists were successful in making *ḥadīth* the primary material of Islamic law.[56]

The impact of *uṣūl* on *furūʿ* is contested.[57] I think the material I cover here shows that *uṣūl* had little effect on actual legal rules. This bears out

[54] The exact definition of *ijmāʿ* is difficult. There is, in fact, no agreement on Shāfiʿī's understanding of it. See, for example, Johansen, *Contingency*, 29–30, and the notes there. See also Lowry, *Early Islamic Legal Theory*, chapter 7. For a good summary discussion of *ijmāʿ*, see Berkey, *The Formation of Islam*, 146–48. In note 12 on 147, Berkey refers the reader to Devin Stewart's excellent, more detailed discussion of *ijmāʿ* in his *Islamic Legal Orthodoxy*, 25–59.

[55] In the context of *uṣūl al-fiqh*, *naṣṣ* means a foundational text, or an explicit textual ruling: "[i]n the technical vocabulary of *uṣūl al-fiqh*, the term refers to a text whose presence in either Ḳurʾān or Ḥadīth must be demonstrated to justify an alleged ruling." *EI*, s.v. "Naṣṣ" See also Kamali, *Principles of Islamic Jurisprudence*, index, s.v. *naṣṣ*.

[56] The traditionists were also instrumental in making *isnād* criticism the primary method of choosing among contradictory *ḥadīth*. Melchert, "Traditionist-Jurisprudents and the Framing of Islamic Law," 399–402.

[57] See Weiss, ed. *Studies in Islamic Legal Theory*, "Alta Discussion," 385–429. Crone also discusses this point in *Roman, Provincial and Islamic Law*, 26.

the observation that the founders were working with a fully developed system of law that incorporated the regional and personal variations mentioned above. In later texts of *furūʿ*, authors of the classical period continue to discuss virtually all the same questions, but they build on the works of their predecessors by adding new details and cases, either to re-examine earlier discussions or to react to social reality. Over the course of the 4th/10th century, the groups of scholars who followed the teaching of one of the founders evolved into the Sunni schools of law.[58]

Types of Fiqh *Texts*

We can divide *fiqh* texts into three categories, *furūʿ*, *uṣūl*, and *ikhtilāf* (or *khilāf*). A text that is purely *furūʿ* would be a compilation of legal rules, an *uṣūl* text would concern the theoretical underpinnings for arriving at those rules, and a work of *ikhtilāf* would record differences of opinion among scholars, either of the same *madhhab* or between and among different *madhhab*s. There is enormous variation in each category, and any one text can include more than one category. For example, Abū Yūsuf's *Āthār* is a collection of traditions drawn mainly from Abū Ḥanīfa, although occasionally from another early authority, without any comment.[59] In Shaybānī's *Āthār*, he too relates traditions from Abū Ḥanīfa (there is some overlap between these and the traditions in Abū Yūsuf's *Āthār*), and he usually adds that the tradition represents Abū Ḥanīfa's opinion, with which he himself agrees. At other times he relates a tradition and then adds a detail, a clarification, or an explanatory tradition from another authority.[60] In his *al-Jāmiʿ al-ṣaghīr* (*The Small Collection*), which is a book of *furūʿ*, Shaybānī states a particular problem and then notes whether he, Abū Ḥanīfa, and Abū Yūsuf agree or disagree on how it should be resolved. He will, for example, bring up their agreement or disagreement about the essential elements of a marriage contract, or the appropriateness of a marriage portion,

---

[58] For the development of the schools of law, see the bibliography in *EI*, s.v. "*Madhhab*." See also Wael Hallaq, *Authority, Continuity and Change*, especially Chapters 2 and 3.

[59] *Āthār* (traditions) is the term usually used to refer to traditions which are not related on the Prophet's authority. See Calder, *Studies in Early Muslim Jurisprudence*, 13 where he translates *āthār* as "authority statements."

[60] See, for example, Shaybānī, *Āthār*, 85, no. 401; 94, no. 439.

or, in the case of a divorce, whether a particular statement a husband makes to his wife results in a single or a triple divorce. He includes no traditions and no reference to any other scholars.

In the texts attributed to Mālik, Shāfiʿī, and Ibn Ḥanbal, *furūʿ* and *uṣūl* are combined; in particular, all three use traditions to support their rulings, but not in the same way. Mālik, presented with a problem on which there is *ikhtilāf* and traditions that support different points of view, chooses those that agree with Medinese practice. He also feels free to reject all the traditions he knows in favor of that practice. Shāfiʿī applies the methodology he outlines in his *Risāla* and, in the absence of traditions with sound *isnād*s, argues for his position on a particular issue by employing *qiyās*. Ibn Ḥanbal undergirds all his opinions with traditions and refuses to take a stand on an issue if he cannot base it on a tradition. Their works can be described as *fiqh-ḥadīth* works and demonstrate the increasing importance of traditions as a source for giving legal rulings.

In the classical period this importance of traditions meant that collecting traditions with sound *isnād*s became a separate discipline, and studying traditions became a vital part of the training of all jurists. In addition, the development of the schools of law led to each school having its own teaching institutions, a curriculum based on the works of its founder (or founders in the case of the Ḥanafīs), and the interpretation and enlargement of these works by the subsequent scholars identified with each school tradition.[61] The authors of later *furūʿ* works built upon the work of their predecessors, the commentaries and interpretations of their teachers, and those of their teachers' teachers.[62] One aspect of this development was the production of *mukhtaṣar*s. A *mukhtaṣar* is primarily a teaching tool, a handbook that is a distillation of the law for the purpose of training students or use as a handy reference tool for judges. And *mukhtaṣar*s in turn generated commentaries. A work that expands on a *mukhtaṣar* and explores the law in more detail is a *mabsūṭ*.[63] These terms are not necessarily reflected in

[61] See Calder, *Studies in Early Muslim Jurisprudence*, Chapter 7, "Literary Format and Social Context." For a clear summary overview of the development of legal literature, see *EI*, s.v. "Sharīʿa" (also by Calder).

[62] For the development of the teacher-student relationship in the classical period, see Makdisi, "*Ṣuḥba* et *riyāsa* dans l'enseignement médiéval"; and more generally the articles in *Law and Learning in Medieval Islam*, edited by Joseph E. Lowry et al.

[63] "The literature of *furūʿ* may be analyzed as displaying two major types: *mukhtaṣar* and *mabsūṭ*, the former term designating an epitome or digest of the law, the latter an

the titles of particular works, although they may be, and the length and complexity of both *mukhtaṣar*s and *mabsūṭ*s vary.[64] In addition to these two types of work, a number of scholars produced works of *ikhtilāf* in which they discussed disagreements among the scholars of the different schools and sometimes the varying opinions within one school.[65] Prominent scholars produced works in all categories, and a number of works combined the several categories.

expansum or broad exploration of the law's details"; Calder, "Law," 986. For a brief overview of the different kinds of legal literature, see Schacht, *Introduction*, "The Original Sources," 112–15.

[64] See *EI*, s.v. "Mukhtaṣar."

[65] See *EI*, s.v. "Ikhtilāf."

CHAPTER ONE

WOMEN IN THE QUR'ĀN

> And if you fear that you will not deal fairly by the orphans, marry of the women, who seem good to you, two or three or four; and if you fear that you cannot do justice (to so many) then one (only) or (the captives) that your right hands possess. Thus it is more likely that you will not do injustice (4:3).

> Men are in charge of women, because Allah has made the one of them to excel the other, and because they spend of their property (for the support of women). So good women are the obedient, guarding in secret that which Allah has guarded. As for those from whom you fear rebellion, admonish them and banish them to beds apart, and scourge them. Then, if they obey you, seek not a way against them. Lo! Allah is ever High, Exalted, Great (4:34).

> Women who are divorced shall wait, keeping themselves apart, three (monthly) courses. And it is not lawful for them that they should conceal that which Allah has created in their wombs if they are believers in Allah and the Last Day. And their husbands would do better to take them back in that case if they desire a reconciliation. And they (women) have rights similar to those (of men) over them in kindness, and men are a degree above them. Allah is Mighty, Wise (2:228).

These three verses—the first addressed to men planning to marry, the second a statement about relations between husband and wife, and the third about divorce and possible reconciliation—are among those most often cited as emblematic of what the Qur'ān has to say about women in Islamic society. The first is used to show that Islam permits polygamy and the second and third to show the superiority of men over women. These are oversimplifications. In this chapter I shall examine these and other verses concerned with women to provide background for the issues that came to the fore in legal discussions. One of the main difficulties with introducing material from the Qur'ān is that so much of it is open to different interpretations that it is hard to "start" anywhere: it is usually easy to see what it says (although even here there are exceptions), but frequently harder to say what it means. Qur'ān commentaries are available to interpret every word of the Qurʾān, but they too present problems of understanding.[1]

To make my start, therefore, I will discuss a number of verses about women and family life. If the verses can be understood on their own—however superficially—I will merely draw attention to them. If they cannot be understood without some explanation, I will provide a context for them drawn from the *Kitāb asbāb al-nuzūl* (*Book of occasions of revelation*) compiled by Wāḥidī (d. 468/1075).[2] Collections of occasions of revelation are based on the assumption that particular verses of the Qurʾān were revealed to the Prophet to guide him in response to a particular set of circumstances or events that were part of his life. Each "occasion" is the subject of at least one *ḥadīth* that tells a story, sometimes about the Prophet's own life, sometimes about the life of a Companion. When the occasion is about the Prophet's own life, he receives guidance from a revelation that explains to him what he must (or must not) do. When the occasion is about the life of a Companion, that person usually comes to him with a particular problem and asks how to handle it. The Prophet then answers, on the basis of a verse (or verses) of the Qurʾān revealed to guide him in the matter at hand. Sometimes several traditions tell the same story about the occasion, but with different transmitters and different details. Other times entirely different stories are told to explain the same verse.[3] Wāḥidī's work is one of the earliest collections of this kind of material.[4] One purpose for such collections is that an occasion of revelation is "part of the documentation used by legal scholars to understand how a Qurʾānic law is to be applied."[5] In the verses devoted to women, their lawful behavior

---

[1] See *EQ*, s.v. "Exegesis of the Qurʾān."

[2] For occasions of revelation (*asbāb al-nuzūl*), see *EQ*, s.v. "Occasions of revelation." For Wāḥidī, see *EI*, s.v. "Wāḥidī, Abuʾl-Ḥasan ʿAlī b. Aḥmad."

[3] See *EQ*, s.v. "Ḥadīth and the Qurʾān."

[4] Some of the translations of the Qurʾān into English include commentary that explains the occasion or purpose of various verses. Pickthall introduces each Sūra with a summary of its contents, which often includes occasions of revelation. Ahmed Ali's translation includes explanatory material in footnotes, as does the Arabic-English Qurʾān put out by the King Fahd Holy Qurʾān Printing Complex in Medina (1410/1989–90).

[5] See *EQ*, s.v. "Occasions of revelation." In this article Andrew Rippin says of the genre: "Historically, it is not certain how the compilations of the *asbāb al-nuzūl* occurred. The reports may have originated within the context of the life story of Muḥammad … they may have been found among the stock of material used by the popular preachers in early Islam … they may have been part of the documentation used by legal scholars to understand how a qurʾānic law was to be applied … or they may have been a form of exegesis in and by themselves."

is almost invariably the main concern, and the traditions Wāḥidī cites focus on changing or correcting pre-Islamic practices. Wāḥidī offers "... material relevant to eighty-five sūras of the Qurʾān."[6]

For the verses I mention that are not covered by Wāḥidī, I rely on the all-inclusive commentary on the Qurʾān by Ṭabarī (d. 310/923).[7] Ṭabarī's commentary is a vast compendium of traditions, definitions of difficult words and phrases, grammatical analysis, and often, but not always, his own opinion of the best understanding of a verse.[8] It is noteworthy that Ṭabarī's *Tafsīr* includes the traditions found in Wāḥidī's *Asbāb al-nuzūl*, along with thousands of additional ones. The sheer amount of material in Ṭabarī's commentary makes it hard to select and summarize in the kind of overview I am providing here, so for the most part Wāḥidī's choices seemed a good guide to selecting explanatory traditions. But I will also turn to Ṭabarī at the end of the chapter to illustrate the general character of pre-modern Qurʾān interpretation. I do not include modern approaches to the interpretation of the Qurʾān, for I am seeking only to provide a context for the material I cover in the subsequent chapters of this volume.

Two more points should be noted. I have organized the material in this chapter thematically and have not made an attempt at chronology. In post-Qurʾānic legal development, chronology is important only if a later verse abrogated an earlier one.[9] Where that is the case, I will mention it. Otherwise, a jurist who bases his discussion of, for example, divorce on relevant verses of the Qurʾān will have all of them in mind. And I quote a number of verses rather than simply referring to them by number. A common problem with modern discussions of the Qurʾān in English is that authors will say something regarding a verse, and readers looking the verse up in a different translation wonder whether they are looking at the same verse. This is, of course, a problem of translation, but it also reflects the difficulty of interpreting the original Arabic. I have relied on Pickthall's translation because it seems to me to remain the one that most accurately reflects the legal content of the verses considered here and

[6] Ibid.

[7] For Abū Jaʿfar Muḥammad b. Jarīr b. Yazīd al-Ṭabarī, see *EI*, s.v. "al-Ṭabarī." For his commentary (*tafsīr*), see *EQ*, s.vv. "Exegesis of the Qurʾān," especially 110–11 and "Ḥadīth and the Qurʾān," especially 388.

[8] For a description of the contents of Ṭabarī's *tafsir*, see *EI*, s.v. "*Tafsīr*."

[9] See *EQ*, s.v. "Abrogation."

because it is readily available in inexpensive paperback.[10] I have modernized some of Pickthall's vocabulary without changing its meaning, but stayed close enough to his original for a reader to follow both of us.

There is general agreement that the rules and regulations about family life found in the Qurʾān reformed many of the social practices of pre-Islamic Arabia that prevailed during the Prophet's lifetime. While there is not complete agreement on what these practices were, Avner Giladi has summed up the current state of our knowledge of this period by saying, "It has been suggested that at the time of the Prophet, the family structure within the Arabian tribal system went through a transition from matrilineal-matrilocal, which was common in central Arabia and influential to a certain degree, during the early Islamic period, to patrilineal-patriarchal-patrilocal, a form dominant in Mecca even before the time of Muḥammad."[11] Giladi's is a useful working statement because it explains the fact that the verses in the Qurʾān relevant to the position of women in society were meant to maintain a patriarchal family. At the same time they were meant to alter or eliminate those customs current that were deemed detrimental to family stability and to the well-being of women and children. Further, the statement goes some way to explaining the Qurʾānic response to the Arabian tribal system of the time. There are other aspects of the environment within which the Prophet guided his community and which we can roughly call the rest of the Near East—the cities and towns, as well as the rural areas adjacent to Arabia. Many Arabs traveled back and forth between the cities and towns of the neighboring countries, and a number of Arabs also lived in them. Thus the understanding that early Muslims had of some of the rules and regulations found in the Qurʾān may also be set against customs prevalent outside the Arabian peninsula.[12]

[10] *The Meaning of the Glorious Koran*, translated by Muhammad Marmaduke Pickthall, is available in a number of editions. For a full discussion of Pickthall's, as well as all other translations, see *EQ*, s.v. "Translations of the Qurʾān."

[11] *EQ*, s.v. "Family." See also, *EQ*, s.vv. "Community and Society"; "Marriage and Divorce"; "Patriarchy."

[12] See for example, Doumato, "Hearing Other Voices: Christian Women and the Coming of Islam," especially, pp. 190–91; Crone, *Roman, Provincial and Islamic Law*, especially Chapter 1.

Marriage

The majority of the verses in the Qur'ān about marriage address the roles men play, as guardians of women or as potential grooms and husbands. To summarize: a woman is given in marriage by her guardian (4:3) to a groom who must provide her with a marriage portion (4:4, 24; 5:5). This is not like a bride price—a payment from the groom to the bride's father—but is a gift to the bride herself.[13] It remains hers to keep unless she voluntarily remits some of it to her husband (4:4). If a couple divorce before they have had sexual intercourse, the husband owes his wife half the stipulated marriage portion (2:237). If one has not been stipulated, he owes her a divorce gift (*mut'a*, 2:236).

Whom to Marry

Those women a man is permitted to marry and how many women he may marry are described in Sūra 4 (verses 3, 4, 19, 22–24) and in Sūras 2:221 and 5:5. In 4:3 (quoted above), a man is permitted to be married to up to four women at the same time if he is able to treat them equally. If not, he is instructed to marry one woman only or perhaps female slaves.[14] The interpretation of this verse is complicated by the connection

[13] Again, I use the expression "marriage portion" because I have found in conversations with colleagues in other fields that it accurately expresses the gift in question and is more widely understood than bridal gift. Dowry (and its variant, dower) is not accurate. See *EQ*, s.v. "Bridewealth," which Motzki considers the most accurate translation of *mahr* or *ṣadāq*, terms used interchangably in legal texts. See *EI*, s.vv. "Mahr"; "Ṣadāḳ."

[14] In the Arabic phrase, *illā mā malakat aimānukum, or (the captives) that your right hands possess*, is understood to refer to female slaves, but whether these are slaves captured in battle, household slaves already in the man's possession, or another person's slaves is open to interpretation. So is the question of whether the verse says a man should marry female slaves or take them as concubines instead. Ṭabarī understands the phrase to mean that a man who cannot be just to wives and orphans should take his own slaves as concubines. The Qur'ān commentator Jaṣṣāṣ (d. 370/981), however, understands the phrase to mean that a man lacking the financial resources to marry free women should seek the slaves of others in marriage (*Aḥkām al-Qur'ān*, 2:50–52). The phrase is also used in 4:24. In his article, "Wal-muḥṣanāt mina n-nisā'i illā mā malakat aimānukum (Koran 4:24) und die koranische Sexualethik," Motzki discusses this phrase. For the second part of 4:3 (*and if you fear that you cannot do justice (to so many) then one (only) or (the captives) that your right hands possess*), he offers the following translation: "If you fear that you cannot be just to several wives, then take one [bride], or [rather than several wives] slave women [as concubines]." My translation of the German. See 210.

it makes between a man's treatment of the orphans in his care and his treatment of potential wives who may or may not be orphans (see below). A girl or a woman is referred to as an orphan if she has neither father nor husband. In that case, a responsible relative is expected to take care of her in her best interests until she has reached puberty or been given in marriage. A number of verses urge guardians to behave responsibly toward their wards and turn over their wealth to them when they reach maturity and can, therefore, be expected to handle it themselves.[15] For example, 4:6 says: *Prove orphans until they reach marriageable age; then if you find them of sound judgment, deliver them their fortune; and devour it not in haste before they grow up.* It then urges those guardians who are rich to abstain from using their wards' wealth to care for them, and those who are poor, to care for them by using it sparingly (*Whoever of the guardians is rich, let him abstain generously from taking the property of orphans; and whoever is poor let him take thereof in reason (for his guardianship)*. It ends by ordering guardians to have witnesses present when they hand over orphans' fortunes (*And when you deliver their fortune to orphans, have (the transaction witnessed in their presence)*.[16]

There are two underlying assumptions of 4:3: one, the man in charge of giving a female orphan in marriage is her guardian and she is his ward, and two, a bride receives a marriage portion.[17] If she has wealth of her own, her guardian might wish to marry her himself without giving her a marriage portion, or he might prevent her from marrying so he can keep control of her wealth, but a guardian must not do either of these things.[18] Wāḥidī reports a tradition from ʿĀʾisha that this verse was revealed regarding the guardian of a wealthy female orphan who

[15] A person is of marriageable age who has reached physical maturity. For children or minors, see *EI*, s.v. "Ṣaghīr"; for adults, *EI*, s.v. "Bāligh."

[16] See *EQ*, s.vv. "Guardianship"; "Orphans," for reference to verses, both from the Meccan and Medinan periods, that exhort believers to treat orphans ethically. See also *EI*, s.v. "Yatīm."

[17] See Chapter 2 and references there for discussion of the extent of a guardian's authority over the marriage of his ward. See also Stern, *Marriage in Early Islam*, Chapters VI and VII; and Watt, *Muḥammad at Medina*, Excursus J, "Marriage and Family in Pre-Islamic Times" for a discussion of women in the pre-Islamic period arranging their own marriages.

[18] See also 4:127, which reinforces the prohibition against withholding the marriage portions of female wards: *They consult you concerning women. Say: Allah gives you decree concerning them, and the Scripture which has been recited to you (gives decree), concerning female orphans to whom you give not that which is ordained for them though you desire to marry them …*

might not have anyone else to represent her rights or to make sure that her guardian did not marry her [solely] for her wealth and then beat her and treat her with cruelty. This verse orders guardians not to marry these orphans, but to marry instead other women who are lawful to them.[19] In a second interpretation that Wāḥidī attributes to Ibn ʿAbbās, men might shun the wealth of orphans, but allow themselves license regarding wives and marry whomever they wished. The verse means that a man's concern for his wives should parallel his concern for the orphans in his care. Therefore, he should marry only as many women as he is capable of treating justly, because wives are as vulnerable as orphans.[20] In the context of concluding a marriage contract either with a woman or on her behalf, to *do justice* means to provide her with her full marriage portion, which is hers to keep, unless she freely makes her husband a gift of part of it: *And give to the women, (whom you marry) free gift of their marriage portions; but if they of their own accord remit to you a part thereof, then you are welcome to absorb it (into your wealth)* (4:4).[21] Ṭabarī mentions three other interpretations of 4:3, which I will discuss below.

A man is permitted to marry Jewish and Christian women in 5:5: *the virtuous women of those who received the Scripture before you*. He is also permitted to marry female slaves if he cannot afford to marry free women: *And whoso is not able to afford to marry free, believing women, let them marry from the believing maids whom your right hands possess* (4:25).[22] However, even though they may not require as large a marriage portion as a free wife, slave wives are to be treated with equal consideration: *so wed them by permission of their folk and give them their marriage portions in kindness, they being honest, not debauched or of loose conduct* (4:25).

Whom Not to Marry

In 4:19, a man is forbidden to inherit the widows of deceased kinsmen along with the rest of their estates, either by claiming the right to marry

[19] Wāḥidī, 95. See also Ṭabarī's discussion at the end of this chapter. This is one of the best-known verses of the Qur'ān and remains one of the most difficult to interpret. See *EQ*, s.v. "Guardianship" and Motzki, "Wa'l muḥṣanāt mina n-nisā'i ."

[20] See Wāḥidī, 95.

[21] For fuller discussion of this verse, see *EQ*, s.v. "Guardianship."

[22] See also 24:32 and *EQ*, s.vv."Concubine"; "Slaves and Slavery."

these widows himself or by preventing them from remarrying and taking their wealth with them into new marriages: *It is not lawful for you forcibly to inherit the women (of your deceased kinsmen), nor (that) you should put constraint upon them that you may take away a part of that which you have given them.* … Wāḥidī says that a number of Qurʾān commentators report that among the Medinese, in pre-Islamic times and in the early period of Islam, when a woman's husband died, his son or another of the deceased's agnate relatives would throw a cloak over her and thereby claim a right to be her guardian. He could then marry her himself for no marriage portion, marry her off to someone else without securing a marriage portion for her, or, if she had money or property, prevent her from remarrying unless she ransomed herself from him.[23]

The further regulation of forbidden marriages deals with relationship by birth (uterine, consanguine, and germane siblings)[24] and with a category referred to as "foster" relationships. These are created by suckling: a man and a woman suckled by the same wet nurse are "milk" siblings.[25] In pre-Islamic Arabia the only female relatives a man was forbidden to marry were his mother and sister, both consanguine and foster. The Qurʾān considerably extended those forbidden in the maternal line, and it added women forbidden in the paternal line.[26] These categories include women a man's father has previously married (*and marry not those women whom your fathers married* [4:22]), and women too closely related to him by consanguinity, foster relationship, or marriage. Those related by consanguinity include a man's mother, daughters, sisters, and maternal and paternal aunts and nieces: *Forbidden to you are your mothers, and your daughters, and your sisters, and your father's sisters, and your mother's sisters, and your brother's daughters and your sisters daughters* (4:23). Those related to a man by foster

[23] Wāḥidī mentions a specific woman by name (Kabīsha bt. Maʿn al-Anṣārī) and also says that several women went to the Prophet to complain of their treatment, and this verse was revealed in response. See 97–98. Ṭabarī mentions Kabīsha bt. Maʿn al-Anṣārī in connection with this verse. See Ṭabarī, *Tafsīr*, 8:106 and the editor's note.

[24] Uterine siblings have the same mother; consanguine, the same father; germane, the same parents.

[25] See *EQ*, s.vv. "Fosterage"; "Wet-nursing"; *EI*, s.v. "Raḍāʿ."

[26] See references in previous note, as well as *EQ*, s.vv. "Lactation"; "Prohibited Degrees." See also Watt, *Muḥammad at Medina*, 280-81. See Bell, *Commentary*, 1:113 where he compares the Qurʾānic regulations to the Mosaic code. See also Lev. 18:6–18.

relationship are those related through suckling—his wet nurse and any women also nursed by her, who thereby become his foster sisters. So 4:23 continues: *and your foster-mothers, and your foster-sisters. …* Women too closely related to a man by marriage are his mothers-in-law, daughters-in-law, and stepdaughters of wives with whom he has had sexual intercourse. Again 4:23 continues: *and your mothers-in-law, and your step-daughters who are under your protection (born) of your women to whom you have gone in—but if you have not gone in to them, then it is no sin for you (to marry their daughters)—and the wives of your sons. …*[27] Finally, in 4:23, a man must no longer be married to two sisters at the same time: *And (it is forbidden to you) that you should have two sisters together, except what hath already happened (of that nature) in the past.*

In 4:24 a man is forbidden to wed married women, with the exception of slave captives (*And all married women are forbidden to you save those captives whom your right hands possess*).[28] After the Battle of Ḥunayn in 8/630, the Muslims pursued the enemy to Awṭās, where they were victorious and took a number of prisoners. Some of the Muslim fighters were worried that the female prisoners they enslaved had husbands. This verse (*save those captives whom your right hands possess*) gave the Muslims license to assume that captivity ended the women's marriages, and therefore it would be licit to consider them slave concubines.[29] Then the verse emphasizes again (as in 4:3 and 4:4) that in a lawful marriage, women are to be given their full marriage portions: *Lawful to you are all beyond those mentioned, so that you seek them with your wealth in honest wedlock, not debauchery. And those of whom you seek content (by marrying them), give to them their portions as a duty.*

---

[27] If a man concludes a marriage contract with a woman, but divorce takes place before consummation, her daughters have not become his stepdaughters, and he may lawfully marry them.

[28] The term *muḥṣanāt* is translated here as "married women." A person who possesses the quality of *iḥṣān* is *muḥṣan* (fem. *muḥṣana*) and thus is morally respectable, either because he (or she) is lawfully married or has never committed unlawful intercourse. See Schacht, *Introduction*, 125 and Burton, "The Meaning of 'Iḥṣān.'"

[29] See Wāḥidī, 98–9. See also Wensinck, *Concordance*, vol. 8, "Awṭās" for references in *ḥadīth* collections to this event. The explanation that this part of 4:24 was revealed in response to the Muslims' question about whether sexual intercourse with the pagan women taken prisoner at Awṭās was licit is always attributed to the Companion Abū Sa'īd al-Khudrī (d. 74/693). In accordance with 2:221, they were forbidden to marry them: *Wed not idolatresses til they believe. …*

Slave Concubines

In general, in addition to marrying slaves, a man is permitted to own slave concubines.[30] However, he is not allowed to force his female slaves into prostitution: *Force not your slavegirls to whoredom that you may seek enjoyment of the life of the world, if they would preserve their chastity* (24:33). Wāḥidī gives several possible occasions for the revelation of this verse. They involve one or more female slaves belonging to ʿAbd Allāh b. Ubayy, who seems for a while to have controlled a number of prostitutes.[31] Once they converted to Islam, these women refused to continue working on his behalf.[32]

Marriage Portion

In pre-Islamic Arabia the dowry (*mahr*) was a payment given to the bride's father or to her guardian.[33] The Qurʾān reformed this practice, and several verses stress that the bride receives and keeps her own marriage portion: in 4:4 (also quoted above), we find: *And give to the women (whom you marry) free gift of their marriage portions*; then in 4:24: *And those of whom you seek content (by marrying them), give to them their portions as a duty*; and in 5:5: *And so are the virtuous women of the believers and the virtuous women of those who received the Scripture before you (lawful for you) when you give them their marriage portions and live with them in honor. …*

In cases of divorce the bride retains her marriage portion: *And if you wish to exchange one wife for another and you have given to one of them a sum of money (however great) take nothing from it* (4:20). In cases of divorce before intercourse, the bride retains only half her marriage portion: *If you divorce them before you have touched them and you have appointed to them a portion, then (pay the) half of that which you*

[30] See *EQ*, s.v. "Concubines," where Jonathan Brockopp, points out that 4:3 (*those whom your right hands possess*) is understood by commentators to refer either to marriage with slaves or concubinage. Further, 23:5-6 and 70:29-30 accept the presence of concubines in a man's household, since they urge men to hide their private parts from all except their wives and "those their right hands own."

[31] ʿAbd Allāh b. Ubayy (d. 9/631) was a member of the Khazraj tribe of Medina and one of the "hypocrites" who intrigued against Muḥammad for a number of years. See *EI*, "ʿAbd Allāh b. Ubayy" and references there.

[32] Wāḥidī, 219–21.

[33] In addition, a gift, usually of less value, was sometimes given to the bride herself. This was a *ṣadāq*. See *EI*, s.v. "Mahr."

appointed, unless they (the women) agree to forgo it, or he agrees to forgo it in whose hand is the marriage tie (2:237[34]). If a fixed amount has not been decided upon, when a husband divorces a wife before intercourse, he provides her with a divorce gift (*mutʿa*), ... *the rich according to his means, and the straitened according to his means, a fair provision* (2:236).[35]

Husband and Wife

A number of verses deal particularly with relations between husband and wife. Some are of greater moral than legal interest; 30:21 for example, says: *He created for you mates from your selves that you might find rest in them, and He ordained between you love and mercy.* In 2:187 sexual intercourse is permitted in the month of Ramaḍān after the daily fast has ended: *They [your wives] are raiment for you and you are raiment for them.* Wāḥidī relates several stories of Companions who found it a hardship to refrain from having intercourse with their wives for a whole month and of others who forgot they were not supposed to and told the Prophet that they had had intercourse the previous night. This verse was revealed to clarify the regulations for fasting in Ramaḍān.[36]

In 2:223 we read: *Your women are a tilth for you (to cultivate), so go to your tilth as you will.* ... To explain this verse, Wāḥidī reports that the Companion Jābir [b. ʿAbd Allāh] said that the Jews [of Medina] and the women of the Anṣār used to say that if a man was behind a woman during sexual intercourse, the child would be born cross-eyed, and this verse was revealed to assure the Muslims that this was not the case. Wāḥidī adds that vaginal intercourse in any position is not harmful for a potential child.[37]

Two verses quoted at the beginning of this chapter (4:34 and 2:228) point to the dominance of a husband over his wife. In 4:34, we find

---

[34] The phrase, *in whose hand is the marriage tie* means either the bride's guardian or her husband. It can be understood to mean the bride's guardian because he is the one who negotiates her marriage contract. See Bell, *A Commentary on the Qur'ān*, 1:49. However, Ṭabarī says the best interpretation is that it means her husband, because once a marriage portion has been agreed upon, it belongs to the bride, not to her guardian, and therefore he is not free to dispose of it. See 5:146–58.

[35] For other meanings of the term *mutʿa*, see the entry in *EI* and also *EQ*, s.v. "Temporary Marriage."

[36] Wāhīdī, 30–32. See *EQ*, s.v. "Fasting."

[37] Wāḥidī, 48. See also *EQ*, s.v. "Sex and Sexuality."

men in charge of women and also given license to discipline their wives. To explain the first sentence of this verse (*Men are in charge of woman* ...), Wāḥidī relates a tradition in which a daughter of one of the chiefs of the Anṣār disobeyed her husband, and he slapped her. When her father came with her to the Prophet to complain, the Prophet initially said she could take revenge against her husband, but then this verse was revealed.[38] Wāḥidī does not provide material on the remainder of this verse. I will discuss Ṭabarī's understanding of it below. In 2:228, although the rights of women are affirmed, so is the dominance of the husband: *And they (women) have rights similar to those (of men) over them in kindness, and men are a degree above them*. The main subject of this verse is divorce; however, along with 4:34 it reinforces the dominance of a husband over his wife (again, I will discuss Ṭabarī's understanding of it below).

In 4:128, women who fear mistreatment by their husbands but who do not wish to be divorced are counseled to negotiate a kind of marital truce with them: *If a woman feareth ill-treatment from her husband, or desertion, it is no sin for them both if they make terms of peace between themselves. Peace is better*. Wāḥidī explains this verse with a tradition from ʿĀʾisha, who says it refers to a woman whose husband no longer desires her and wishes to divorce her to marry someone else. But the woman in question might have children in the household or have formed bonds with other members of it, so her husband would be loathe to divorce her and thereby remove her from her accustomed home. In this situation a woman can ask her husband not to divorce her, but rather to remain married to her and in addition to marry someone else. She can offer to relieve him from providing her with maintenance and offer to relinquish her right to have sexual intercourse with him.[39] Although Wāḥidī does not mention her, the Prophet's wife Sawda figures in a number of traditions that explain this verse. According to one found in Ṭabarī's commentary, she feared that

[38] Wāḥidī offers several traditions that are variants on this story. See 100–1. After each of them, the Prophet is reported to have said: "We initially commanded one thing, but God commanded another."

[39] Wāḥidī, 123. On 124, he relates a similar tradition about a specific woman, Bint Muḥammad b. Maslama, whose husband developed an antipathy toward her either because she had aged or for some other reason. She asked him not to divorce her, but to keep her and spend as much or as little time with her as he chose.

the Prophet would divorce her and asked him instead to remain married to her but not allot her any of his private time.[40] In 4:129, men are told that they can never treat all their wives equally, but that they should not ignore any one of them completely.[41]

A woman's menstrual periods figure both in marital relations and in divorce proceedings. In 2:222, husbands are instructed not to have sexual intercourse with their wives while they are menstruating: *They question you (O Muhammad) concerning menstruation. Say: It is an illness, so let women alone at such times and go not in to them till they are cleansed. And when they have purified themselves, then go in to them as Allah has enjoined upon you.*[42] Wāḥidī explains that this verse was revealed in response to queries brought to the Prophet about the way Jews treated menstruating women. In one, the Companion Anas b. Mālik says that the Jews put a woman out of her house during her menstrual period and did not eat, drink, or associate with her. The Prophet was asked about that, and 2:222 was revealed. In another explanation, Wāḥidī says that a number of Qurʾān commentators say that in the *jāhiliyya*, the Arabs did not eat or drink with a menstruating woman and would not live with her in the same house, as the Magians did.[43] The Companion Abu'l-Daḥdāḥ asked the Prophet what they should do about menstruating women and 2:222 was revealed.[44] In cases of divorce, a woman's *ʿidda* (the period of time she must wait after divorce and before remarriage) is reckoned in terms of menstrual periods.

[40] Ṭabarī, 9:277–78. In Ibn Saʿd's biographical notice on her, several traditions say that the Prophet had already divorced her, and she asked him to take her back so she could be among his wives in the Hereafter. See Ibn Saʿd, 10:155–57; Also see *EI*, s.v. "Sawdah bt. Zamʿa"; and *EQ*, s.v. "Wives of the Prophet."

[41] *You will never be able to deal equally between (your) wives, however much you wish (to do so). But turn not altogether away (from one), leaving her as in suspense. Leaving her as in suspense*, Ṭabarī says, means neither divorcing her, nor having sexual intercourse with her. See 9:284–96. He quotes a number of traditions that point to the fact that it is impossible for a man to care equally for his wives, but he is still obliged to be as fair as possible to all of them.

[42] See *EI*, s.v. "Ḥayḍ" and *EQ*, s.v. "Menstruation" where the word *adhan*, translated above as "illness," is discussed at some length in the context of ritual purity. Other possible translations are "pollution" and "harm."

[43] See *EQ*, s.v. "Magians."

[44] Wāḥidī, 46–47. For full discussions of menstruation see *EI*, s.v. "Ḥayḍ" and *EQ*, s.v. "Menstruation."

Divorce

In general, the Qur'ān allows a husband to pronounce a unilateral divorce against his wife. At the same time, the verses that regularize divorce procedures are meant to protect a woman from being abandoned, and, should she be pregnant, they establish the paternity of (and hence responsibility for) any unborn children. Protection from abandonment is accomplished first through a woman's control of her marriage portion (see again, 4:4) and second by means of her *ʿidda*. In 4:20, for example, a husband who wishes to divorce his wife is instructed to make sure that she retains her full marriage portion: *And if you wish to exchange one wife for another and you have given to them a sum of money (however great), take nothing from it.* The verse ends with a question: *Would you take it by the way of calumny and open wrong?*[45] In 2:228, a woman's *ʿidda* is fixed at three menstrual cycles: *Women who are divorced shall wait, keeping themselves apart, three (monthly) courses.* Or, if a woman does not menstruate, her *ʿidda* lasts three months: *And for such of your women as despair of menstruation, if you doubt, their period (of waiting) shall be three months, along with those who have it not* (65:4). Further in 65:4, if a woman is pregnant, her *ʿidda* ends with her delivery: *And for those with child, their period shall be till they bring forth their burden.* In 65:1, men are urged to pronounce divorce at a moment that makes it easy to reckon a woman's menstrual cycle and hence count the three menstrual periods until her *ʿidda* ends: *When you (men) put away women, put them away for their (legal) period, and keep your duty to Allah, your Lord.*[46]

During a divorcée's *ʿidda*, her husband can take her back. However, he can do so only twice: *Divorce must be pronounced twice and then (a woman) must be retained in honour or released in kindness* (2:229). After a third divorce, a couple can remarry only if the wife has first

[45] The verse 4:21 emphasizes the exhortation in 4:20 with a rhetorical question: *How can you take it (back) after one of you have gone in unto the other, and they have taken a strong pledge from you?*

[46] The occasion of revelation most often offered for this part of 65:1 is about the Companion ʿAbd Allāh b. ʿUmar (son of the Caliph, ʿUmar b. al-Khaṭṭāb) who divorced his wife while she was menstruating. In order to make it easy to reckon three menstrual cycles, the Prophet ordered him to return to her and, if he still wished to divorce her, wait a full menstrual cycle and then divorce her just after the end of her period and before having intercourse with her. See Wāḥidī, 289. In legal discussions, this timing is usually referred to as *ṭalāq al-sunna*.

been married to and divorced from another husband: *And if he has divorced her (the third time), then she is not lawful to him thereafter until she has wedded another husband* (2:230). During a woman's *ʿidda*, her husband should decide whether or not he wishes to return to her. Once he has reached a decision, two men should witness the fact that he will resume the marriage or that it has come to an end: *Then when they have reached their term, take them back in kindness or part from them in kindness, and call to witness two just men among you, and keep your testimony upright for Allah* (65:2).[47] Also, once a woman's *ʿidda* ends, she should not be prevented from remarrying: *And when you have divorced women and they reach their term, place not difficulties in the way of their marrying their husbands if it is agreed between them in kindness* (2:232).[48]

Although women should not be prevented from remarrying, men are urged to act with propriety toward those who are waiting an *ʿidda*: *There is no sin for you in that which you proclaim or hide in your minds concerning your troth with women* (2:235). Ṭabarī explains that this means that a man who wishes to marry a woman who will soon be free should not say so in so many words, but he may intimate his interest in becoming her next spouse by saying such things as, "You are beautiful," or "I wish to marry." He might also say to her guardian, "Do not place anyone ahead of me with her."[49] The second part of the verse says: *And do not consummate the marriage until (the term) prescribed is run*. Here, Ṭabarī offers several possible meanings. The one he supports is that a man who has intercourse with a woman before her *ʿidda* has ended commits adultery.[50]

---

[47] See also, 2:231: *When you have divorced women, and they have reached their term, then retain them in kindness or release them in kindness.*

[48] Either a woman's relatives might wish to stop her from returning to a husband from whom she has been revocably divorced, or her now former husband might try to stop her from marrying another man. See Watt, *Companion*, 42; Bell, *Commentary*, 1:48. For the first explanation, see Wāḥidī, 50: the Companion Maʿqil b. Yasār gave his sister in marriage to a man who subsequently divorced her, but after the end of her *ʿidda*, he wished to remarry her. Even though she was amenable, Maʿqil told the Prophet that he refused to give his sister in marriage to this man again, and then this verse was revealed.

[49] Ṭabarī, 5:95–96.

[50] The other possibilities are (2) that a man should not preclude a woman from marrying anyone else during her *ʿidda*; (3) that he should not directly tell her not to marry anyone else, (4) or that he should not marry a woman in secret during her *ʿidda*. See Ṭabarī, 5:105–13. Ahmed Ali's translation of this verse reads: *And do not resolve upon marriage till the fixed term of waiting is over*. This translation supports possibility (2) in Ṭabarī's commentary.

Since her husband may return to her at any moment, a woman who has been revocably divorced remains in her marital home during her *ʿidda*: *Expel them not from their houses nor let them go forth unless they commit open immorality* (65:1). If a divorcée is pregnant, regardless of whether her divorce is revocable or final, in accordance with 65:6 she receives both maintenance and lodging in her husband's home at his expense, until she delivers: *Lodge them where you dwell, according to your wealth, and harass them not so as to straiten life for them. And if they are with child, then spend for them till they bring forth their burden.*[51]

This description of divorce procedures is based on the assumption that a husband has made a unilateral declaration of divorce using some form of a word composed from the root letters *ṭ, l, q*, as in "*Anti ṭāliq*" (you are divorced). Several other statements that can effect a divorce are also regulated in the Qurʾān.

Ẓihār *and* Īlāʾ

A man can separate himself from his wife by taking one of two oaths, an oath of *ẓihār* or an oath of *īlāʾ*. These are both assumed to be pre-Islamic procedures, which are at the same time disapproved of and regulated in the Qurʾān. In the case of *ẓihār*, a man swears that his wife is to him "like the back of his mother."[52] By means of this statement, he forbids himself sexual relations with his wife. The Qurʾān treats his statement as an extrajudicial oath and provides a man with the means to expiate it if he wishes to return to his wife. He may either manumit a slave or feed sixty poor people. *Ẓihār* is condemned in the Qurʾān in 58:2: *Such of you as put away your wives (by saying they are as their mothers)—they are not their mothers; none are their mothers except those who gave them birth—they indeed utter an ill word and a lie.*[53] Then it is regulated in 58:3–4: 3: *Those who put away their wives (by saying they are as their mothers) and afterwards would go back on that*

---

[51] See Chapter 3 below for the question of lodging and maintenance for a woman who has been definitely divorced and is not pregnant.

[52] See *EI*, s.v. "Ṭalāq"; *EQ*, s.v. "Marriage and Divorce."

[53] It is also condemned in 33:4: … *nor hath He made your wives whom ye declare (to be your mothers) your mothers.* … For a discussion of the oath of *ẓihār*, along with that of *īlāʾ*, by means of which a man swears to abstain from having sexual relations with his wife, see Hawting, "An Ascetic Vow and an Unseemly Oath? *Īlāʾ* and *Ẓihār* in Muslim Law."

which they have said, (the penalty) in that case (is) the freeing of a slave before they touch one another. ... 4. And he who finds not (the wherewithal), let him fast for two successive months before they touch one another; and for him who is unable to do so (the penance is) the feeding of sixty needy ones. ... Wāḥidī identifies the woman whose concerns led to the revelation of these verses as the woman referred to in the title of this Sūra (*She that disputeth*). She is Khawla bt. Thaʿlaba, who complained to the Prophet that her husband had separated himself from her permanently by means of this oath. These verses provided a way for Khawla's husband to expiate his oath and return to her.[54]

A man who takes an oath of *īlāʾ* swears to abstain from sexual intercourse with his wife for four months. At the end of this period he should not leave his wife in a state of uncertainty, but either resume sexual relations with her or divorce her. *Īlāʾ* is mentioned in 2:226–27: *Those who forswear their wives must wait four months; then if they change their minds, lo! Allah is Forgiving, Merciful. And if they decide upon divorce, (let them remember that) Allah is Hearer, Knower.* Wāḥidī provides two traditions describing the pre-Islamic practice of *īlāʾ* that offer the reason for the revelation of these verses. In one, the Companion Saʿīd b. al-Musayyib relates that *īlāʾ* was a harmful pre-Islamic practice whereby a man who did not want his wife himself, but did not want another man to marry her, would swear never to approach her. Thus she would be left without sexual relations and without a husband, so God set a time limit for this oath. In the other, the Companion Ibn ʿAbbās relates that in the pre-Islamic period men would swear an oath of *īlāʾ* for one or two years, or possibly more. Then God set a time limit of four months. An oath of abstinence for less than four months does not constitute *īlāʾ*.[55]

Takhyīr

"The choice" (*takhyīr*) (see verses 33:28–29) is closely associated with ʿĀʾisha and with events in the Prophet's family life, so it will be discussed below. In such a divorce, a man gives his wife the option of initiating divorce proceedings if she wishes to do so.

---

[54] Wāḥidī, 273. There is also a reference to *ẓihār* in 33:4: ... *nor hath [H]e Allāh made those whom ye declare (to be your mothers) your mothers.* ... For Khawla bt. Thaʿalaba, see Stern, *Marriage in Early Islam*, 127–28.

[55] Wāḥidī, 49.

Liʿān

The procedure of *liʿān* is described in 24:6–9. A man who wants to divorce his wife and at the same time deny the paternity of a child with which she is pregnant can publicly accuse her of adultery. In turn, she can avert the punishment for adultery by swearing she is innocent. If she does so, the husband is punished for slander as it is assumed that he cannot provide the eyewitness proof[56] needed to prove his accusation: 24:6: *As for those who accuse their wives but have no witnesses except themselves; let the testimony of one of them be four testimonies, (swearing) by Allah that he is of those who speak the truth;* 24:7, *And yet a fifth, invoking the curse of Allah on him if he is of those who lie.* 24:8, *And it shall avert the punishment from her if she bear witness before Allah four times that what he says is indeed false,* 24:9, *And a fifth (time) that the wrath of Allah be upon her if he speaks truth.*

Wāḥidī offers two occasions of revelation for these verses. In the first, on the authority of Ibn ʿAbbās, Hilāl b. ʿUmayya complains to the Prophet that he has found his wife with another man and is distressed that 24:4 forbids him to act unless he can provide four witnesses to her behavior (*And those who accuse honourable women but bring not four witnesses, scourge them (with) eighty stripes …*). At first the Prophet rebuffs him, but then the verses delineating *liʿān* are revealed, and Hilāl, pleased, says that he had been hoping for guidance from his Lord. Here Wāḥidī says: "and he (i.e., Ibn ʿAbbās) mentioned the rest of the tradition."[57] The "rest of the tradition" can be found in many sources,[58] with varying detail. In some versions Hilāl's wife does not swear a fifth time and departs. The unspoken assumption is that she is guilty. In others, she does swear a fifth time, and then the Prophet separates the couple and at the same time suggests that if the child she bears has no physical resemblance to Hilāl, it is not in fact his.[59]

---

[56] See 24:10–20 for the necessity of providing four eyewitnesses for an accusation of adultery, and below for "the affair of the lie," which refers to an accusation of adultery made against ʿĀʾisha.

[57] Wāḥidī, 212–13. For this *ḥadīth*, see Schacht's article "Ṭalāq" in the first edition of *EI*. This article summarizes the development of the doctrine of *liʿān* and gives a description of this and other *ḥadīth*s used to explain the occasions of revelation of these verses. This portion of the article "Ṭalāq" has not been reproduced in the second edition of the *EI*.

[58] See Wensinck, *Concordance*, 8, "Hilāl b. ʿUmayya al-Wāqifī."

[59] For one example, see Bukhārī, *Ṣaḥīḥ*, 3:414–15, no. 5309.

In a second *ḥadīth*, also on the authority of Ibn ʿAbbās, an anonymous member of the *anṣār* wonders what to do if a husband finds his wife with another man, since he incurs the punishment for slander if he accuses her without four witnesses. He decides to ask the Prophet about this, and these verses are revealed.[60]

Khulʿ

Khulʿ[61] is the word used to refer to a divorce initiated by a wife rather than her husband. Although the word is not used in connection with divorce per se in the Qurʾān, two verses, 2:229 and 4:35, are understood to refer to such a divorce. As we saw above, the first part of 2:229 decrees that a man must pronounce a divorce twice and then either remain married to a woman or divorce her a third and final time, so that she is free to marry someone else. The second part of the verse refers to a woman who wishes to end her marriage. It allows her to ransom herself by offering to buy her freedom from her husband by returning her marriage portion to him. However, there is some suggestion in the Qurʾān that her husband might demand a larger sum: *And it is not lawful for you that you take from women any of that which you have given them; except (in the case) when both fear that they may not be able to keep within the limits (imposed by) Allah. And if you fear that they may not be able to keep the limits of Allah, in that case it is no sin for either of them if the woman ransom herself* (2:229). To explain this verse, Ṭabarī includes a version of the story most often told to define *khulʿ*: the wife of the Companion Thābit b. Qays came to the Prophet to say that she could not bear Thābit. The Prophet ordered her to return to Thābit the garden he had given her as a marriage portion and ordered Thābit to separate from her.[62]

In 4:35, arbitration is recommended for a couple who are not getting along. Although here too the verse does not refer to *khulʿ* directly, it is

---

[60] Wāḥidī, 212–13.

[61] This word is used once in the Qurʾān in 20:12 (in the imperative of Form I to mean "remove" or "take off") when the Lord speaks to Moses and commands: "*Take off your shoes. …*" For its use as a legal term to refer to a divorce procedure initiated by a wife, see Lane, *Arabic-English Lexicon, at kh, l,ʿ*.

[62] See Ṭabarī, 4:538–85 for this and (several) other stories about the Prophet separating incompatible couples after ordering the wife to return her marriage portion to her husband.

understood as a possible outcome in cases where the arbitrators are unable to reconcile the couple to each other: *And if you fear a breach between husband and wife, appoint an arbiter from his folk and an arbiter from her folk. If they desire amendment, Allāh will make them of one mind.* Part of Ṭabarī's explanation of the verse is that a couple might not "desire amendment" if a breach occurs between husband and wife, either when the wife is refractory, and she ceases to carry out the duties to her husband that God has prescribed for her, or when the husband is no longer retaining his wife with honor or releasing her with kindness (in accordance with the first part of 2:229). At that point, either the *qāḍī* appoints an arbitrator to represent each spouse, or each of them (or his or her agent) chooses an arbitrator. Ṭabarī goes on to report different views on what the arbitrators actually do. If the husband is the oppressor, the imam (i.e., the *qāḍī*) should remind him of his duty to his wife. If the wife is refractory and fails in her duty to her husband, God has allowed him to compensate himself through the revelation of 2:229, or he can divorce her. Ṭabarī thinks that the arbitrators can separate the couple if the husband has authorized them to do so, but they cannot take money from the wife (to ransom herself) without her consent.[63]

Children

Relations with Parents

A number of Qur'ānic statements about children speak of the affection between parents and children and of the importance for children of honoring and caring for aging parents.[64] In 31:33 we find: *O Mankind! Keep your duty to your Lord and fear a Day when the parent will not be able to avail the child in anything, nor the child to avail the parent.* And in 17:23: *Your Lord has decreed that you worship none save Him, and (that you show) kindness to parents. If one of them or both of them attain to old age with thee, say not "Fie" to them nor repulse them, but speak to them a gracious word.*[65] In return, parents are expected to value and care for their children. Thus the Qur'ān condemns the pre-Islamic

[63] See Ṭabarī, 8: 319–31.
[64] See *EI*, s.v. "*Ṣaghīr*"; *EQ*, s.v. "Children."
[65] In 4:36, kindness to parents is included with the exhortation to show kindness to others as well. See also 2:83 and 31:14.

practice of sacrificing infants to false gods. For example, in 6:137 we find: *Thus have ... (so-called) partners (of Allah) made the killing of their children to seem fair to many of the idolators. ...*[66] It also condemns infanticide in response to economic pressure: *Slay not your children fearing a fall to poverty* (17:31).[67] Finally, it condemns eliminating daughters and saving sons (who were more highly valued) in 81:8–9 where female infanticide is singled out in the midst of the description of the signs of the end of the world: *And when the girl-child that was buried alive is asked for what sin she was slain.*[68]

The main legal rulings about children are about nursing and weaning infants, and these rulings are found in verses that regulate divorce.[69] Thus 2:233, which refers to a divorcing couple who have a child, says that if mothers wish to, they should nurse their infants for two full years: *Mothers shall suckle their children for two whole years (that is) for those who wish to complete the suckling.* During this time, it is the duty of the child's father to provide support for both; 2:233 continues: *The duty of feeding and clothing nursing mothers in a seemly manner is upon the father of the child.* If a mother prefers to wean a child before the end of the two-year period, a wet nurse can be hired in her stead: *If they desire to wean the child by mutual consent (and after) consultation, it is no sin for them; and if you wish to give your child out to nurse, it is no sin for you, provided that you pay what is due from you in kindness.*[70]

Adoption

Adopting a child who thereby takes his adopted parent's name and is in every way considered a son (or daughter) is forbidden by the Qur'ān in 33:4–5. In 33:4, we find: *Allah has not assigned to any man two hearts within his body, nor has he made those whom you claim (to be your sons) your sons.* And in 33:5: *Proclaim their real parentage. That will be more*

---

[66] See also 6:140.

[67] See also 6:151.

[68] See *EQ*, s.v. "Children"; and *EI*, s.v. "Ṣaghīr." See also, 16:58–59 against killing female infants by exposing them and burying them alive.

[69] An exception is 46:15 where, in the context of a man's reverence for his parents and his God, thirty months are given as the time period within which a child is conceived, born, and nursed

[70] See *EQ*, s.v. "Wet-Nursing." See Qur'ān 31:14 for the period of nursing lasting for the first two years of life. See 65:6 for another reference to hiring a wet nurse.

equitable in the sight of Allah. And if you know not their fathers, then (they are) your brethren in the faith, and your clients.[71] Before these verses were revealed, the Prophet himself had an adopted son, Zayd b. Ḥāritha. In his youth, Zayd was captured in battle and sold to a relative of the Prophet's wife Khadīja. Zayd then came into Khadīja's possession, and at some point she gave him to Muḥammad, who subsequently manumitted and adopted him. Zayd was married to the Prophet's maternal cousin Zaynab bt. Jaḥsh. When the Prophet wished to marry her himself (this incident is discussed further below), Zayd divorced her. Since a father cannot marry his son's wife, the Prophet's marriage to Zaynab underscored the point made in 33:5 that there was thenceforth to be no adoption in Islam and those who had been adopted were to be treated as clients.[72] This prohibition is reiterated in 33:40: *Muḥammad is not the father of any man among you, but he is the messenger of Allah and the Seal of the Prophets; and Allah is Aware of all things.*

Wāḥidī explains that the first part of the sentence, quoted from 33:4 above, by saying it refers to a Fihrite who was an intelligent man and remembered everything he heard. The Quraysh used to say of him that only someone with two hearts could remember that much, and he used to say of himself that he reasoned with both hearts, and thus his reasoning was superior to that of Muḥammad's. On the day of the Battle of Badr in which he participated, he was seen wearing one shoe and carrying another. When asked about this, he said he had been unaware of the fact that he was not wearing both shoes. Then everyone knew that if he had really had two hearts, he would not have forgotten the shoe in his hand.[73] Ṭabarī also mentions this interpretation, but says that the best interpetation of the verse is that it refers to Zayd b. Ḥāritha, regarding whom God provided a parallel: just as a man cannot have two hearts, he cannot be the son of more than one father.[74] For 33:5, Wāḥidī says Ibn ʿAbbās used to say: "We used to call Zayd b. Ḥāritha, Zayd b. Muḥammad until *Proclaim their real parentage. That will be more equitable in the sight of Allah* was revealed.[75] The Prophet's

[71] For "clients" (*mawālī*), see *EI*, s.v. "Mawlā"; *EQ*, s.v. "Clients and Clientage."
[72] See *EI*, s.vv. "Zayd b. Ḥāritha"; "Zaynab bt. Jaḥsh." See also *EQ*, s.vv. "Children"; "Family of the Prophet"; "Wives of the Prophet."
[73] Wāḥidī, pp. 236–37.
[74] Ṭabarī, *Tafsīr* (Beirut, 1987), 10:75.
[75] Wāḥidī, 237.

marriage to Zaynab is connected to several other verses of the Qurʾān that are discussed below.

Despite the formal ban on adoption, a number of verses exhort believers to care for orphans.[76] Perhaps the most famous is 2:177, which says in part: *righteous is he who believes in Allah and the Last Day and the angels and the Scripture and the Prophets; and gives his wealth, for love of Him, to kinsfolk and to orphans and the needy and the wayfarer.* … Further, as we saw above, 4:3 exhorts their guardians not to exploit orphan girls, and 4:6 is about managing orphans' wealth solely for their benefit and turning it over to them once they reach maturity.

Widows and Heirs

The ʿ*idda* of a widow is longer than that of a divorcée. In 2:234 it is set at four months and ten days. After this period of time has elapsed, she is free to remarry: *Such of you as die and leave behind them wives, they (the wives) shall wait, keeping themselves apart, four months and ten days. And when they reach the term (prescribed for them) then there is no sin for you in aught that they may do with themselves in decency.*[77] As a "sharer," that is as an heir designated in 4:12, the widow inherits a portion of her late husband's estate, out of which she is expected to support herself during her ʿ*idda*.[78]

In addition to widows, mothers, grandmothers, daughters, granddaughters, and sisters all inherit from a deceased relative, either as "sharers," who are specifically mentioned in 4:11, 12 and 176, or as agnates. Once the sharers receive their fixed percentages, the remainder of the estate is divided up among the agnatic heirs in a fixed order.[79] Although as a general rule women inherit proportionally less than men do, the Qurʾān seems to have regularized and improved their status. One of the traditions Wāḥidī relates as the occasion of

[76] See *EI*, s.v. "*Yatīm*"; *EQ*, s.v. "Orphans."

[77] In 2:235, men are cautioned against proposing to a widow before her ʿ*idda* has ended, although they may intimate to her that they will wish to do so when appropriate. They are also cautioned against reaching a secret agreement with her before the allotted period of time is up. See *EQ*, s.v. "Widow."

[78] See *EQ*, s.vv. "Widow"; "Inheritance."

[79] A nearer agnate will eliminate one more distantly related. The rules of inheritance (ʿ*ilm al-farāʾid*) are complex. For a clear explanation of the Qurʾānic rules, see *EQ*, s.v. "Inheritance." For an overview of the historical development of inheritance regulations in the pre-modern period, see *EI*, s.v. "*Mīrāth*."

revelation for 4:11 is of a woman widowed by the death of her husband at the Battle of Uḥud. She came to the Prophet to say that her two daughters had been left destitute by their paternal uncle, who had seized their wealth and their inheritance as booty. Once the verse has been revealed, the Prophet summons the uncle and orders him to give to each of his nieces one-third of his late brother's wealth and to give his widow one-eighth, after which he may take the rest for himself.[80]

The Prophet's Wives

The Prophet's wives became models for all women and have a special status among the believers.[81] They are never actually mentioned by name in the Qur'ān, but their participation in the Prophet's life made them actors in the ongoing process of revelation, and they are the subject of a number of verses. When the Prophet died, he left nine widows. In addition, he married other women (in several cases these were women whose marriage contracts were not completed) and had one or possibly two concubines.[82] However not all his wives played an equal role in subsequent legal discussions. His first wife Khadīja, who died in 619, looms large in the Prophet's life in Mecca when his mission was beginning. Although she plays an important role in the popular imagination, she does not figure significantly in the rules and regulations for daily life, most of which were developed after her death, in the last ten years of Muḥammad's life.

Several verses in Sūra 33 refer to Muḥammad's wives. In v. 6, for example, they are given special status: *The Prophet is closer to the believers than themselves, and his wives are their mothers.* Other special

[80] Wāḥidī, 97.

[81] See *EQ*, s.v. "Wives of the Prophet" and references there. Also see *EI* entries for these women under each of their names. They are depicted as loving, kind, and charitable, but also as typical women who were jealous of each other and quarreled among themselves.

[82] In addition, several women who offered themselves to the Prophet never actually became his wives. In 33:50–52, the Prophet is granted special privileges regarding the women he is permitted to marry and the number of wives he is permitted to have at the same time. Further, he is relieved of the need to treat all his wives equally. These privileges are for the Prophet alone and do not extend to other believers. See *EQ*, s.v. "Wives of the Prophet" (8); Abbott, *'Ā'isha the Beloved of Mohammed*, 59–61; Watt, *Muhammad at Medina*, Excursus L, Muḥammad's Marriages; Stern, *Marriage in Early Islam*, passim.

aspects of the Prophet's wives are mentioned in vv. 30 and 31. In v. 30, their divine punishments for lewd behavior will be double that of other women: *O you wives of the Prophet! Whichever of you commits manifest lewdness, the punishment for her will be doubled. ...* In v. 31, their divine reward for virtuous behavior will be double that of any other woman: *And whichever of you is submissive to Allah and His messenger, and does right, We shall give her reward twice over, and We have prepared for her a rich provision.*

Sūra 33 also contains rules for the modest dress and seclusion of the Prophet's wives from all but close relatives. In v. 33, for example, we find an exhortation to modest dress and restrained public behavior: *And stay in your houses. Do not adorn yourselves with the adornment of the Time of Ignorance, ...*[83] Two verses order the physical seclusion of the Prophet's wives. In v. 53, they are to be secluded indoors; in v. 59, out of doors. In v. 53, they are to remain behind a curtain (*ḥijāb*) when believers visit them at home to ask favors of them: *And when you ask of them (the wives of the Prophet) anything, ask it of them from behind a curtain. That is purer for your hearts and their hearts.* In v. 59, the Prophet is ordered to instruct both his wives and all other believing women to cover themselves when they go out: *O Prophet! Tell your wives and daughters and the women of the believers to draw their cloaks close round them (when they go out). That will be better, so that they may be recognized and not annoyed.*[84] Wāḥidī reports that the believing women used to leave their houses at night because there were no indoor plumbing facilities, and the Hypocrites would interfere with them and harass them.[85] In a second report, if the undesirable elements of Medinese society who were out of doors at night saw a veiled woman, they would assume she was not a slave and leave her alone. If they saw an unveiled one, they would assume she was a slave and accost her.[86] Those from whom the Prophet's wives (and by extension other women) need not seclude themselves are close male relatives and their own male slaves.

[83] This verse initially referred to the Prophet's wives, but was then extended to all women. See *EQ*, "Wives of the Prophet (5)"; Stowasser, *Women*, 95–96.

[84] The initial reason women were to cover themselves out of doors was to be recognized. However, as the custom evolved, the reason became not to be recognized. For modern discussion of these verses, see *EI*, s.v."Ḥidjāb," *EQ*, s.v. "Veil"; Stowasser, *Women*, 127–31.

[85] For the Hypocrites, see *EI*, s.v. "Munāfiḳūn"; *EQ*, s.v. "Hypocrites and Hypocrisy."

[86] Wāḥidī, 245. See also Stowasser, *Women*, 91–92.

The two wives of the Prophet associated with particular Qur'ān verses are Zaynab bt. Jaḥsh and 'Ā'isha bt. Abī Bakr. As mentioned above, Zaynab was married to the Prophet's adopted son Zayd b. al-Ḥāritha. In 4/626, Zayd divorced her because the Prophet wished to marry her. This marriage and God's command that it take place are the subjects of 33:36 and 37. God's commands must be obeyed: v. 36 says: *And it becometh not a believing man or a believing woman, when Allah and His Messenger have decided an affair (for them) that they should (after that) claim any say in their affair* ..., and in v. 37: *And when you said ... keep your wife to yourself, and fear Allah. And you hid in your mind that which Allah was to bring to light, and you feared mankind whereas Allah had a better right that you fear Him. So when Zeyd had performed the necessary formality (of divorce) from her, We gave her to you in marriage, so that (henceforth) there may be no sin for believers in respect of wives of their adopted sons.* ...

According to Ṭabarī, the Prophet went one day to Zayd's house to find him, but Zayd was not home. Zaynab invited the Prophet to wait until Zayd's return, but the Prophet realized immediately that he himself wished to marry her and withdrew. When Zaynab told Zayd what had happened, Zayd offered to divorce her, but the Prophet told him not to. Once these verses were revealed, Zayd did divorce Zaynab, and after her *'idda* had ended, the Prophet married her. Ṭabarī explains the passage: *And you hid in your heart that which Allah was to bring to light, and you feared mankind whereas Allah had a better right that you fear Him*, by saying that the Prophet was aware of his attraction to Zaynab and knew that he was destined to marry her, but feared criticism, because hitherto adopted and consanguine sons had been considered equal. This marriage of the Prophet's has attracted a great deal of attention. Some pre-modern commentators unashamedly discuss Zaynab's beauty and the Prophet's attraction to her. Others are apologetic. Modern detractors are sarcastic about the ease with which the Prophet's personal desires were fulfilled by his revelations.[87] Of legal

[87] Ṭabarī, *Tafsīr* (Beirut, 1987), 10 (section 12), 10–11. Reasons for the Prophet's marriage to Zaynab have been much discussed in both pre-modern and modern Qur'ān commentaries, as well as in many works on the Prophet's life. Some follow Ṭabarī's description, which includes details about how Zaynab was wearing a revealing garment when the Prophet arrived unexpectedly, and he saw how beautiful she was and was immediately attracted to her. Others stress (and Ṭabarī also mentions) that Zayd and Zaynab were not compatible, and the Prophet rescued them from an unhappy

interest is the fact that from then on, as mentioned above, formal adoption was forbidden.

The "*ḥijāb* verse" (33:53), which imposed seclusion on the Prophet's wives indoors, was revealed in the context of the wedding banquet celebrating the marriage of Zaynab and the Prophet.[88] The first part of v. 53 says: *O you who believe! Enter not the dwellings of the Prophet for a meal without waiting for the proper time, unless permission be granted to you. But if you are invited, enter, and, when your meal is ended, then disperse. Linger not for conversation. Lo! That would cause annoyance to the Prophet. …* As we just saw, the verse continues: *And when you ask of them (the wives of the Prophet) anything, ask it of them from behind a curtain.* The verse ends with the injunction that believers must not annoy the Prophet and must not marry his widows, who, as we saw above, are designated as *mothers of the believers*: *And it is not for you to cause annoyance to the messenger of Allah, nor that you should ever marry his wives after him.*

Two incidents in the family life of the Prophet involve ʿĀʾisha.[89] The first is often referred to as the "affair of the lie." In 5/627, ʿĀʾisha had accompanied the Prophet on his expedition against the Banūʾl-Muṣṭaʿliq[90] and was accidentally left behind as the caravan was returning to Medina. She was found and brought home by a young Muslim (Ṣafwān b. al-Muʿaṭṭal al-Sulamī).[91] The fact that she had been alone in his company led a number of Companions to suggest that their encounter could not have been innocent and to urge the Prophet to divorce her. Although this incident is not referred to directly in the Qurʾān, Sunni Qurʾān commentators say it is the occasion for the revelation of 24:11–20, verses which they believe were revealed to clear ʿĀʾisha of any wrongdoing. Verse 11 inveighs against slander: *Lo! they who spread the slander are a gang among you.* Verse 13 demands four witnesses for an accusation of adultery: *Why did they not produce four witnesses? Since they produce not witnesses, they verily are liars in the sight of*

---

marriage by marrying Zaynab, who had always wanted to be his wife, and allowing Zayd to marry someone else. For references to these discussions, see the bibliography to the article on Zaynab in *EI*; and cf. Abbott, *ʿĀʾisha the Beloved of Muhammad*, 16–19; Sonbol, "Adoption in Islam"; Stowasser, *Women*, 87–90.

88 But see Stowasser, *Women*, 90–91, for an alternate explanations of this verse.

89 See *EQ*, s.v. "ʿĀʾisha bint Abī Bakr."

90 See *EQ*, s.v. "Expeditions and Battles."

91 For his role in this incident, see *EI*, s.v. "Ṣafwān b. al-Muʿaṭṭal."

Allah.[92] Verses 12 and 14–20 admonish those who are willing to listen to unproven allegations and act upon them.

The second incident involving ʿĀʾisha is the occasion for the revelation of 33:28–29.[93] These verses are said to have been revealed in response to domestic discord in the Prophet's household. His wives, or at least some of them, seem to have wanted more worldly goods than he was able to provide and to have badgered him to the point where he secluded himself from all of them for a month.[94] To put a stop to their demands, the Prophet was instructed to offer his wives the choice of leaving him: *O Prophet! Say to your wives: If you desire the world's life and its adornment, come! I will content you and release you with a fair release* (33:28). *But if you desire Allah and His messenger and the abode of the Hereafter, then lo! Allah has prepared for the good among you an immense reward* (33:29). Before offering ʿĀʾisha this choice, he urged her not to make a hasty decision once she had heard the verses, but to consult her parents first. However, she immediately chose to remain with the Prophet, and his other wives followed suit.[95] This option, which gives a wife the opportunity to choose divorce, is called *takyīr* (see Chapter 3).

The beginning of Sūra 66 also refers to domestic discord in the Prophet's household. Several of his wives were involved, but the narratives that explain this discord do not always refer to the same women or the same incident. In one, for example, related by Wāḥidī, the Prophet's wife Ḥafṣa found him in her dwelling with his slave concubine Māriya.[96] The Prophet swore to Ḥafṣa that if she would not share her discovery with ʿĀʾisha, he would no longer have sexual relations with Māriya. Ḥafṣa promised but subsequently told ʿĀʾisha anyway. The Prophet then refused to spend time with any of his wives and withdrew from them for one month. Then God revealed 66:1: *Oh Prophet! Why do you ban that which Allāh has made lawful for you seeking to please your wives?* In a second story related by

[92] See Wāḥidī, 214–19; and *EQ*, s.v. "ʿĀʾisha bint Abī Bakr." For a full discussion of this incident in ʿĀʾisha's life, see Abbott, *ʿĀʾisha the Beloved of Mohammed*, 29–38.

[93] But see below for the connection of these verses with 66:1–5.

[94] This is one possible explanation. Several others are also possible; see Stowasser, *Women*, 96; and *EQ*, s.v. "Wives of the Prophet."

[95] For more details of the situation in the Prophet's household surrounding the revelation of these verses, see Abbott, *ʿĀʾisha the Beloved of Muhammad*, 51–56.

[96] See *EI*, s.vv. "Māriya"; "Ḥafṣa."

Wāḥidī, the Prophet was particularly fond of honey, and to eat more of it, he spent more time than usual with whichever wife had some. Several other wives, angry at such favoritism, agreed secretly among themselves to complain that he exuded an unpleasant smell when he came to them. After hearing repeated complaints and finally being told by one of his wives what the secret was, he withdrew from all of them until 66:1 was revealed. In the context of the first story, 66:2 enables the Prophet to expiate his oath not to have sexual relations with Māriya (*Allah has made lawful for you absolution from your oaths* ...); and Wāḥidī relates that 66:3: *When the Prophet confided a fact to one of his wives and when she afterward divulged it and Allah apprised him thereof,* ... lets him know what has been going on behind his back. Then, again according to Wāḥidī, 66:4 was revealed: *If you two turn to Allah repentant, you have cause to do so for your hearts desired (the ban): and if you aid one another against him (Muhammad), then lo! Allāh, even He is his protecting friend.* ...[97] In 66:5, the Prophet's wives are threatened with divorce: *It may happen that his Lord, if he divorce you, will give him in your stead wives better than you.* ...[98]

Other Issues

Veiling

The verse that enjoins women to cover themselves is 24:31:

> Tell the believing women to lower their gaze, guard their private parts, and to display of their adornment only that which is apparent, and to draw their veils over their bosoms, and not to reveal their adornment save to their own husbands or fathers or husbands' fathers, or their sons or their husbands' sons, or their brothers or their brothers' sons or sisters' sons, or their women or their slaves, or male attendants who do not have any need of women, or children who know nothing of women's nakedness. And let them not stamp their feet so as to reveal what they hide of their adornment. ...

[97] Wāḥidī, 291–293.

[98] See *EQ*, s.v. "Wives of the Prophet" where Barbara Stowasser discusses both 33:28–29 and 66:1–5. In her discussion of 66:1–5, Stowasser points out that "[t]here is a great deal of overlap in the details of the quoted *asbāb al-nuzūl* (occasions of revelation) materials, and some sources even collapse the occasions of revelation of *Q* 33:28–29 and *Q* 66:1–5."

Just before this verse and usually understood to go with it, 24:30 says: *Tell the believing men to lower their gaze and guard their private parts.* Together these verses exhort Muslims to behave and dress with decorum. What that means for women has been subject to many interpretations. As the religious scholars of the community worked on gathering material with which to emulate the life of the Prophet, 24:31 was linked with 33:59 (*Tell your wives and daughters and the women of the believers to draw their cloaks close around them*), and the two together were taken as the basis for "*ḥijāb*" for women in general, not just the Prophet's wives. Initially, *ḥijāb* referred to the curtain that concealed the Prophet's wives from inappropriate male visitors in their homes (33:53), but it rapidly took on the connotation of concealment outside as well and became the word for the concealing garment worn by women outside the house and for the physical barrier they place between themselves and outsiders.[99] Subsequent discussion focused on what parts of a woman needed to be covered rather than what she needed to wear to cover them. The word Pickthall translates as "*nakedness*" is *ʿawrāt*, literally *pudendum* or genitals, but figuratively those parts of the body that must be covered in public as well as those parts that must not be uncovered during prayer.[100] Ṭabarī says the best understanding of *[t]hat which is apparent* of their adornment, is that the phrase means their faces, their hands, and the part of their arms up to the middle of their forearms, the part of their arms the Prophet had permitted them to show. The reason, he continues, why this is the best understanding of the phrase is because of the general consensus that every person must cover his *ʿawra* during prayer, and a woman must uncover her face and her palms during prayer and otherwise have the rest of her body covered.[101] As for *what they hide of their adornment*, that, Ṭabarī says, refers to ankle bells, which could be heard if they stamped their feet.

No early Islamic texts are extant that enjoin veiling for all women, but there is evidence that in some cities in Arabia, as well as in the

[99] See *EQ*, s.v. "Veil"; and *EI*, s.v. "Ḥidjāb."

[100] See *EQ*, s.v. "Modesty."

[101] See Ṭabarī, *Tafsīr* (Beirut, 1986–87), 18:94. Ṭabarī's interpretation of the meaning of verse is not as strict as those of later commentators, who recommended that women cover more and more of themselves when not in the privacy of their home, except in certain special circumstances, such as when they were witnesses in court or required medical treatment. For some examples of later commentaries, see Stowasser, "The Status of Women in Early Islam," 11–43.

cities of the rest of the Middle East conquered by the Arab Muslim armies, upper-class women veiled themselves in public. How soon or how completely urban Muslim women started to veil themselves in public is open to question.[102]

Witnessing

In 2:282, if a written record is to be drawn up of a debt, the record should be witnessed by two men or by one man and two women: *And call to witness from among your men, two witnesses. And if two men be not (at hand) then a man and two women, of such as you approve as witnesses, so that if one errs (through forgetfulness) the other will remember.* Ṭabarī says very little about the fact that two women replace one man. He says that *such as you approve as witnesses* means they must be moral and upright.[103] Otherwise, he does not discuss any intrinsic female weakness, but rather the grammar and syntax of this sentence, and then states that if one of the women forgets, the other will remind her.[104] This equivalence of one man and two women is not mentioned elsewhere in the Qur'ān, but later discussions apply it to other contexts (see below, Chapter 5).

Ḥadd *Punishments*

Ḥadd punishments are prescribed for five acts forbidden in the Qur'ān:[105] unlawful intercourse,[106] false accusation of unlawful intercourse (*qadhf*),[107] drinking wine, theft, and highway robbery. Although in theory both women and men may perpetrate any of these forbidden acts, the two for which women are specifically mentioned along with men are theft and unlawful sexual intercourse.[108] In 5:38, male and female thieves receive equal punishment (*As for the thief, both male and female, cut off their hands.*). In 17:32, there is a general statement condemning adultery: *And come not near to adultery. Lo! It is an*

[102] See Doumato, "Hearing Other Voices," especially 183–85 where she shows that veiling and seclusion among Christian women of the upper classes was common in 6th-century Najran.
[103] They must possess the quality of *ʿadl*, trustworthiness. See *EI*, s.v. "ʿAdl."
[104] Ṭabarī, 4:61–69.
[105] See *EI*, s.v. "Ḥadd."
[106] See *EI*, s.v. "Zinā."
[107] See *EI*, s.v. "Ḳadhf."
[108] See *EQ*, s.vv. "Adultery and Fornication"; "Flogging."

abomination and an evil way.[109] In 4:15, if four witnesses testify to a woman's sexual misconduct, she is to be confined to her house until death or *until Allah appoints for them* [i.e., women guilty of sexual misconduct] *a way*. This verse is understood to have been abrogated by 24:2, which stipulates one hundred lashes as punishment for both men and women who commit adultery: *The adulterer and the adulteress, scourge each one of them (with) a hundred stripes.*[110] False accusation of adultery (*qadhf*) is punished with eighty lashes, and the accuser is thereafter not considered a reliable witness: *And those who accuse honourable women but bring not four witnesses, scourge them (with eighty stripes and never (afterward) accept their testimony* ... (24:4). As we saw above, the occasion of revelation for this verse was the accusation against ʿĀʾisha.[111] The penalty of stoning is popularly assumed to be the Qurʾānic punishment for adultery. It is not found in the Qurʾān; it is found in a number of traditions about the practice of the Prophet and the early caliphs.[112]

Discussion

Most of the verses we have just gone over address men and their treatment of women.[113] A girl or a woman is given in marriage by one or another male guardian, and 4:3 is directed to these guardians. Similarly, 4:19 assumes that if a woman is widowed, a relative of her late husband becomes her guardian. With the exception of *takhyīr* and *khulʿ* divorces, men initiate divorce and women accept it. As far as relations between the spouses are described: *Men are in charge of women* (4:34), and *men are a degree above them* (2:228).

However, these verses are not just a list of rules and commands without a moral dimension. Kevin Reinhart says of Qurʾānic discourse

[109] See also 25:68. In 17:32, *zinā* is usually translated as adultery, but can also mean fornication.

[110] See *EQ*, s.v. "Adultery and Fornication." Abrogation of one Qurʾān verse by another is mentioned in 2:106: *Such of Our revelations as We abrogate or cause to be forgotten, we bring (in place) one better or the like thereof.* See *EQ*, s.v. "Abrogation"; *EI*, "Naskh."

[111] The punishment for female slaves is half that for free women: *And if when they (female slaves) are honourably married, they commit lewdness they shall incur the half of the punishment (prescribed) for free women (in that case)* (4:25).

[112] For an examination of what early texts say about stoning, see Burton, "Law and Exegesis: The Penalty for Adultery in Islam."

[113] In 33:30–33, the Prophet's wives are addressed directly.

that the Qur'ān assumes that "humans know the good and nonetheless often fail to follow it," and that "the good has the utility of guaranteeing success and reward." Further, there are three reasons to behave ethically: "keeping a promise made primordially [with the Creator], paying back what is owed by acting well, and fear of punishment—all motivate the Qur'ān's audience to act ethically."[114] In 4:3 and 4:19, guardians are urged to behave honorably in dealing with their wards. Verse 4:3 ends: *Thus it is more likely that you will not do injustice.* And 4:19 ends: *But consort with them in kindness, for if you hate them, it may happen that you hate a thing wherein Allah has placed much good.* Although 4:34 is devoted to establishing the authority of a husband over his wife, it ends with an exhortation: *Then if they obey you, seek not a way against them. Lo! Allah is ever High, Exalted, Great.* In 2:228, the rights of women are mentioned (*And they (women have rights similar to those (of men) ...*), as well as the degree that men are above them (*and men are a degree above them*) and the final sentence is a reminder to the believers: *Allah is Mighty, Wise.*

These exhortations, which come at the end of each verse, are often overlooked by modern scholars, or considered irrelevant to the question of the (unequal) status of women. However, they were not considered irrelevant by earlier scholars, and leaving them out ignores an entire dimension of the Qur'ān and the concerns of what Reinhart refers to as its "audience." I will illustrate this by summarizing what Ṭabarī says about each of the three verses at the head of this chapter. His commentary, and the traditions he uses to make his points, reinforce the ethical exhortations expressed at the end of each verse.

Ṭabarī reports five interpretations of 4:3. All of them construe the verse as a corrective to pre-Islamic practice that is in the interests of women's well-being. In the first of the five, Ṭabarī reports that one group of Qur'ān commentators says that the verse means that if you (i.e., guardians who are kinsfolk of the orphans in your care) fear you will not be just to these orphans by seeing to it that they receive their fair marriage portions in full, do not marry them, but instead marry other women (e.g., not relatives) whom God has made lawful and pleasing to you, between one and four. If you fear you cannot be fair to more than one woman, marry only one, *or (the captives) that your right hands possess.* The Arabic phrase *illā mā malakat aimānukum*, "or

[114] *EQ*, s.v. "Ethics and the Qur'ān."

those whom your right hands possess," is understood to mean "slaves," but whether slaves captured in battle, household slaves already in a man's possession, or another person's slaves is one of the problems with the verse.[115]

A number of traditions, on the authority of ʿĀʾisha, support this explanation, with slightly different emphases. In one, for example, she says that "orphans" refers to those orphans in a guardian's care. He might desire their wealth and beauty, but wish to marry them for less than their fair marriage portions. Thus he is forbidden to marry them unless he can act justly toward them by giving them their full marriage portions, and he is ordered (instead) to marry other women. In another tradition, ʿĀʾisha explains that a female orphan in the care of her male guardian participates with him in his wealth, and he might wish to marry her both for her beauty and for her money, but give her a smaller marriage portion than she would receive from another suitor. If he cannot manage to give her what she deserves, he should marry other women who are not in his care. In a third tradition, ʿĀʾisha explains that a guardian might marry an orphan in his care whom he does not like merely for her money and mistreat her, so he (i.e., the guardian) was admonished in this regard.[116]

According to the second interpretation, 4:3 prevents a man from marrying more than four wives in order to protect the wealth of any orphans in his care. Some Qurayshites used to marry ten women—sometimes more or fewer; then when they found themselves impoverished, they would turn to the wealth of the orphans in their care and either spend it, use it to sustain their current wives, or use it to marry other women. These Qurayshites were told that if they needed their orphans' money, they should marry no more than four wives, and if they still needed their orphans' money, they should marry only one

---

[115] Ṭabarī, 7:540–41. Ṭabarī interprets *(the captives) that your right hands possess* to mean that a man should take as concubines his own slaves rather than seek to marry slaves belonging to others. It is most likely, Ṭabarī continues, that a man will not oppress his own slaves, since such women constitute part of his own wealth and property and need not be granted the same rights as free women. Jaṣṣāṣ has a different interpretation of the phrase, *aw mā malakat aymānukum*: that a man should seek to marry slaves if he cannot bear the financial burden of free wives. In this case, Jaṣṣāṣ refers to the slaves of others, since one spouse can never own the other. See Jaṣṣāṣ, Aḥkām, 2:55–61.

[116] Ṭabarī, 7:532–33, no. 8457 and no. 8461. This interpretation is like the tradition from ʿĀʾisha that Wāḥidī uses to underline the Qurʾān's insistence that a woman receive a fair marriage portion (see Wāḥidī, 95).

woman, or *those captives that your right hands possess.* Several traditions illustrate this view; two are on the authority of Ibn ʿAbbās. In one, he said that a man is restricted to four wives so that he will not spend the wealth of orphans. In the second, Ibn ʿAbbās reports that for as long as God intended, men made use of the wealth of orphans to marry (presumably before the revelation of the verse), and then He forbade that.[117]

A third interpretation is that people used to avoid wrongdoing with regard to the wealth of orphans in order not to act unjustly, but they would not avoid wrongdoing with regard to wives. Therefore, 4:3 tells them that in the same way they feared being unjust to orphans, they should fear being unjust to wives. Therefore they should marry between one and four, not more, or *(the captives) that your right hands possess.* One of the traditions cited by Ṭabarī to support this position is attributed to the Successor Qatāda, who said the verse means that if you fear oppressing orphans and that weighs upon you, you should be equally fearful of an accumulation of wives. In the *Jāhiliyya*, men married ten, or more wives, so God restricted the number to two, three, or four, or one only, if men could not be just to more, or *(the captives) that your right hands possess.*[118]

For the fourth interpretation, Ṭabarī provides one tradition on the authority of the Successor Mujāhid, who said that if a man avoids wrongdoing in exercising control over the orphans in his care and in preserving their wealth, and avoids it faithfully and in a trustworthy manner, he should also avoid unlawful intercourse and marry other woman lawfully, two, three or four; or, if he cannot be just, one only, or *(the captives) that your right hands possess.*[119]

Finally, for a fifth interpretation of this verse, Ṭabarī explains that if men fear that they will not be just toward [certain] orphans who are in their care, they should not marry them, but marry instead the orphans of others who are [also] lawful for them. Ṭabarī supports this interpretation with two traditions of slightly different import. In one, ʿĀʾisha says that a man might marry an orphan in his care who has no other guardian and no rival for her hand who would marry her for herself and not only for her money. In consequence, her guardian might beat

117 Ṭabarī, 7:535, nos. 8464, 8465.
118 Ṭabarī, 7:536–37, no. 8468. See also Wāḥidī, 95.
119 Ṭabarī, 7:539, no. 8575.

her and treat her badly. In the second, the Successor Ḥasan al-Baṣrī says the verse means that a guardian should marry those orphans from among his relatives who are lawful for him, two, three, or four, and if he fears that he cannot be just, only one, or *(the captives) that your right hands possess.*[120]

These five interpretations emphasize ethical treatment of wives or orphans or both. Ṭabarī chooses and restates the third position, which emphasizes both and is in keeping with the concerns of the "Qurʾān's audience." Thus, Ṭabarī says, if a man fears he cannot be just to orphans, he should fear the same thing with regard to his wives and marry only as many as he can treat fairly, between one and four. If a man cannot treat one wife justly, then he should not marry at all, but instead take slave concubines. He connects appropriate treatment of orphans in 4:3 with that laid out in 4:2.[121] The reason why this is the best interpretation, Ṭabarī says, is because in the previous verse God forbade consuming the wealth of orphans and mixing it in with other monies. Those who fear God will, therefore, be equally fearful of transgression in matters related to both wives and orphans.

Despite Ṭabarī's extensive survey, this remains a difficult verse. It is noteworthy that Ṭabarī's discussion has not been a source for the views put forward in modern secondary literature either about marriage in pre-Islamic Arabia or about the rationale for the revelation of the verse. Stern, for example, concludes that in pre-Islamic Medina, "it was not customary for a man to marry more than one woman at a time, but that divorce and remarriage was a very common experience."[122] Further, she says that polygamy was not the rule in pre-Islamic Mecca, where, "[t]he outstanding feature appears to be the looseness of marriage ties in general and the lack of any legal system for regulating procedure."[123] Watt, who agrees with her, says that it is reasonable to assume that there are "good grounds for holding that in pre-Islamic Arabia and especially in Medina, it was unusual for a man to have more than one wife living with him in his house."[124] Both add that the

[120] Ibid., no. 8477.

[121] *Give unto orphans their wealth. Exchange not the good for the bad (in your management thereof), nor absorb their wealth into your own wealth. Lo! that would be a great sin.*

[122] Stern, *Marriage in Early Islam*, 62.

[123] Ibid., 70.

[124] Watt, *Muhammad at Medina*, 276.

absence of any real evidence of polygamous households in pre-Islamic Arabia supports the "traditional account" of the revelation of 4:3, according to which the verse was revealed after a number of Muslim men were killed in the battle of Uḥud, leaving many widows and girls of marriageable age without male guardians. Polygamy would have been a way of providing them with husbands. If so, Ṭabarī does not mention it.[125]

On 4:34, Ṭabarī begins his discussion with an interpretation of the first sentence. It means, he says, that men are responsible for disciplining their wives and for guiding them with regard to their duty to God and to their husbands. God has set husbands over wives because husbands provide wives with a marriage portion and expend their wealth on them and satisfy their need for provisions. Ṭabari supports his interpretation with a number of traditions, including the one related by Wāḥidī as the occasion for the revelation of this statement. For the second sentence, Ṭabarī says that *good women* means women who are upright in their religion and do good [rather than evil]. He continues, the word *obedient* means obedient to God and to their husbands. [G]*uarding in secret*, according to Ṭabarī's interpretation, means "guarding in [the] absence] of their husbands." That is to say, when their husbands are away, they guard their own private parts and their husbands' wealth. [T]*hat which Allah has guarded* means that Allah guards the women in leading them toward this behavior. In the next sentence, Ṭabarī glosses the word *rebellion* as "refractoriness." [A]*dmonish them* means admonish them with words, by reminding them of the Qur'ān and of their duty to their husbands. [B]*anish them to beds apart* means refrain from sexual intercourse with them.[126] [S]*courge them* means beat them, but in a way that is not agonizing. Ṭabarī provides a tradition on the authority of Ibn ʿAbbās, who said that "in a way that is not agonizing" means hitting them with a toothpick or something similar.

[125] Neither does Jaṣṣāṣ, who is particularly concerned with the legal import of the Qur'ān. Also, see above, note 14 for Motzki's translation of this verse, which he bases on comparing it to other places in the Qur'ān where wives and concubines are mentioned together. He points, for example, to 4:25, where a man who cannot afford to marry free women is urged to marry slaves instead. He also points out that linking the verse to Uḥud suggests that many unmarried men took orphans under their protection, which cannot be assumed, and that certainly marrying a slave instead of an orphan would not affect orphans one way or another.

[126] For the phrase, *banish them to beds apart*, see Lane, *Arabic-English Lexicon*, at *ḥ, j, r*.

The phrase, *[T]hen, if they obey you, seek not a way against them*, Ṭabarī says, means that once his wife has ceased to be refractory, her husband should take no further action against her. He cites a poignant tradition on the authority of the Successor Sufyān b. ʿUyayna that supports this interpretation: Sufyān b. ʿUyayna said that if a wife is amenable to sexual intercourse with her husband, he cannot demand that she love him, because her heart is not in her hands.[127] Certainly this verse provides a husband with disciplinary options, but at the same time Ṭabarī points to a wife's "obedience" meaning first obedience to God and second, to her husband. The verse ends with a statement of God's majesty.

On 2:228, we saw above that the first sentence regulates a divorcée's *ʿidda* (*Women who are divorced shall wait, keeping themselves apart three [monthly] courses*). For the first part of the second sentence (*And it is not lawful for them that they should conceal that which Allah has created in their wombs if they are believers in Allah and the Last Day*), Ṭabarī presents three interpretations. In one, a divorcée should not hide the truth about her menstrual periods; in another, she should not hide a pregnancy; and in a third, she should not hide either. The motive suggested for a divorcée's secrecy is her wish to be rid of her husband. Therefore she would announce that she had menstruated three times before she really had to end her *ʿidda* quickly and give her husband less time to return to her. If she were pregnant, she might, following a practice of women in the *Jāhiliyya*, wish to attribute the child to a subsequent husband and hence try not to give the husband on whose behalf she was observing the *ʿidda* any motive (such as caring for her and her child) for returning to her. As for the second part of the sentence (*if they are believers in Allah and the Last Day*), Ṭabarī says it means that it is immoral for believing women to hide what is in their wombs because that harms their husbands.[128] The sentence *And their husbands would do better to take them back in that case if they desire a reconciliation*[129] means, he says, that husbands should return to their wives during their *ʿidda*s.

For *And they (women) have rights similar to those (of men) in kindness,* Ṭabarī explains that women owe their husbands obedience, and

[127] Ibn ʿUyayna seems to mean that although a woman might be able to control her behavior, she cannot force herself to love someone. Ṭabarī, 8:290–318.

[128] See Ṭabarī, 4:527.

[129] *[I]n that case* suggests that the divorcée might be pregnant. The Arabic says only *in that* (*fī dhālika*).

in turn they themselves are owed connubial companionship and kind treatment. In general, the best meaning of the verse is that men should return to their wives only if they really want to, not in order to harm them. On the rest of the sentence (*and men are a degree above them*), Ṭabarī reports disagreement. Some say that this phrase means that men are a degree above women because of the superiority God granted them in matters such as inheritance and undertaking *jihād*. Others say it refers to men's superiority because women obey men and not vice versa; others, that a wife is punished if she slanders her husband, but that if her husband slanders her, he can go a step further and institute the procedure of *liʿān*. Still others say that it means a husband forgives his wife some of her duties to him and is lenient toward her, while at the same time he fulfills his obligations toward her.[130] Like 4:34, this verse ends with a statement reminding believers of God's majesty.

This brief outline of the majority of verses in the Qur'ān about women's lives depicts a woman who is a member of a patriarchal household. She is at all times under the care and control of a male guardian. When she is a minor, he manages any assets she has. If she is fortunate, he manages her assets responsibly, and he turns them over to her once she has reached physical and mental maturity.[131] Whether she is a minor or an adult, he is in charge of concluding a marriage contract on her behalf. When she passes into the care of her husband, she owes her husband absolute obedience. However, women have rights as well as men, and men are urged to treat the women in their care well. It is here that the three legal qualifications of recommended, neutral, and disapproved of come into the legal material that I describe in subsequent chapters.

[130] Ṭabarī, 4:499–538.

[131] See *EI*, s.v. "Ṣaghīr" for minors and s.v. "Bāligh" for adults. A boy is assumed to be an adult when he reaches puberty, usually at fifteen years of age; a girl is an adult when she begins to menstruate.

CHAPTER TWO

MARRIAGE IN THE FORMATIVE PERIOD

Introduction and Sources

It is hard to say when and to what extent the picture the Qur'ān paints of women's lives became a reality. The information we have about the early Islamic community is found in traditions collected after the Prophet's death. We have just seen the way some of them were used to explain the verses covered in the previous chapter. The jurists described here and in the next chapters used these explanations along with other traditions in their discussions of how to incorporate Qur'ānic norms into Muslim lives.

In this chapter I describe what the early Ḥanafīs, Mālik, Shāfi'ī, and Ibn Ḥanbal said about various aspects of a valid marriage. I have selected what I think are the most important issues that are touched on by at least one of the Ḥanafīs and by each of the other three jurists, which makes it possible to compare and contrast their views. It should be noted though that in one sense this gives a false picture, because even though they all cover the same broad topics, they do not always take up exactly the same points; some details found in one text are not in others.

For Ḥanafī *fiqh* I have used the following works. Abū Yūsuf's *Āthār*, which is a collection of Kufan traditions, mainly on the authority of Abū Ḥanīfa, but other authorities are also quoted. Of the works attributed to Shaybānī, I have used four: his *Āthār*, his *al-Jāmiʿ al-ṣaghīr* (The small collection), his version of Mālik's *Muwaṭṭa'*, and, to a lesser extent, his *Kitāb al-ḥujja 'alā ahl al-Madina* (The book of disputation with the Medinese). Shaybānī's *Āthār*, as we noted in the introduction, is similar to Abū Yūsuf's, and they often quote the same tradition to explain a particular point. But Shaybānī also relates opinions of Abū Ḥanīfa's based on other early authorities, and again as we noted, he sometimes adds his own agreement (or disagreement). His *al-Jāmiʿ al-ṣaghīr* is a different kind of text. It is an eliptic discussion of particular points of law followed by a statement of whether he, Abū Ḥanīfa, and Abū Yūsuf agree or disagree on how a particular problem should be handled.

Kitāb al-ḥujja is a polemical work in which Shaybānī discusses points of disagreement between Medinese and Kufan scholars.[1] He begins by stating Abū Ḥanīfa's opinion of a particular problem. Then he gives Mālik's, which usually disagrees with Abū Ḥanīfa's (if not entirely, then on a particular aspect of a given problem). Finally, he discusses both opinions and quotes a number of traditions to back up Abū Ḥanīfa's. Shaybānī's version of Mālik's *Muwaṭṭa'* is one of two full-length versions of this work. It too is polemical: Shaybānī states Mālik's position on an issue and then says whether he and other Ḥanafī scholars do or do not agree with it. He often uses traditions to support his own or Abū Ḥanīfa's opinion.

For Mālikī *fiqh*, I have used the version of Mālik's *Muwaṭṭa'* compiled by the Cordovan jurist Yaḥyā b. Yaḥyā (d. 234/848).[2] It is longer than Shaybānī's *Muwaṭṭa'* and covers many more questions. Each question is introduced either by a tradition related on Mālik's authority or by a statement of what Mālik said, sometimes followed by one or more traditions, sometimes not.[3] The *Mudawwana*, which I have also used here to establish Mālik's doctrine, is by the North African Mālikī scholar Saḥnūn b. Sa'īd al-Tānūkhī (d. 240/854) and contains replies to questions he asked an Egyptian student of Mālik's, Ibn al-Qāsim al-'Utaqī (d. 191/806). Saḥnūn also includes traditions and opinions from the Egyptian Mālikī scholar Ibn Wahb (d. 197/812). Saḥnūn's purpose in compiling the *Mudawwana* was to establish Mālik's position on points of law about which he himself was uncertain and to check his own knowledge of Mālik's doctrine with a scholar (Ibn al-Qāsim) who had studied with Mālik himself.[4]

In his *Kitāb al-umm*, Shāfi'ī discusses all the topics mentioned in the previous works, usually at much greater length and in much greater complexity. The presentation of doctrines in *Kitāb al-umm* is more

---

[1] For a description and discussion of this work, see Calder, *Studies in Early Muslim Jurisprudence*, Chapter 5, "Early Ḥanafī Texts."

[2] For other versions of the *Muwaṭṭa'* (most of which are no longer extant or available only in manuscript fragments), see *EI*, s.v. "Mālik b. Anas"; and *GAS*, 1:458–64. See *EI*, s.v. "Yaḥyā b. Yaḥyā," for this scholar's influence in bringing Mālikī doctrines to al-Andalus. Yaḥyā b. Yaḥyā did not hear the *Muwaṭṭa'* directly from Mālik, but from students of Mālik.

[3] Goldziher's description and comparison of Shaybānī's and Yaḥyā b. Yaḥyā's versions of the *Muwaṭṭa'* is still useful. See *Muslim Studies*, 2:198–209.

[4] For the *Mudawwana*, see *GAS*, 1:465–66. For Saḥnūn, *GAS*, 1:468–71; and *EI*, s.v. "Saḥnūn"; for Ibn Wahb, *GAS*, 1:466.

orderly than that found in the texts of the Ḥanafīs and Mālik. Shāfiʿī often introduces a topic by quoting relevant Qurʾān verses and traditions from the Prophet to support his positions on particular issues. However, he does not do this consistently.

For Ibn Ḥanbal's doctrines, I have used four versions of his *Masāʾil*.[5] Unlike the *Muwaṭṭaʾ* or *Kitāb al-umm* and more like Shaybānī's *al-Jāmiʿ al-ṣaghīr*, Ibn Ḥanbal's *Masāʾil* are not meant to lay out the basics of law in any area. Each compiler asks Ibn Ḥanbal a question on which he knows there is *ikhtilāf* (disagreement) to learn what Ibn Ḥanbal thinks about a particular issue, or which of several traditions he supports.

I introduce each topic with several traditions found in the *Muṣannaf*s of ʿAbd al-Razzāq and Ibn Abī Shayba that highlight the particular problems associated with each topic. ʿAbd al-Razzāq was a leading traditionist in the Yemen. He studied with Mālik in Medina, and Ibn Ḥanbal traveled to Ṣanʿāʾ to study traditions with him. Ibn Abī Shayba was a traditionist who lived and studied both in Baghdad and Kufa and was a teacher of Bukhārī, Muslim, Abū Dāwūd, and Ibn Māja. In addition to being a useful way to highlight early and ongoing *ikhtilāf* among jurists, a comparison of these two tradition collections with the *fiqh* texts of the formative period brings home the fact that both groups of scholars were working with the same material, the record of the *sunna* of the Prophet and the way the Companions and Successors understood it.

Marriage

Ideally, a girl or a woman is given in marriage by her guardian, her *walī*; she is betrothed to a groom who is not too closely related to her and is her equal in status, in the presence of witnesses, and she receives a marriage portion. Each of these conditions is a topic of discussion in legal literature. If a girl or a woman has never been married, she is referred to as a virgin, a *bikr*. One who has been married is referred to as an *ayyim* or a *thayyib* (the terms are used interchangeably). The distinction depends on the marriage contract itself, since *ayyim* or *thayyib*

[5] There are six extant collections of Ibn Ḥanbal's *Masāʾil*, one by each of his sons, one by a colleague, and three by students. The contents overlap, but each version includes material not found in the others. See *GAS*, 1:507–08.

can also be used of a woman for whom a previous marriage contract has been concluded, but who has never lived with a husband, or who has lived with him but not had sexual intercourse. The former would be the case if a girl or a woman has been given in marriage to a man who dies before the couple have had sexual relations, or if either spouse is a child and too young for sexual intercourse, the latter, if he or she had a disability that prevented it.[6]

A marriage contract can be concluded for a girl at any age, so a considerable amount of time may elapse between the contract and the moment when a wife actually takes up residence with her husband. If, for example, a girl's father arranges a marriage for his daughter when she is an infant, she will not live with her husband until she has reached puberty. The earliest age at which she might be expected to reach puberty is nine. In a famous tradition on the authority of ʿĀʾisha, she says: "The Prophet married me when I was a girl of six or seven years of age, and he had intercourse with me when I was nine years of age."[7]

A Woman's Guardian

1. ʿĀʾisha said: "The Prophet said: 'There can be no marriage without a *walī*, and the *sulṭān* is the *walī* of the one who has no other.'"[8]
2. ʿĀʾisha said: "The Prophet said: 'Women should be consulted about their private parts.' She said: "I said: 'O Messenger of Allah, they are shy.' He said: 'The *ayyim* has the right to [speak up for] herself, whereas the *bikr* is shy, and her silence is tantamount to her consent.'"[9]

---

[6] The disabilities most often cited are leprosy for both men and women, sexual malfunction for men, and any physical condition that makes vaginal intercourse impossible for women. For a full discussion of these and other disabilities, see Rispler-Chaim, *Disability in Islamic Law*, Chapter 3, "People with disabilities and marriage."

[7] Nine years of age is considered the youngest age at which a girl may begin to menstruate. See again *EI*, s.v. "Ḥayḍ"; *EQ*, s.v. "Menstruation."

[8] Ibn Abī Shayba, *Muṣannaf*, 3:272, no. 15. For this use of "*sulṭān*," see EI, s.v. "Sulṭān." In legal texts from the formative period, this word is used in an abstract sense to mean "political authority." In the context of this tradition and in reference to problems of marriage and divorce in general, it means the *qāḍī*. See, for example, Ibn Ḥanbal, *Musnad*, 6:47, where a version of this same tradition is found. ʿAbd Allāh b. Aḥmad b. Ḥanbal, who compiled his father's *Musnad*, adds a note that Ibn Ḥanbal said that the word meant "*qāḍī*" because the *qāḍī* is the one in charge of women's private parts and legal judgments (*aḥkām*, "the application of legal rules to concrete cases." *EI*, s.v.).

[9] Ibn Abī Shayba, *Muṣannaf*, 3:277, *bāb* 7, no. 1.

3. ʿĀʾisha said: "The Prophet said: 'If a woman has not been given in marriage by one of her *walīs*, her marriage is void.' The Prophet repeated [the word] 'void' three times. [He continued:] 'If the couple have had intercourse, she receives a marriage portion in accordance with what her husband regarded as lawfully his. If they cannot agree (i.e., a woman with her *walīs*, or the *walīs* among themselves), the *sulṭān* is the *walī* of the one who has no other.' "[10]

These three traditions refer to the necessity of a male guardian to conclude a marriage contract on behalf of a bride. Unless otherwise stated, it is taken for granted that a woman's *walī* is related to her. The first tradition points to the fact that if she is without male relatives, the *sulṭān* (meaning the *qāḍī*) is in charge of giving her in marriage. The second tradition states that although a bride needs her *walī*'s permission to marry, he should consult her before concluding a marriage contract for her. It also makes a distinction between a *bikr* and a *thayyib*. A *bikr* is presumed to be shy about potential sexual relations; a divorcée or a widow is expected to speak up for herself on the basis of her experience. The third tradition deals with a marriage contract that is not valid. It cannot, in accordance with this tradition, be allowed to stand. If the husband (mistakenly) regarded his marital right to intercourse with the bride as lawful, she must receive a marriage portion. Although it is not stated as a general principle, all legal texts assume that every act of intercourse with a free woman requires either a marriage portion or a *ḥadd* punishment for adultery or fornication. The last sentence of this tradition suggests that if the marriage is invalid as the result of a quarrel between a woman's *walīs*, it should be referred to the *qāḍī*.[11] If a marriage is not valid, there are two possibilities: it can be validated retroactively, or the couple must be separated.

Fiqh texts take up each of these issues, often in conjunction with additional ones. Considerable attention, for example, is devoted to a woman's guardian. If he is a relative (rather than the *qāḍī*), which one? And, a related question, what is the extent of his authority? In an ideal situation, a woman's guardian is her father. If he cannot act because he

[10] Ibid., 3:272, no. 1.

[11] The problem referred to here is that of two or more of a woman's *walīs* giving her in marriage without it being clear which one was first. If they cannot figure it out among themselves, the *qāḍī* should sort it out for them. This particular problem would come up only if a potential bride has no father or grandfather, and several male relatives were equally qualified to be her *walī*.

is on a long journey or is deceased, another of her agnate relatives acts in his stead. The extent of a guardian's authority over a woman's marriage depends on her age and status and on his relationship to her. As noted above, she can be given in marriage when she is a minor. But she can also be given in marriage when she has reached puberty and is still a *bikr*, or when she has reached puberty and is a divorcée or a widow. Most jurists say that if a woman is a minor, the only guardian who can give her in marriage is her father, or, in his stead, her paternal grandfather. Once she has reached puberty, other guardians can also do so.

The nature of a woman's consent also receives attention. If she is a *bikr*, as we just saw, she is presumed to be too shy to articulate her interest in a marriage; instead, she may show it by her silence (as suggested in the second tradition above), or by laughing or weeping if either of these is known to be her way of acquiescing. In a tradition from the Companion ʿAṭāʾ, he reports that whenever anyone sought the hand of one of the Prophet's daughters, he would seat himself next to her curtain and then say: "A particular man (i.e., he would name the man) wishes to become engaged to you. If she was silent, he would go ahead with the marriage. But if she made a motion with her hand, that is, if she struck the curtain, he would not."[12]

If, on the other hand, a woman is a *thayyib*, she must give verbal consent to any impending marriage contract before it is concluded for her. A widely cited example of the Prophet's insistence that a *thayyib* be consulted before she is given in marriage is the story of the widow Khansāʾ bt. Khudhām, whose husband was killed at the Battle of Uḥud. Her father then gave her in marriage against her will. When she complained to the Prophet, he revoked the marriage and told her to marry instead whomever she wished.[13]

---

[12] Ibn Abī Shayba, *Muṣannaf*, 3:277–78, no. 3 See also Lane, *t*, ʿ, *n*, where he explains and translates the phrase used here, *ṭaʿanat fī'l-khidr*, "said, in a trad., of any one of the Prophet's daughters, when demanded in marriage, as denoting her disapproval, means '*She entered within the khidr* [or curtain]: or, as some say, *she struck the khidr with her hand*. See *EQ*, s.v. "Veil" for a discussion of 33:53 and seclusion of the Prophet's wives and daughters.

[13] See Ibn Saʿd, *Kitāb al-ṭabaqāt al-kabīr*, 8:333–34; Mālik, *Muwaṭṭaʾ*, 3:143–44; Shāfiʿī, *Kitāb al-umm*, 5:17; Stern, *Marriage in Early Islam*, 34–35; Wensinck, *Concordance*, 8, s.v. "Khansāʾ bt. Khudhām." For other versions of the story of Khansāʾ bt. Khudhām and other *thayyib*s who appealed to the Prophet after being given in marriage against their will, see ʿAbd al-Razzāq, *Muṣannaf*, 6:146–47, nos. 10303–07.

A Woman's Father as Guardian

A father's authority is based on the underlying assumption that he has his daughter's best interests at heart and knows better than anyone else how to secure them. He can give her in marriage without consulting her; he can retain part of her marriage portion for himself; and, if divorce occurs before the marriage is consummated, he can exempt the groom from a *mutʿa* (divorce gift) payment.[14]

Despite the Prophet's declaration in the third tradition above and the story of his behavior regarding the marriages of his own daughters, there were lengthy discussions among Sunni jurists about whether a father *must* consult his *bikr* daughter before giving her in marriage, whether he *should* do so even if he does not have to, or whether he should do so once she has reached puberty. Mālik and the Mālikīs give fathers virtually unlimited authority over their daughters' marriages. In the *Muwaṭṭaʾ*, Mālik refers to the practice of the Successors al-Qāsim b. Muḥammad and Sālim b. ʿAbd Allāh, who, he says, used to give their virgin daughters in marriage without asking their permission, and he adds, "That is our practice regarding the marriage of virgins."[15]

Shaybānī prefers to limit a father's authority. For example, in his version of the *Muwaṭṭaʾ*, he cites a variant of the second tradition (above) in which the Prophet says: "The *ayyim* has more right to herself than her *walī*, and the *bikr* is consulted about herself. In the case of the *bikr*, her silence is tantamount to her consent."[16] In other words, she *should* be consulted. Shaybānī says he supports this tradition and that it is Abū Ḥanīfa's doctrine as well, both for women whose *walī*s are their fathers and women whose *walī*s are other men.

In his discussion of a father's authority in *Kitāb al-umm*, Shāfiʿī does not disagree with Mālik, but at the same time he agrees with Shaybānī. He says that regardless of the fact that a father *can* give his

---

[14] See Qurʾān 2:236; and explanation in Chapter 1. See ʿAbd al-Razzāq, *Muṣannaf*, 6: 221; and Ibn Abī Shayba, *Muṣannaf*, 3:327–28 for traditions that allow a bride's father to reserve something of the marriage portion for himself. See also, Saḥnūn, *Mudawwana*, 2:159–61 for discussion of circumstances in which Mālik thought it was permissible for a woman's guardian to retain some of her marriage portion for himself.

[15] Mālik, *Muwaṭṭaʾ*, 3:126–27.

[16] Shaybānī, *Muwaṭṭaʾ*, 220. Mālik quotes this same tradition in Yaḥyā b. Yaḥyā's version of the *Muwaṭṭaʾ* (3:126), but he ignores it.

bikr daughter in marriage without consulting her, the Prophet's *sunna* recommends that he do so.[17] If a father consults his daughter about a marriage, for example, he can find out whether she is content with it, or has a disease that only she knows about, or whether she dislikes the groom. Shāfiʾī also brings in another possibility: he urges a father to have his *bikr* daughter's nearest female relative—her mother, or another woman to whom she might reveal her innermost thoughts—ask her about the marriage.[18] A father, Shāfiʾī says, should be in no hurry to give a daughter in marriage without informing her to whom exactly she is to be married. Indeed, it is reprehensible for him to give her in marriage to a man he knows is displeasing to her. However, if he does so anyway, the marriage is valid. Further, Shāfiʾī points out, if a marriage is valid when a father gives his daughter in marriage to someone she dislikes, it is certainly valid if he gives her in marriage without consulting her. A father has this unlimited authority over the marriages of his *bikr* daughters, both those who are minors and those who are adults. If he did not have this authority over their marriages at all ages, Shāfiʾī continues, a father's authority would be no greater than that of any other *walī*.[19] Ibn Ḥanbal agrees with Mālik and Shāfiʾī, but reluctantly. When asked whether a father could give his *bikr* daughter in marriage without consulting her, he replied: "If her father gives her in marriage without her consent, that is a valid marriage. However, I prefer that he consult her."[20]

A number of traditions on the subject urge that a father consult a *bikr* before giving her in marriage, regardless of whether he is obliged to.[21] But others echo the views expressed by Mālik and Shāfiʾī, that fathers need not consult their *bikr* daughters. For example, in Ibn Abī Shayba's *Muṣannaf*, he reports that Mālik cited the same practice we saw above in the *Muwaṭṭaʾ*, although this time as a statement from al-Qāsim b. Muḥammad and Sālim b. ʿAbd Allāh rather than as their practice: they used to say: "If a father gives his *bikr* daughter in marriage,

[17] Shāfiʾī quotes the tradition: "The *ayyim* has more right to herself than her guardian, but the *bikr* is consulted about herself, and her silence is tantamount to her consent," on the authority of Mālik.

[18] In Abū Dāwūd's *Sunan*, we find a *matn* that takes up Shāfiʿī's point about asking the women of her family whether a girl wishes to be married to a particular man: "The Prophet said, 'Ask women for advice about their daughters.' " *Sunan*, 3:81.

[19] Shāfiʿī, *Kitāb al-umm*, see 5:17–18.

[20] See Spectorsky, *Chapters*, 143, §1.

[21] Wensinck, *Concordance*, s.vv., "*ayyim*"; "*bikr*."

that is valid for her, even if she dislikes it." Further, Ibn Abī Shayba reports that the Successor Ḥasan al-Basrī used to say: "When a father gives his daughter in marriage it is valid, regardless of whether she is a *bikr* or a *thayyib* and regardless of whether she is displeased with the marriage."[22]

Agnate Guardians

Whenever a woman, of any age or station, has neither father nor husband, she is referred to as a *yatīma*, or an "orphan." In this case her nearest male agnate becomes her *walī*, and she is his ward. As noted above, such a *walī*'s authority is more limited than a father's. For one thing, only the Mālikīs say he can give a minor girl in marriage. The other jurists say he must wait until she has reached puberty, and, in addition, he cannot give his ward in marriage without her explicit consent.

Discussions of a woman's agnates assume that she has a number of them; the questions raised are usually about the principle on which their precedence is based. In the *Mudawwana*, Ibn al-Qāsim reports that when asked whether a woman's paternal grandfather or her brother had the most right to give her in marriage, Mālik said her brother did. If her brother is unavailable, then his son, her nephew, takes precedence over her grandfather. If a woman has both a father and a son, then her son has more right to give her in marriage, because, according to Mālik, he is the one who prays over her at her funeral.[23] Shaybānī says if a woman's father is unavailable, her grandfather is her *walī*, and her grandfather goes before her brother because he takes precedence in inheritance. Shaybānī says that that is also Abū Ḥanīfa's opinion.[24]

Shāfiʿī agrees with Shaybānī and Abū Ḥanīfa, but makes a slightly different argument: he too gives a woman's paternal grandfather the same authority as her father (and after him, his father, then his father's

[22] Ibn Abī Shayba, *Muṣannaf*, 3:278, no. 7. An interesting additional detail is found in a tradition in ʿAbd al-Razzāq's *Muṣannaf* where a *thayyib* living in her father's household is treated the same way a *bikr* is: "Ibrāhīm [al-Nakhaʿī] said, 'As for the *bikr*, her father does not consult her; as for the *thayyib*, if she is part of his household, he does not consult her. If she is not, he does.' " See ʿAbd al-Razzāq, *Muṣannaf*, 6:144, no. 10293.

[23] See Saḥnūn, *Mudawwana*, 2:161–62. For several traditions about who has the most right to pray over a woman at her funeral, see Ibn Abī Shayba, *Muṣannaf*, 3:241–42.

[24] See Shaybānī, *Kitāb al-ḥujja*, 3:123ff. See also *EI*, s.v. "Mirāth."

father, etc.). In the absence of grandfathers, guardianship moves to a woman's brothers, first her full brothers, then her paternal half-brothers. Shāfiʿī does not mention the question (brought up in the *Mudawwana*) of who prays over a woman at her death or the opinion shared by Shaybānī and Abū Ḥanīfa that a woman's grandfather (or great grandfather) becomes her *walī* because he takes precedence in inheriting from her. Instead, he emphasizes her lineage, her *nasab*.[25] He points out that a woman's maternal relatives can also act as her *walī*s, but only if they too are agnates. Her agnates are responsible for blood-money if she injures anyone, and they are part of her tribe, the genealogy of which is traced through them.[26] Several different orders of agnate are reported from Ibn Ḥanbal, who, like Shāfiʿī, emphasizes a woman's *nasab*.[27]

The Necessity of a Guardian

Whenever a woman has no agnates, or they cannot or will not act on her behalf, we saw that the *qāḍī* becomes her guardian. This rule is given in the third tradition quoted above. It is also the case that if a woman's *walī* refuses to give her in marriage, she can appeal to the *sulṭān*.[28]

As a rule, a woman does not give herself in marriage. In *Muwaṭṭaʾ Shaybānī*, Mālik quotes a tradition in which ʿUmar b. al-Khaṭṭāb says: "It is not valid for a woman to marry without the permission of her *walī*, or a responsible relative, or the *sulṭān*." Shaybānī himself quotes a variant of the third tradition above and says: "There can be no marriage without a *walī*, and if the potential bride and her *walī* quarrel, then the *sulṭān* is the *walī* of the one who has no other." However, Shaybānī also points out that Abū Ḥanīfa held that if a woman married herself to someone who was her equal in status (*kafāʾa*) and did not accept an inadequate marriage portion, then her marriage was valid.[29]

---

[25] See *EI*, s.v. "Ḥasab wa-nasab." Tribal superiority is usually described with the double terms *ḥasab wa-nasab*. Singly, the two words are often used interchangeably to mean "rank." Strictly speaking, *ḥasab* refers to the tribal valor expected of someone of noble descent (*nasab*).

[26] See Shāfiʿī, *Kitāb al-umm*, 5:14–15. For the collective responsibility of a person's agnates who must pay his (or her) blood-money, see *EI*, s.v. "ʿĀḳila."

[27] See Spectorsky, *Chapters*, s.v. index "Agnate(s)."

[28] See Saḥnūn, *Mudawwana*, 2:161–65; and Ibn Abī Shayba, *Muṣannaf*, 3:281 for examples.

[29] See Shaybānī, *Muwaṭṭaʾ*, 221. Shaybānī adds here that proof of the validity of a marriage contract a woman concludes for herself is found in the tradition from ʿUmar: ʿUmar mentioned a "responsible relative" and thus was not referring to a woman's *walī*.

In his *Kitāb al-ḥujja*, Shaybānī elaborates on this position of Abū Ḥanīfa's by pointing to the fact that after the Prophet dissolved her marriage, he instructed Khansāʾ bt. Khudhām to marry whomever she wished.[30]

Shāfiʿī states emphatically that a woman can never be her own *walī*. He quotes the Prophet, "The marriage contract of any woman who concludes it without the permission of her *walī* is invalid." Then he adds that this tradition makes it clear that the *walī* must be a man and that since a woman cannot be her own *walī*, she certainly cannot be a *walī* for someone else.[31] Ibn Ḥanbal implies a similar view when he says that if a woman gives herself in marriage in the presence of two witnesses, but in the absence of her *walī*, he cannot send his consent in writing after the fact. To be valid, the marriage contract must be concluded again.[32]

Although in the *Muwaṭṭaʾ* Mālik quotes ʿUmar b. al-Khaṭṭāb ("It is not valid for a woman to marry without the permission of her *walī*, or a responsible relative, or the *sulṭān*"),[33] in the *Mudawwana*, he is reported as having made an exception in the case of a lowly woman. There, Ibn Wahb reports that Mālik said: "As for a lowly woman such as a manumitted slave, a black woman or a recent convert to Islam, as long as the marriage is not hidden and is widely known, that is less important in my opinion than it would be for a woman of substance."[34]

Forbidden Degrees (Raḍāʿ)

1. The Prophet said: "Nursing forbids what birth does."[35]
2. Ibn ʿAbbās was asked about a man who has both a wife and a slave concubine. If one of them nurses a boy and the other a girl, can the boy legally marry the girl? He said: "No! The semen is the same."[36]

---

[30] Shaybānī, *Kitāb al-ḥujja*, 3:98–104. See also 3:105–22, where Shaybānī relates a number of traditions that support Abū Ḥanīfa's position that a woman can conclude her own marriage contract as well as act as a marriage guardian for other women and for her male and female slaves.

[31] Shāfiʿī, *Kitāb al-umm*, 5:19.

[32] See Spectorsky, *Chapters*, 93, §8.

[33] See Shaybānī, *Muwaṭṭaʾ*, 221; and Mālik, *Muwaṭṭaʾ*, 3:127.

[34] Saḥnūn, *Mudawwana*, 2:166. See *Kitāb al-umm*, 7:222–23 for Shāfiʿī's vigorous attack on Mālik for differentiating between lowly and noble women.

[35] ʿAbd al-Razzāq, *Muṣannaf*, 7:476, no. 13952. This is one example of this *matn*. There are several others on 476–77. For those in the Six Books, see Wensinck, *Handbook*, s.v. "Nursing."

[36] Ibn Abī Shayba, *Muṣannaf*, 3:423, no. 1.

3. Ibn al-Musayyab said: "Nursing takes place only in infancy."[37]
4. ʿĀʾisha said: "The Prophet said: 'One or two acts of nursing do not establish foster-relationships.' "[38]

As we saw in the previous chapter, *raḍāʿ*, suckling or nursing, is the term used to refer to relationships that forbid a man and a woman to marry. These can be relationships established by consanguinity and marriage, as well as by foster relationships, which are those established by nursing (again, most obviously, that of a boy and girl nursed by the same wet nurse who thereby become "milk" siblings). Verses 4:22–24 of the Qurʾān mention those women a man is forbidden to marry. In 4:23, those forbidden by nursing are a man's wet nurse and any woman also nursed by her. Over time this particular foster relationship was extended until it virtually paralleled the relationships delineated by consanguinity. This is encapsulated in the first tradition above.[39]

Laban al-faḥl (literally, sire's milk) is the expression used to refer to the fact that a mother's milk was created by her husband's semen, or in the case of a female slave, by her owner's. It is illustrated by the second tradition above in which the two women are not co-wives, and hence not related to each other, but because their milk is due to sexual intercourse with the same man, the two children in question are milk siblings. The concept of *laban al-faḥl* also reinforces the first tradition above and means that relatives of the husband (or master) of the wet nurse are, along with those of his wife, within the forbidden degrees. A widely reported tradition that demonstrates this point is one in which ʿĀʾisha refuses to be unveiled in the presence of the Companion Aflaḥ b. Abi ʾl-Quʿays when he comes to visit her. He reminds her that his brother's wife was her wet nurse and therefore he is her uncle, but she points out that it was the wife not the husband who nursed her. The Prophet then arrives at ʿĀʾisha's dwelling and agrees with Aflaḥ that he is her foster uncle.[40]

A number of traditions address the question of whether it is permissible for a woman to nurse a grown man in order to establish an

[37] ʿAbd al-Razzāq, *Muṣannaf*, 7:465, no. 13907.

[38] Ibid., 7:469, no. 13925.

[39] It is not clear when this extension took place. For a discussion of the evolution of early thinking about 4:23, see Burton, "The Interpretation of 4:23 and the Muslim Theories of Naskh" and idem, *The Sources of Islamic Law*, 156–58.

[40] See Ibn Abī Shayba, *Muṣannaf*, 3:387, no. 3, for one version of this story. For other examples and variants of this same story in the Six Books, see Wensinck, *Concordance*, s.v. "*Laban al-faḥl*"; and Wensinck, *Handbook*, s.v. "Nursing."

artificial foster relationship. Traditions that allow it are usually regarded as efforts to ease the *ḥijāb* regulations imposed by the Qurʾān. This is part of the point of the tradition about ʿĀʾisha and Aflaḥ in the previous paragraph. In another tradition, Sahla bt. Suhayl, wife of the Companion Abū Hudhayfa, complains to the Prophet that a man named Sālim, whom they had considered a son before the Qurʾānic injunction against adoption, could no longer be part of their household and come freely into her presence. The Prophet suggests that she suckle him in order to make him her foster son.[41]

Traditions that say it is not permissible for a woman to nurse a grown man stress that mother's milk is meant for infants. The third tradition above illustrates this point. The fourth, addresses the question of whether foster relationships must be based on an ongoing nursing relationship. This question comes up in traditions about nursing adults as well as infants. Still other traditions emphasize that as long as the nursling is an infant, even if only a drop of milk enters its belly, a foster relationship is established.[42]

In the *Muwaṭṭaʾ* we find a number of traditions similar to the four quoted above. For example, Mālik reports the tradition of the Prophet informing ʿĀʾisha that Aflaḥ b. Abi ʾl-Quʿays was her foster uncle and therefore allowed into her presence. At the end of the version in the *Muwaṭṭaʾ*, ʿĀʾisha says: "Nursing forbids what birth does."[43] Mālik also reports a version of the story of Abū Hudhayfa's wife Sahla telling the Prophet of her concern that she could no longer regard Sālim as a foster son. Mālik reports this tradition on the authority of Zuhrī, who, when asked whether nursing adults was permissible, said that ʿUrwa b. Zubayr had informed him that the Prophet told Sahla to nurse Sālim five times, after which she considered him her foster son. ʿUrwa continues by saying that ʿĀʾisha adopted the practice of having her nieces nurse men whom she wished to allow into her presence. However, the other wives of the Prophet disapproved and said: "No, by God, we think what the Prophet ordered Sahla bt. Suhayl to do was a dispensation (*rukhṣa*) only for her. …"[44]

---

[41] See ʿAbd al-Razzāq, *Muṣannaf*, 7:458–59, no. 13884.

[42] See, for example, Saḥnūn, *Mudawwana*, 2:405–6; Ibn Abī Shayba, *Muṣannaf*, 3:386, nos. 1–7.

[43] Mālik, *Muwaṭṭaʾ*, 3:238–39.

[44] Ibid., 3:245–46. See also ʿAbd al-Razzāq, *Muṣannaf*, 7:459, nos. 13885 and 13886, for the possibility that this was a special dispensation for Sālim. For "dispensation," see *EI*, s.v. "Rukhṣa."

Mālik relates these traditions without comment, but his own opinion is that only nursing that takes place within the first two years of a child's life establishes a foster relationship and that no minimum number of feedings is required: Yaḥyā said: "I heard Mālik say, 'Regardless of the number of times nursing occurs, as long as it takes place within the first two years of a child's life, a foster relationship is established. After a child is two years old, nursing is only eating and does not establish a foster relationship.'"[45] Further, after relating a tradition in which ʿĀʾisha says: "In what was revealed of the Qurʾān, ten well-attested acts of nursing established a foster relationship, then the ten were replaced by five, and then the Prophet died while five were being recited in the Qurʾān," Yaḥyā reports that Mālik said: "This is not our practice."[46]

In his version of the *Muwaṭṭa'*, Shaybānī agrees that as long as nursing occurs within the first two years of a child's life, even one instance of it establishes a foster relationship, because God said: *Mothers shall suckle their children for two whole years: (that is) for those who wish to complete the suckling* (2:233). Nursing thereafter, Shaybānī says, does not establish relationships within the forbidden degrees.[47]

Shāfiʿī agrees with Mālik that only nursing within the first two years establishes a foster relationship, but, unlike Mālik, he adduces the tradition on ʿĀʾisha's authority to uphold the rule that no fewer than five acts of nursing are required.[48] Ibn Ḥanbal concurs that only nursing in infancy establishes a foster relationships,[49] but he is hesitant about the traditions supporting a minimum of five acts of suckling, since he clearly knows others that point to one or two acts of suckling, or even a drop of milk entering an infant's belly.[50]

---

[45] Mālik, *Muwaṭṭa'*, 3:243.

[46] Ibid., 3:249.

[47] However, although he himself disagrees, he notes that Abū Ḥanīfa, as a precaution (*yaḥtāṭu*), included the six-month period after a child's first two years and said that a foster relationship was created by nursing that took place within the first two years of life plus an additional six months, and that is thirty months. Shaybānī, *Muwaṭṭa'*, 251; and see Qurʾān 46:15, … *and the bearing of him and the weaning of him is thirty months*.… For the notion of "precaution," see Schacht, *Introduction*, 123.

[48] Shāfiʿī, *Kitāb al-umm*, 5:29. See also 7:224, where Shāfiʿī points out that the *isnāds* for the traditions on which Mālik bases his position are not as strong as those that insist on five separate acts of nursing to create a relationship within the forbidden degrees.

[49] "If an adult nurses, his nursing does not establish a foster-relationship; rather, it is simply eating." Spectorsky, *Chapters*, 111, §67.

[50] His son ʿAbd Allāh reports: "I asked my father, 'Do one or two acts of suckling establish foster-relationship?' He said, 'I hesitate about this.' I said, 'There are sound

Another issue that comes up in connection with foster relationships is whether illicit sexual relations establish the same relationships that legal ones do. Mālik and Shāfiʿī said they do not, because what God forbade was actually *marriage* within the forbidden degrees. Therefore fornication or adultery, and marriage with two women too closely related to each other do not forbid the same things that lawful marriages do.[51] Abū Ḥanīfa and Ibn Ḥanbal disagree, and both say that even lustful behavior that does not involve intercourse sets up a barrier to lawful sexual relations. Ibn Ḥanbal says: "If a man buys a female slave and then touches her, kisses her, or undresses her out of lust, she is forbidden to his son."[52]

Equality (Kafāʾa)

1. ʿUmar b. al-Khaṭṭāb said: "We forbid the private parts of noble women to anyone except their equals."[53]
2. The son of ʿUbayd b. ʿUmayr said: "A woman of the … tribe of Kināna married a *mawlā* in Iraq. There was disagreement about [the validity] of this matter [i.e., the marriage], so the issue was brought before ʿUbayd b. ʿUmayr, who ruled the marriage was valid."[54]
3. Kathīr b. Ṣalṭ said: "A *mawlā* of ours who married an Arab woman was brought before the Caliph, ʿUmar b. ʿAbd al-ʿAzīz … and he said, 'Abū Kathīr's *mawlā* has overstepped his limits.'"[55]
4. Ḥasan al-Baṣrī said: "I asked Ibn Abī Laylā about *kafāʾa* in marriage, and he said, 'In religion and in rank.' I asked, 'In means (*māl*)?' and he said, 'No.'"[56]

As we saw, the Qurʾān refers to the women a man should marry: preferably free, believing women, or, if he cannot afford a free woman's marriage portion, a believing slave. A man may also marry free Jewish and Christian women. But the Qurʾān does not say which men women should be given to in marriage, even as it urges guardians to treat their

---

traditions to this effect.' He said, 'Yes, but I do not allow the assumption of a foster-relationship on the basis of them.'" See Spectorsky, *Chapters*, 111, §66 and 170, §90.

[51] See Mālik, *Muwaṭṭaʾ*, 3:141 and 142; and Shāfiʿī, *Kitāb al-umm*, 5:25.

[52] See Shaybānī, *Kitāb al-ḥujja*, 3:367–68; and Spectorsky, *Chapters*, 106, §46. For a more detailed discussion of the legal effects of illicit and licit sexual relations, see Schacht, "Adultery as an Impediment to Marriage."

[53] ʿAbd al-Razzāq, *Muṣannaf*, 6:152, no. 10324.

[54] Ibid., 6:153, no. 10327. The Successor ʿUbayd b. ʿUmayr (d. 68/721) was originally from Mecca. He is said to have been the first *qāṣṣ* (*See EI*, s.v. "Qāṣṣ").

[55] See Ibn Abī Shayba, *Muṣannaf*, 3:466, no. 3.

[56] Ibid., 3:467, no. 8.

wards with fairness. In *fiqh* texts about marriage, the choice of an appropriate groom is discussed in terms of *kafāʾa*,[57] and the four traditions quoted above reflect its most common components: lineage, social class, wealth, and piety.[58]

In the first tradition, the statement attributed to ʿUmar b. al-Khaṭṭāb expresses the pre-Islamic values of tribal ranking. A woman from a pre-eminent tribe should not be given in marriage to a man from a lesser one. In the second and third traditions, the question is whether an Arab woman should be married to a *mawlā*. In this context, *mawlā* means a non-Arab convert to Islam,[59] and the answers—no, as well as yes—reflect the fact that in the formative period of Islam, the Arab Muslims did not easily relinquish belief in the importance of Arab superiority, despite the principle that all Muslims theoretically are equal before God.[60] The most forceful statement of this principle is in Qurʾān 49:13: *O mankind! Lo! We have created you male and female and have made you nations and tribes that ye may know one another. Lo! the noblest of you, in the sight of Allah is the best in conduct.*[61] The fourth tradition, like the first, points to the importance of equal tribal rank and stresses that it far outweighs the importance of wealth.[62]

We have already discerned hints of concern for lineage in Shāfiʿī's insistence that in the absence of her father, only a woman's agnates, who represent her *nasab,* should give her in marriage because the genealogy of her tribe is traced through them. His reference to *kafāʾa* itself is brief, and he mentions only *nasab* (along with *ḥasab*)[63] as an issue and thus bears out the sentiment of the fourth tradition, that

---

[57] See *EI*, s.vv. "Kafāʾa"; "Nikāḥ."

[58] See Farhat Ziadeh, "Equality (*kafaʿah*) in the Muslim Law of Marriage."

[59] See EI, s.v. "Mawlā."

[60] See Crone, *Roman, Provincial and Islamic Law,* for a study of the development of the status of *mawālī*. For the status of the *mawlā* these traditions refer to, see 91, n. 11.

[61] For an understanding of this verse in the context of tribal attitudes, Goldziher's discussion in *Muslim Studies* remains useful. See 1, Chapter 2, "The Arabic Tribes and Islam," especially 70–78. For several different contexts for the occasion of revelation of this verse, see Wāḥidī, 264–65.

[62] For a discussion of this point as well as the importance of the principle of *kafāʾa* in pre-Islamic Arabia, see Bravmann, *Spiritual Background*, Chapter XII, "Equality of Birth of Husband and Wife (*kafāʾah*), an Early Arab Principle," 301–10.

[63] *EI*, s.v. "Ḥasab wa-nasab."

wealth is not important: a reduced marriage portion does not mean reduced *nasab*.[64]

Kafāʾa is not discussed in Mālik's *Muwaṭṭaʾ*, but in the *Mudawwana*, Ibn al-Qāsim describes the case of a woman whose father or *walī* refuses to give her in marriage to a man of her choice who is her equal in religion but beneath her in tribal and personal standing *(ḥasab* and *sharaf)*.[65] The question is: if she brings the matter to the *qāḍī*, can he give her in marriage and ignore the objections of her father or her *walī*? Ibn al-Qāsim says that according to Mālik's doctrine, the *qāḍī* can. Further, Saḥnūn says that he asked Ibn al-Qāsim about a woman who wished to marry a man who was her equal in religion but not in wealth. Again, if her father or *walī* refuses to give her in marriage, can the *qāḍī*? Ibn al-Qāsim replies that he did not hear anything specifically about this question from Mālik, but that he had asked him generally about a *mawlā* marrying an Arab, and Mālik's response was to say there was no harm in it and to quote 49:13.[66]

Mālik's attitude is not shared by Abū Ḥanīfa, Shaybānī, or Ibn Ḥanbal, who are much closer to Shāfiʿī in their interest in having a woman marry someone who is her tribal equal. At the same time they also show an interest in wealth and do not endorse the sentiments of the fourth tradition. In *al-Jāmiʿ al-ṣaghīr*, Shaybānī reports that Abū Ḥanīfa said: "The Quraysh are each other's equals, and the Arabs are each other's equals. Among the non-Arabs, whoever has two Muslim parents or grandparents are each other's equals." Abū Ḥanīfa adds: "A man is not an equal at all, if he cannot produce a marriage portion or maintenance."[67] In his *Āthār*, Shaybānī quotes the first tradition above approvingly and adds that if a woman *does* marry a man who is not her

[64] See Shāfiʿī, *Kitāb al-umm*, 5:15.

[65] See *EI*, s.v. "Sharaf": "In pre-Islamic Arabia and in early Islam, *sharaf* and *madjd* both denote 'illustriousness acquired by oneself" (as opposed to *nasab*, for example, which is inherited). The personal standing of the male members of a woman's tribe would be due to their valor in battle, and her standing would reflect their achievements. See further, Bravmann, *Spiritual Background*, Chapter XII, "Equality of Birth of Husband and Wife (*kafāʾah*), an Early Arab Principle."

[66] Saḥnūn, *Mudawwana*, 2:163.

[67] Shaybānī, *Al-Jāmiʿal-ṣaghīr*, 140–41. Above, we noted Abū Ḥanīfa's concern for a woman's marriage portion where he was willing to consider valid a marriage a woman concluded for herself without a *walī* as long as she had married an equal and received a marriage portion. He adds here concern about a potential husband's ability to support his wife.

equal, and her *walī* brings the matter to the *qāḍī*, the *qāḍī* ought to separate the couple.[68]

Ibn Ḥanbal echoes Abū Ḥanīfa and Shaybānī. Asked about an Arab man who gives his daughter in marriage to a *mawlā*, he says: "I would separate the two of them." Then he adds: "Arabs are of equal standing with each other, and the Quraysh are of equal standing with each other."[69] Asked again about a marriage between a *mawlā* and an Arab woman, he responds by asking rhetorically: "If a man whose father accepted Islam yesterday marries a Hashimite woman, does that man allege that he is her equal?"[70] Further, Ibn Ḥanbal says that when a woman named Fāṭima bt. Qays asked the Prophet whether she should marry a certain Muʿāwiya, the Prophet replied: "Muʿāwiya is destitute; he has no wealth."[71]

Witnesses to a Marriage[72]

1. The Prophet said: "There can be no marriage without a *walī* and two trustworthy witnesses."[73]
2. Ibrāhīm [al-Nakhaʿī] said: "The minimum prerequisites for a marriage are four: a man to get married, another to give [the bride] in marriage [to him], and two witnesses."[74]
3. Ṭāwūs said: "A woman who had become pregnant was brought before ʿUmar [b. al-Khaṭṭāb], and she said, 'I married with my mother and my sister as witnesses.' ʿUmar separated the couple, warded off the *ḥadd* punishment from them, and said, 'There can be no marriage without a *walī* and witnesses.'"[75]
4. Regarding a man who asked a woman's *walī* for her hand in marriage and then married her in the presence of one man and two women, Zuhrī said, "If they announced it, then I think it is a valid marriage; [that is] if they announced it and did not keep it a secret."[76]

Discussions of witnessing a marriage contract revolve around three problems: whether witnesses are necessary, their qualifications, and

---

[68] Shaybānī, *Āthār*, 95. Shaybānī also notes that Abū Ḥanīfa agrees that the *qāḍī* separates the couple.
[69] Ibn Hāniʾ, *Masāʾil Aḥmad b. Ḥanbal*, 200, no. 992.
[70] Spectorsky, *Chapters*, 61, §6.
[71] Ibid., §8.
[72] See *EI*, s.vv. "Shāhid"; *EQ*, "Witnessing and Testifying."
[73] ʿAbd al-Razzāq, *Muṣannaf*, 6:196, no. 10473.
[74] Ibn Abī Shayba, *Muṣannaf*, 3:274, no. 23.
[75] Ibid., 3:273, no. 14.
[76] ʿAbd al-Razzāq, *Muṣannaf*, 6:196, no. 10474.

their role in making a marriage public. The first of these traditions is a variant of the initial one quoted above about a woman's guardian, in which the Prophet states the necessity of a *walī* to conclude a marriage contract. In this case the second part of the statement refers to the requirement of witnesses for a valid marriage contract (and not, as above, to the fact that the *sulṭān* is the *walī* of the one who has no other). The second tradition states the minimum prerequisites for a valid marriage contract. The third depicts ʿUmar upholding the fact that inadequate witnessing made the contract invalid, but assuming, nonetheless, that the wife really knew no better and therefore not ordering that she be punished for illicit intercourse.[77] The fourth describes an approach to valid marriage contracts that seems to view them as political and communal acts that are validated by being generally known as well as by formal witnessing. Thus as long as no attempt was made to hide the marriage, it can be allowed to stand. All these views of witnessing a marriage contract are found in *fiqh* texts.

In the *Muwaṭṭaʾ*, Mālik relates a tradition in which ʿUmar reacts with less leniency than he shows in the third tradition above: when told about a marriage witnessed by only one man and one woman, he says: "That is a secret marriage, and I do not allow it. Had I been there, I would have stoned [them]."[78] Mālik adds no explanation for this tradition, but Shaybānī, in his version of the *Muwaṭṭaʾ*, goes into greater detail. First, he quotes the same tradition and then says: "We adopt this (i.e., ʿUmar's position) because marriage is not permissible with fewer than two witnesses, and only one man and one woman witnessed this marriage which ʿUmar rejected. Further, it is a secret marriage because it was inadequately witnessed. If it had been adequately witnessed by two men, or by one man and two women, then it would have been valid, even though it was concluded in secret. It would have been valid because what makes a secret marriage invalid is that it occurs without witnesses; however, if the witnessing is adequate, then it is a public marriage, even though they kept it secret."[79] Shaybānī adds here that ʿUmar accepted

[77] See *EI*, s.v. "Shubha." *Shubha* literally means "resemblance" and in law refers to an illicit act that resembles a licit one. It can be translated as 'uncertainty', meaning uncertainty about the law or about the facts of the case. Here, ʿUmar gives the woman the benefit of the doubt and therefore she is not punished. For traditions urging Muslims to try to avoid inflicting *ḥadd* punishments, see *EI*, s.v. "Ḥadd"; and Wensinck, *Handbook*, s.v. "Punishment."

[78] Mālik, *Muwaṭṭaʾ*, 3:144.

[79] Shaybānī, *Muwaṭṭaʾ*, 218.

one man and two women as witnesses for a marriage contract and that he himself also accepts one man and two women, as does Abū Ḥanīfa. Two issues are present in Shaybānī's statement: first, validating a marriage by adequate witnessing, and second, validating it by making it public. He thinks a contract is valid only if there are two witnesses, regardless of whether there is widespread knowledge that it has taken place.[80]

In the *Mudawwana*, Mālik is reported to have held the opposite: he objected to the validity of a marriage if the witnesses kept it secret, but accepted its validity even if there were no witnesses but the marriage was made public. Saḥnūn reports that he asked Ibn al-Qāsim the following question: "[What] if a man is given in marriage without witnesses and the one who gave him in marriage confirms that he did so without witnesses? Is it permissible for two witnesses to affirm what has happened after the fact and for the contract to be valid according to Mālik's doctrine?" Ibn al-Qāsim answers that yes, this is what Mālik thought.[81]

In *Kitāb al-umm*, Shāfiʿī agrees with Shaybānī that a marriage must be witnessed. He reports that Ibn ʿAbbās said: "There can be no marriage without two just witnesses and a responsible *walī*," and he also relates the tradition from ʿUmar that a man along with only one woman does not provide adequate witnessing. Then he himself emphasizes that the two witnesses must be trustworthy. He adds that if the witnesses (and the couple) keep the marriage secret, even though that is reprehensible, the marriage is still valid.[82]

Ibn Ḥanbal agrees with Shāfiʿī and quotes a slight variant of the second tradition above; he says that the minimum prerequisites for a valid marriage are: "A suitor, someone to give the bride in marriage and two witnesses."[83] Unlike Shaybānī, he equates making a marriage public with witnessing it: "[A]sked about a man who gave his daughter in marriage to her paternal cousin without witnesses, but the neighbors knew that he had given her in marriage, even though he had not invited them to witness this fact, he answered: 'The marriage is not lawful until it is made public by means of witnesses.'"[84] Further, when asked

[80] Another issue here is Shaybānī's assumption that Qurʾān 2:282 means that two women equal one man in all instances where two witnesses are required. See Chapter 5 for discussion of this question.
[81] Mālik, *Mudawwana*, 2:192.
[82] Shāfiʿī, *Kitāb al-umm*, 5:22.
[83] See Spectorsky, *Chapters*, 62, §17.
[84] Ibn Hāniʾ, *Masāʾil*, 199.

whether a marriage is secret if the contract was concluded by a *walī* in the presence of two witnesses, Ibn Ḥanbal says: "It is preferable that a marriage be made public and not kept secret, that it be concluded by a *walī* and that the tambourine be played at it, so that it becomes well known and acknowledged."[85]

Ibn Ḥanbal refers here to the wedding banquet, or *walīma*, which normally involves guests, feasting, and also music of some kind.[86] In the *Muwaṭṭaʾ*, Mālik quotes a tradition in which the Prophet says: "When any one of you is invited to a *walīma*, let him attend." And in the *Mudawwana*, we find a tradition in which the Prophet and several of his Companions pass by the dwellings of the Banū Zurayq and hear playing and singing. The Prophet asks what is happening, and when he is told that a marriage is taking place, he approves and says that if the tambourine is heard and smoke is seen (presumably for preparation of food for the banquet), the marriage is valid, and thus an example neither of fornication nor of secret marriage.[87] In his discussion of witnesses to a marriage, Shāfiʿī does not mention the *walīma*, but elsewhere in *Kitāb al-umm* he devotes a section to it in which he discusses a number of traditions about the obligation to accept an invitation to a *walīma*, including the tradition Mālik quotes on the authority of the Prophet ("When any one of you is invited to a *walīma*, let him attend").[88]

The reports from Mālik and Ibn Ḥanbal conflate two issues. As noted above, a marriage contract can be concluded for a couple at any age. So, for example, the father of a prepubescent girl may conclude a marriage contract for her long before she is old enough to take up residence in her husband's house. This contract, according to the Ḥanafīs and Shāfiʿī, must be witnessed. Mālik does not emphasize formal witnesses for the contract as much as he does the fact that it should be

[85] See Spectorsky, *Chapters*, 92, §5.

[86] See EI, s.v. "ʿUrs." The *walima* is normally held by the bridegroom after the bride has taken up residence in his house or after the marriage has been consummated. See Stern, *Marriage in Early Islam*, 89–91 for stories about wedding banquets held on the occasion of several of the Prophet's marriages, as well as those of some of his Companions.

[87] Saḥnūn, *Mudawwana*, 2:194.

[88] See Shāfiʿī, *Kitāb al-umm*, 6:181. Shāfiʿī discusses an invitation to a *walīma* along with invitations to other happy events, such as the birth of a child or a circumcision. Attending these celebrations is less important than attending a wedding banquet, which he considers an obligation, a *ḥaqq* (for which see *EI*, s.v. "Ḥuḳūḳ"). Even if one is fasting, it is possible simply to attend and not eat. See *EI*, s.v. "ʿUrs."

widely known that a particular couple are legally married when the bride takes up residence with her husband, as signaled by the wedding banquet referred to in the *Mudawwana*. Ibn Ḥanbal seems to treat witnesses as a necessary but not sufficient condition: to make a marriage valid, he wants both witnesses and a public announcement; he shifts the emphasis away from the formal witnesses of the contract to the importance of the communal knowledge that a bride has removed to her husband's house.

Marriage Portion

Amounts

1. Yaḥyā b. Saʿīd said: "Muḥammad b. Ibrāhīm related to me saying, 'The marriage portions of the Prophet's wives and daughters was 500 dirhams.' "[89]
2. Shaʿbī said that ʿAlī said: "No marriage portion should be less than ten dirhams."[90]
3. On the authority of Nāfiʿ, ʿUmar forbade that women's marriage portions be more than 400 dirhams.[91]
4. Al-Ḥasan al-Baṣrī said: "Whatever the spouses are agreed upon is a satisfactory marriage portion."[92]

Another element in an ideal marriage is a woman's marriage portion.[93] In Chapter 1, we saw that the verses in the Qurʾān about a woman's marriage portion stress that it be given to her voluntarily (4:4. 4:24, 5:5) and that she retain it in the case of divorce (4:20). If divorce occurs before a couple have consummated their marriage, but after a marriage portion has been agreed upon, the wife receives only half of it, unless she agrees to forego it (2:237). In a case of divorce before consummation, if a marriage portion was not specified in the marriage contract, the husband owes his wife a divorce gift (*mutʿa*), *the affluent according to their means, the poor in accordance with theirs* (2:236). But no amounts are mentioned.

The traditions above are only a small sample of the many opinions that prevailed about an appropriate marriage portion. In the first, the

[89] Ibn Abī Shayba, *Muṣannaf*, 3:313, no. 13.
[90] Ibid., no. 14.
[91] Ibid., 3:318, no. 15.
[92] Ibid., no. 7.
[93] See *EI*, s.v. "Mahr."

marriage portion of the Prophet's wives and daughters is reported as 500 dirhams. However, other traditions report that their marriage portions were 480 dirhams, and others report different amounts as well as gifts. For example, 'Alī is sometimes said to have given the Prophet's daughter Fāṭima a suit of armor, or a few household appurtenances. He is also said to have sold a camel for 480 dirhams and then, in accordance with the Prophet's instructions, to have spent two-thirds of the money on perfume and the other third on clothing.[94]

The second and third traditions above indicate efforts to establish respectively a minimum and a maximum marriage portion. In contrast, the fourth tradition indicates that the marriage portion can be whatever the spouses agree upon. Another example of "whatever the spouses agree upon" is a tradition in which Ibn al-Musayyab said: "If she is satisfied with a leather whip, then that constitutes a marriage portion."[95]

Fiqh texts mention other numbers. In Abū Yūsuf's *Āthār*, he reports that Ibn 'Umar used to give his daughters in marriage for 1,000 dirhams.[96] In *Muwaṭṭa' Shaybānī*, Shaybānī says that the minimum marriage portion is ten dirhams, and that Abū Ḥanīfa agrees, because that is the smallest amount that can be demanded as compensation for the loss of a hand. In the *Muwaṭṭa'*, Mālik mentions a minimum amount of one quarter of a dinar (three dirhams), because, he says: "That is the minimum compensation for stolen goods."[97] Shāfi'ī wants to establish a maximum rather than a minimum amount, which he sets at 500 dirhams, like the first tradition above, but he supports it with a tradition on the authority of 'Umar b. al-Khaṭṭāb that this was the amount received by the Prophet's wives and daughters. Ibn Ḥanbal is unwilling to fix an amount and says, in accordance with the fourth tradition above, that the marriage portion is whatever the parties agree upon.[98] A woman's appropriate, or "fair," marriage portion, is the amount a wife can claim if no sum has been specified in the marriage contract concluded for her. It is the amount that the women of her family might expect to receive and is generally based on the status of

[94] Ibn Sa'd, *Ṭabaqāt*, 8:115–16 and 12–13, for different traditions about Fāṭima's mariage portion.
[95] Ibn Abī Shayba, *Muṣannaf*, 6:317, no. 5.
[96] Abū Yūsuf, *Āthār*, no. 1021.
[97] Shaybānī, *Muwaṭṭa'*, 214–15; Mālik, *Muwaṭṭa'*, 3:133.
[98] See Spectorsky, *Chapters*, s.v. index, "Dower."

the family, although other factors may enter in, such as the individual qualities of the bride (e.g., beauty, wealth), and the financial situation of the groom.[99]

If a potential groom has no financial resources, it is possible for him to marry on the basis of a pledge to do something. The most famous example of this is found in a story of the Prophet giving a woman in marriage to a man who was destitute, but who knew some verses of the Qurʾān by heart that he could teach her. In a version of it found in the *Muwaṭṭaʾ*, a woman comes to the Prophet and offers herself to him. The Prophet does not respond, at which point a man who had been sitting with him stands up and says: "O Messenger of God, marry me to her, if you have no need of her." The Prophet responds by asking whether the man has anything to offer as a marriage portion. He replies that he has nothing except his waist wrapper. The Prophet urges him to search for something else, "even an iron ring." When the man still can't find anything, the Prophet asks whether he knows any chapters of the Qurʾān by heart. He names some, at which point the Prophet says: "I marry you to her on the basis of what you know of the Qurʾān."[100] However, Mālik himself does not say this is Medinese practice.

Shāfiʿī says that anything that can be bought, sold, or hired for a price is a lawful marriage portion. It must be a known quantity, and it must be something specific that can be sold immediately or at some future date. In addition, a marriage portion can be a garment a man sews for his wife, a house he builds for her, a service he performs for her for one month, or some particular action he performs on her behalf. It can also consist of his teaching her specific verses of the Qurʾān.[101]

Ibn Ḥanbal, in accordance with the fourth tradition above, says the marriage portion can be whatever the parties agree upon. On the

---

[99] See, for example, Saḥnūn, *Mudawwana*, 2:236; and Shāfiʿī, *Kitāb al-umm*, 5:68.

[100] Mālik, *Muwaṭṭaʾ*, 3:128–29. Many traditions recount this story, but with varying detail. See, for example, ʿAbd al-Razzāq, *Muṣannaf*, 6:174, no. 10394; Ibn Abī Shayba, *Muṣannaf*, 3:317; Ibn Ḥanbal, *Musnad*, 5:330. In a number of these traditions, it is possible to understand either that the potential husband can teach his bride verses of the Qurʾān, or that he may marry her simply on the basis of knowing them. For different versions of the tradition, see Wensinck, *Concordance*, s.vv. "*ṣadāq*" and "*mahr*"; Wensinck, *Handbook*, s.v. "Marriage," 146.

[101] Like Mālik, Shāfiʿī includes the tradition about the Prophet marrying a couple for a marriage portion of what the man knew of the Qurʾān, but he does not present it tosupport his inclusion of *teaching* the Qurʾān as a possible marriage portion. Shāfiʿī, *Kitāb al-umm*, 5:59–60.

question of a marriage portion of the Qurʾān, he points to the possibility of understanding the tradition to mean that the man simply knew some verses of the Qurʾān and therefore was a worthy husband, or that he was meant to teach them to his wife. However, he is not in favor of a marriage portion consisting of verses of the Qurʾān, regardless of whether the husband merely knows them or promises to teach them to his wife.[102]

Neither Abū Ḥanīfa nor Shaybānī mention a marriage portion of verses from the Qurʾān. In *al-Jāmiʿ al-ṣaghīr*, Shaybānī expresses concern that a marriage portion have a monetary value. He says that if a free man marries a woman for a marriage portion of serving her for a year, she receives instead the price of his service.[103]

Deferred and Immediate Payment of the Marriage Portion

1. Al-Shaʿbī said: "There is an immediate marriage portion and the remainder is deferred until death or divorce."[104]
2. Sufyān al-Thawrī said: "She receives her entire marriage portion all at once if she asks for it, both the immediate and the deferred portions, unless he has specified a time [for payment of the deferred portion].[105]
3. Qatāda said: "A woman can demand her marriage portion from her husband as long as the couple have not had intercourse. If they have, she has no recourse.[106]

Opinion was divided about whether a bride should be given a part or all of her marriage portion before the couple have intercourse. The three traditions above point to the possibility of dividing it into an immediate and a deferred payment, with the deferred payment due at a specified time, or when the husband divorces his wife, or when one spouse dies. In the first of these traditions the division of the marriage portion is taken for granted, as is the fact that the deferred portion becomes the wife's only when the marriage ends. In the second, the wife has the right

[102] Spectorsky, *Chapters*, 151, §20. For a version of this *ḥadīth* in Ibn Ḥanbal's *Musnad*, see 5:330. Ibn Ḥanbal often rejects doctrines by saying they are not found in *ḥadīths*.
[103] Shaybānī, *al-Jāmiʿ al-ṣaghīr*, 149.
[104] Ibn Abī Shayba, *Muṣannaf*, 3:299, no. 6.
[105] ʿAbd al-Razzāq, *Muṣannaf*, 6:296, no. 10902.
[106] Ibid., no. 10903. The point of Qatāda's statement is not that the wife receives no marriage portion, but that if she (or her *walī*) fails to make certain that she received all or part of it before the marriage was consummated, the husband cannot be made to pay it until one of them dies or he divorces her.

to receive her marriage portion all at once, unless a particular time (before divorce or death) is specified for payment of the second part. In the third, the wife must secure her marriage portion before the marriage is consummated, or she loses control over when she receives it.

Shaybānī said that Abū Ḥanīfa saw no harm in a husband's having intercourse with his wife and delaying giving her any of her marriage portion for a year. Ibn Ḥanbal sees no harm in a husband's giving his wife her marriage portion after the couple have had intercourse, as well as in installments. Shāfiʿī says if the marriage has been consummated, the wife is owed her entire marriage portion. Mālik does not mention this problem in the *Muwaṭṭa'*, but in the *Mudawwana* seems to agree with the third tradition above by saying that the wife has the right to demand her full marriage portion before sexual intercourse, but that once the marriage has been consummated, she can demand only her fair marriage portion (which might be smaller than the one she originally agreed to), and she has no recourse against her husband for a larger sum, or for any part of the marriage portion that may have been delayed to a future date.[107]

Two Types of Marriage without a Marriage Portion

In a *shighār* marriage, one man agrees to give his daughter or sister in marriage to another, who in turn agrees to give his daughter or sister in marriage to the first. In this way, by swapping female relatives, they both avoid the cost of a marriage portion. *Shighār* is always described as a pre-Islamic practice that the Prophet forbade. Whenever it is discussed, he is usually quoted as saying: "There is no *shighār* in Islam."[108] The question jurists discussed was what to do if actual instances of it occurred. In the *Muwaṭṭa'*, Mālik merely quotes the Prophet's statement. In the *Mudawwana* however, Ibn al-Qāsim reports that in all instances of *shighār* the marriage is not valid, and both couples are separated. Thus in a case in which a couple have lived together, had intercourse, and borne children, they are still separated, and the wife receives her fair marriage portion. The same thing happens if two

[107] See Shaybānī, *Kitāb al-ḥujja*, 3:231–39; Spectorsky, *Chapters*, 107, §51, 118, §89, 151, §21; Shāfiʿī, *Kitāb al-umm*, 5:58; Saḥnūn, *Mudawwana*, 2: 239–40, 253. For a full discussion of this question in theory and in actual social practice, see Rapoport, "Matrimonial Gifts in Early Islamic Egypt."

[108] For examples, see ʿAbd al-Razzāq, *Muṣannaf*, 6:183–85, nos. 10432–442.

slaves are swapped as brides by their masters. Shāfiʿī agrees with Mālik: the marriage is not valid, and the couples are separated. If they have had sexual intercourse, the wife is owed her fair marriage portion and must wait an *ʿidda* before remarrying. Ibn Ḥanbal agrees that the couples are separated. He says that if they have not had intercourse, the wife receives nothing; if they have, she receives a marriage portion. Shaybānī disagrees and says that a *shighār* marriage *is* valid, the couple (or couples) remain married, and the wife receives her fair marriage portion, no more and no less. And this, he says, is also Abū Ḥanīfa's doctrine.[109]

In a *tafwīḍ* marriage, a man marries a woman who consents to be married without any marriage portion being specified or consents to be married for no marriage portion at all. In this case the marriage is valid, and if the couple have intercourse, the wife is entitled to a fair marriage portion. If they divorce before intercourse, she is entitled to a divorce gift.[110] However, there was disagreement about what happens when the husband dies before the couple have had intercourse. In Shaybānī's *Āthār*, he says that the widow receives both her full marriage portion and her inheritance, and, in addition, she waits an *ʿidda*. This, Shaybānī says, is also Abū Ḥanīfa's opinion.[111] Shāfiʿī and Ibn Ḥanbal agree with Shaybānī and Abū Ḥanīfa.[112] Their opinion is supported by a tradition about a woman named Barwaʿ bt. Wāshiq, who was married in a *tafwīḍ* marriage. When her husband died before having intercourse with her, the Prophet granted her a fair marriage portion and her full inheritance. Mālik disagrees and says that the widow inherits from her late husband, but that since the couple have not had sexual intercourse, no marriage portion is due. This view is supported by a decision of Ibn ʿUmar's: when one of his sons died before having intercourse with his wife, Ibn ʿUmar granted the widow her full inheritance from him but no marriage portion.[113]

---

[109] Mālik, *Muwaṭṭaʾ*, 3:142–43; Saḥnūn, *Mudawwana*, 2:152–55; Shāfiʿī, *Kitāb al-umm*, 5:76–77; Spectorsky, *Chapters*, 99, §25; Shaybānī, *Muwaṭṭaʾ*, 217–18.

[110] See Shaybānī, *al-Jāmiʿ al-saghīr*, 150; Saḥnūn, *Mudawwana*, 2:238; Shāfiʿī, *Kitāb al-umm*, 5:68; Spectorsky, *Chapters*, 66, §46.

[111] See Shaybānī, *Āthār*, 86–87; also Abū Yūsuf, no. 607; and Shaybānī, *Muwaṭṭaʾ*, 222–23.

[112] See Shāfiʿī, *Kitāb al-umm*, 5:68; Spectorsky, *Chapters*, 169, §88.

[113] For Shāfiʿī's discussion, see *Kitāb al-umm*, 5:68f. For Ibn Ḥanbal's opinion, see Spectorsky, *Chapters*, index, s.v. "Barwaʿ bt. Wāshiq." For Mālik, see Shaybānī, *Muwaṭṭaʾ*,

Marriage Portion and Divorce before Consummation

If a marriage portion has been specified and a marriage is dissolved before it has been consummated, there was disagreement on how to figure the half that the wife retains (in accordance with the Qurʾān [2:237]). If she has already received her full marriage portion, Shaybānī reports that Abū Ḥanīfa said she returns to her husband half of it. Ibn Ḥanbal too says she returns to her husband exactly half of what he originally gave her. So does Shāfiʿī, who says that the wife absorbs any increase in the value of the original marriage portion, and the husband is owed only half of what he originally gave her. Mālik, however, says the couple are associated together in any increase (or decrease) in the original amount and that this must be taken into account when it is divided.[114]

If a couple have been alone together, or, as a number of early texts put it, "whenever a door has been locked or a curtain drawn," most jurists assume that they have had intercourse, and the wife is owed her full marriage portion. This is the case unless they are fasting in Ramaḍān, or one or both of them are in a state of *iḥrām* for the Pilgrimage, or the wife is menstruating.[115] However, Shaybānī thinks that if a couple have been alone together, it must always be assumed they have had intercourse. Thus, in a case where a man marries and then divorces a woman claiming that he did not have intercourse with her, Shaybānī, assumes that they have had intercourse (and hence the wife is owed a marriage portion).[116]

222–23; and Saḥnūn, *Mudawwana*, 2:238. For some early traditions about Barwaʿ bt. Wāshiq and the death of her husband before her marriage was consummated, as well as traditions reflecting Ibn ʿUmar's decision, see ʿAbd al-Razzāq, *Muṣannaf*, 6:292–95, nos. 10889–901. For traditions about Barwaʿ in the Six Books, see Wensinck, *Concordance*, 8, s.v. "Barwaʿ bt. Wāshiq."

[114] See Shaybānī, *al-Jāmiʿ al-ṣaghīr*, 146–49, Spectorsky, *Chapters*, 65–66, §41 and §42; Shāfiʿī, *Kitāb al-umm*, 5:62–63; Saḥnūn, *Mudawwana*, 2:226–27.

[115] See Mālik, *Muwaṭṭaʾ*, 3:133–34: Ibn al-Musayyab used to say that if husband and wife are alone together in the husband's house and disagree about whether intercourse has taken place, the wife is believed, but if they have been alone in the wife's house, the husband is believed. But for the view commonly attributed to Mālik, and virtually all other jurists, see Saḥnūn, *Mudawwana*, 2:320–23; and Spectorsky, *Chapters*, 66, §§43–45.

[116] Thus this particular husband cannot marry his former wife's sister before her ʿ*idda* has ended (in accordance with the Qurʾānic rule that a man cannot be married to two sisters at the same time). Shaybānī, *Al-Jāmiʿ al-ṣaghīr*, 144.

Conditions in a Marriage Contract

1. Regarding a woman whose husband married her and agreed to the condition that he not take her out of her house, Shaʿbī did not consider that [condition] valid. He said: "Her husband is her house."[117]
2. Manṣūr b. Ibrāhīm said: "Every condition in a marriage contract is invalid, [such as] a condition that he (i.e., the husband) not marry another wife, or take a concubine and such like, unless he actually says: 'If I do such and such, then she is divorced.' If he does say this, then the condition [he agreed to] is binding."[118]
3. The Prophet said: "The best of conditions that you fulfill are those by means of which you make women's private parts lawful for you."[119]

The first tradition quoted above expresses the view that a wife owes her husband obedience, and if he wishes to take her out of her house, it is his right to do so. The second says that if a husband agrees to a condition without at the same time building in the penalty of divorce for nonfulfillment, it is not valid. The third, on the authority of the Prophet, supports the notion that any lawful condition can be part of a marriage contract.

Fiqh texts reflect these traditions in discussions of whether conditions a wife wishes to include in a marriage contract are valid.[120] In the *Muwaṭṭa*ʾ, Mālik relates that Saʿīd b. al-Musayyab said that if a woman stipulates in her marriage contract that her husband not take her to another town, he can in fact take her to another town if he wishes to. Here, Ibn al-Musayyab echoes the first tradition above. Mālik himself echoes the second tradition and says that if a man undertakes in his marriage contract not to take a second wife or a concubine, the undertaking has no effect unless there are consequences if he does not fulfill it.[121] Shāfiʿī's opinion agrees with the first tradition. He explains that conditions in a marriage contract that contravene things allowed by God in the Qurʾān (such as marrying a second wife or taking a concubine) are not valid. To emphasize his point, he quotes two sayings of the Prophet. The first is the same as the third tradition above: "The best

---

[117] ʿAbd al-Razzāq, *Muṣannaf*, 6:226, no. 10603.

[118] Ibid., 6:225, no. 10600.

[119] Ibn Abī Shayba, *Muṣannaf*, 3:326, no. 3.

[120] As a general rule, even if a condition is part of a marriage contract, like the bride's marriage portion, it is not an essential element of the contract. See *EI*, s.v. "Sharṭ."

[121] The consequences suggested are that nonfulfillment result in divorce or in the necessity of manumitting a slave. Mālik, *Muwaṭṭa*ʾ, 3, 136–37.

conditions that you fulfill are those which make women's private parts lawful to you." The second is: "Muslims are bound by their stipulations, except for those that make lawful what is unlawful and make unlawful what is lawful."[122] Shaybānī accepts conditions as part of a marriage contract, but only if they are lawful. If not, the marriage contract itself is valid, but the condition is not.[123] Ibn Ḥanbal too accepts any condition that is not in itself unlawful. Ibn Ḥanbal uses the same quotation from the Prophet that Shāfiʿī does ("The best conditions that you fulfill are those which make women's private parts lawful to you"), but understands it to mean that any condition that becomes part of a contract and is not in and of itself unlawful is valid. So, for example, when asked whether a woman can insert in her marriage contract the stipulation that her husband not take another wife, or not take a concubine, or not take her out of her house, he replies, "These conditions [if she stipulates them] are all lawful for her, and if he marries [another wife] or takes a concubine, she is given the option of choosing to remain married to her husband if she wishes, or of separating from him if she wishes."[124]

Invalid Marriage Due to Disability or Illness

1. Jābir b. Zayd said: "Four things are not lawful in sale and marriage: leprosy, insanity, elephantiasis and vaginal occlusion."[125]
2. Makḥūl and Zuhrī both said that when a man marries a woman, has intercourse with her, and then finds that she is insane, has leprosy, elephantiasis, or is an imbecile, she can be sent back (*turaddu*), but she is owed her full marriage portion, both immediate and deferred, by means of which her private parts were considered legal. [Payment of] her marriage portion is due from the one who deceived the husband.[126]

---

[122] See Shāfiʿī, *Kitāb al-umm*, 5:73–74.

[123] See Shaybānī, *al-Jāmiʿ al-ṣaghīr*, 147; Shaybānī, *Kitāb al-ḥujja*, 209–14.

[124] Spectorsky, *Chapters*, 183–84, §127.

[125] Ibn Abī Shayba, *Muṣannaf*, 3:310, *bāb* 54, no. 3. *Qarn* is the word I have translated as "vaginal occlusion." According to Rispler-Chaim, *Disability*, it refers to "a protruding tissue or bone that blocks the vagina" (53). "*Ratq*," which I have also translated as "vaginal occlusion," may refer to several possible conditions in which "the meatus of the vagina is sealed by a tissue which prevents penetration, or the absence of an aperture except the *mabal* (*meatus urinarius*, urinary tract); or the *farj* (vagina) being so drawn together that the *dhakar* (penis) can hardly pass or cannot pass at all" (53).

[126] Ibn Abī Shayba, 3:311, no. 9.

3. Zuhrī said: "If a man who has a defect such as insanity, elephantiasis or leprosy marries a woman who was unaware of his condition, she is given the option of separating from him."[127]

Each of the conditions mentioned in these traditions is considered a physical flaw (*ʿayb*) that affects a marriage contract.[128] Elephantiasis,[129] leprosy, and insanity are the three most often mentioned; then, in women, any condition that causes vaginal occlusion preventing sexual intercourse, and in men, sexual dysfunction that makes intercourse and potential procreation impossible. Most legal texts do not refer to all possible physical flaws. The first tradition compares marrying a woman with buying a female slave. Both marriage and sale are invalid if the woman in question has any of these flaws.[130] However, the second tradition makes the point that if a couple have had intercourse, and the husband then realizes the wife has a particular physical flaw, she must receive her full marriage portion. In this case, the woman's guardian, who duped the husband, is responsible for compensating him for the wife's marriage portion. The next tradition deals with flaws the husband may have. Even if the husband was unaware of his problem when the marriage contract was concluded (and presumably married in good faith), the wife has the option of dissolving the marriage.

In his *Āthār*, Shaybānī reports that Abū Ḥanīfa said that if either spouse is found to have a physical flaw, the other does not have the right to opt out of the marriage. Abū Ḥanīfa's view is contrary to any of the traditions above. Shaybānī himself says that he agrees with Abū Ḥanīfa if the wife has a flaw, because her husband can stay with her or divorce her at any time. Further, Shaybānī says, if the husband has a flaw that the wife can tolerate, the couple can remain married. However, if the husband is impotent or a eunuch, the wife does have the option of initiating a divorce from him. In the case of an impotent husband, Shaybānī points out that ʿUmar b. al-Khaṭṭāb gave the wife a time limit of one year. If the couple had not had intercourse in that time, he allowed her to opt out of the marriage. Shaybānī concludes by saying

---

[127] Ibid., no. 1.

[128] See Rispler-Chaim, *Disability in Islamic Law*, Chapter 3, "People with disabilities and marriage."

[129] See *EI*, s.v. "Djudhām."

[130] For invalid contracts, see *EI*, s.vv. "Faskh"; "Fāsid wa-bāṭil."

that a time limit should be set in all instances of unbearable flaws, those even more unbearable than castration or impotence, at the end of which the wife is given the option of initiating a divorce from her husband.[131]

In the *Muwaṭṭaʾ*, Mālik reports and agrees with a version of the second tradition, but adds that the husband has recourse against the wife's *walī* only if he is a relative who is close enough to her to have been aware of any physical flaws she had. Further, Mālik adds that she returns all but the minimum marriage portion by means of which intercourse with her became lawful.[132]

Shāfiʿī says that if a woman has a vaginal condition that makes intercourse impossible, the husband can declare the marriage invalid. He can also declare it invalid if she is insane or has leprosy. If the bride's guardians deny she has leprosy, her husband can always divorce her. If he has intercourse with her and then discovers leprosy, she receives her marriage portion, but he still has recourse against her *walī*. However, if he finds out she had leprosy before intercourse, he can opt out of the marriage and owes her nothing, no marriage portion—not even half of it—and no *mutʿa* payment.[133]

Ibn Ḥanbal agrees with the tradition Mālik mentioned (that ʿUmar said a man who had intercourse with a wife who had leprosy, elephantiasis, or was insane had recourse against her *walī*), but he also agrees with Shāfiʿī's view that the marriage can be invalidated before intercourse.[134]

Mutʿa *Marriage*

1. ʿAṭāʾ b. Abī Rabāḥ said: "I heard Ibn ʿAbbās say, "May God have mercy on ʿUmar: *mutʿa* was a concession from God and a mercy to Muḥammad's community (*umma*). If ʿUmar had not forbidden it, only a scoundrel would need to commit fornication.' "[135]
2. Al-Ḥasan al-Baṣrī said: "*Mutʿa* used to last for three days until God and His Prophet forbade it."[136]

[131] Shaybānī, *Āthār*, 85.
[132] Mālik, *Muwaṭṭaʾ*, 3:130. The assumption here is that her marriage portion was larger than her fair marriage portion would have required.
[133] Shāfiʿī, *Kitāb al-umm*, 5:84.
[134] Spectorsky, *Chapters*, 152, §24.
[135] ʿAbd al-Razzāq, *Muṣannaf*, 7:496–7, no. 14021.
[136] Ibid., 7:505, no. 14043.

3. Al-Zuhrī on the authority of al-Rabīʿ b. Ṣabra al-Juhanī on the authority of his father that on the day of the conquest of Mecca, the Prophet forbade *mutʿat al-nisāʾ*.[137]
4. Ibn Masʿūd said: "Divorce, *ʿidda* and inheritance abrogated it."[138]

Mutʿa marriage, or "marriage of enjoyment," is forbidden by most Muslims, but not by Imāmī Shīʿīs.[139] In a *mutʿa* marriage, a man and a woman (most often a *thayyib*) agree to marry for a specified period of time. The wife receives a marriage portion agreed upon by the couple, but she does not receive maintenance (*nafaqa*) from her husband, and the couple do not inherit from each other unless they include either or both of these provisions in their nuptial negotiations. The contract need not be witnessed, although some traditions on the authority of the Shīʿī imāms consider witnesses desirable. There is much discussion and no general agreement in Shīʿī sources about whether an adult woman in such an arrangement needs a *walī* to give her in marriage. At the end of the specified period, husband and wife separate without formal divorce proceedings and, it is generally agreed, without witnesses. Before she can remarry, the wife waits an *ʿidda* of two menstrual periods rather than the three normal in a permanent marriage contract, and if she does not menstruate, of one and one half months.[140]

Although it may have been widely practiced in the earliest period of Islam, opposition to *mutʿa* marriage prevailed among Sunnīs and the non-Imāmī Shīʿī groups.[141] In the received text of the Qurʾān, 4:24 reads: *And those of whom ye seek content (by marrying them), give unto them their portions as a duty*. But the texts attributed to Ubayy b. Kaʿb, Ibn ʿAbbas, and Ibn Masʿūd read before *give unto them their portions as a duty*, the words *for a definite period*.[142] From the Imāmī

[137] Ibn Abī Shayba, *Muṣannaf*, 3:389, no. 2. On 390 in no. 4, the Prophet forbade *mutʿa* after the Battle of Awṭās, which took place shortly after that of Ḥunayn in 8/630. See Guillaume, *The Life of Muhammad*, 575. Other traditions say the Prophet forbade *mutʿa* marriage when Khaybar was attacked, or conquered. For one of these, see Shaybānī, *Āthār*, no. 433. See *EI*, s.v. "Khaybar" for the Muslim conquest of that oasis in 6/628.

[138] ʿAbd al-Razzāq, *Muṣannaf*, 7:506, no. 14044.

[139] See *EQ*, s.v. "Temporary Marriage"; *EI*, s.v. "Mutʿa."

[140] The shortened *ʿidda* suggests to those against *mutʿa* marriages that the wife in such cases is little more than a slave concubine. See I. K. A. Howard, "*Mutʿa* Marriage reconsidered in the Context of the Formal Procedures for Islamic Marriage."

[141] See *EI*, s.v. "Mutʿa"; and *EQ*, s.vv. "Marriage and divorce"; "Temporary Marriage."

[142] For texts of the Qurʾān attributed to these three Companions, see Arthur Jeffery, *Materials for the History of the Text of the Qurʾān*, 36, 126, 197. For a history of the evolution of the text of the Qurʾān, see *EQ*, s.v. "Codices of the Qurʾān."

point of view, the words *for a definite period* are an integral part of the understanding of 4:24, although Imāmī scholars have different views on whether these actual words are, at the same time, an integral part of the received text.[143]

The four traditions above refer to both Imāmī and Sunni attitudes. In the first, ʿUmar is associated with forbidding *mutʿa* marriage. The Imāmī view is that he forbade something the Prophet had allowed. The second and third traditions express the Sunni view that although *mutʿa* was allowed during the lifetime of the Prophet, at a certain point it was forbidden. The second refers generally to the fact that the Qurʾān, and thus the Prophet forbade it. The third offers a possible time at which it was forbidden; on the day Mecca was conquered (8/630). The fourth tradition alludes to the verses of the Qurʾān that Sunnis believe abrogate *mutʿa* marriage. In the Sunni view, divorce, *ʿidda,* and inheritance are three characteristics of a legal marriage. A legal marriage can be ended by a divorce, which is not the case in a *mutʿa* marriage. Thus in a legal Sunni marriage, if one of the spouses dies, the other inherits, and an appropriate *ʿidda* is either three months for a divorcée or four months and ten days for a widow, unlike that of a woman in a *mutʿa* marriage.[144]

Early Sunni jurists repeat, with some variation, the material found in these five traditions. In his *Āthār*, for example, Abū Yūsuf reports that Ibn Masʿūd said that they (i.e., the Companions) used to complain of celibacy, so the Prophet allowed *mutʿa* marriage for three nights only. Then, however, the verse about marriage abrogated it, along with [the length of time of] the *ʿidda* and [the rules for] inheritance. He also reports that the Prophet forbade it on the day Mecca was conquered.[145] In Shaybānī's *Āthār*, one tradition says that it was forbidden on the day Mecca was conquered, the other that it was forbidden on the day

[143] For a chronological survey and an extremely clear discussion of the development of Imāmī thinking about 4:24, see Robert Gleave, "Shiʿite Exegesis and the Interpretation of Qurʾān 4:24."

[144] See Gribetz, *Strange Bedfellows*, Chapter 1, 6–21 for a discussion of *mutʿat al-nisāʾ* in Sunni *ḥadīth* and in particular 17–18 for the verses of the Qurʾān that refer to divorce, *ʿidda*, and inheritance and therefore, in the Sunni view, abrogate *mutʿa*. For example, 65:1 and 33:49 speak of ending marriage by means of divorce; 2:228 mentions a divorcée's *ʿidda*; 4:12, the amount inherited by a husband when his wife dies. Further, 23:5–6 speak of lawful intercourse, which can take place only with a wife or a slave concubine, and the woman in a *mutʿa* marriage is neither.

[145] Abū Yūsuf, *Āthār*, See nos. 698–701.

Khaybar was attacked. Until that time, according to Ibn ʿUmar, "We were not adulterers"![146] In the *Muwaṭṭaʾ*, Mālik cites a tradition that the Prophet forbade *mutʿa* marriage on the day Khaybar was attacked. He also cites another, which takes for granted the fact that *mutʿa* marriage had been forbidden before the Prophet died: a woman comes to ʿUmar b. al-Khaṭṭāb and informs him about a particular temporary marriage, and he says: "This is a *mutʿa* marriage! Had I been there, I would have had the couple stoned."[147]

Shāfiʿī has a full treatment of the topic. He starts with two traditions that say that the Prophet forbade *mutʿa* marriage on the day of Khaybar; he then goes on to combine consideration of *mutʿa* marriage with consideration of *taḥlīl*, the practice whereby a man marries a woman who has been triply divorced from one husband for the sole purpose of subsequently divorcing her so that she can remarry the first husband.[148] Both *mutʿa* and *taḥlīl* marriage contracts are concluded for a limited amount of time, Shāfiʿī says, and therefore both are illegal. In the case of a *mutʿa* marriage, it is not relevant whether the time frame is long or short: a marriage contract concluded for anything less than the lifetime of the partners is not permissible. If, however, either spouse, or the woman's *walī*, secretly intend a marriage to be temporary, the contract is not invalidated, because, Shāfiʿī says, intention is an interior matter. A person can intend one thing and actually do another, or vice versa; the action is the decisive thing, not the intention.[149] Ibn Ḥanbal agrees with Shāfiʿī that nothing can be done about intentions and says only that a *mutʿa* marriage is reprehensible.[150]

Marriage with Slaves

1. On the question of whether a man already married to a slave could marry in addition a free woman, ʿAṭāʾ said: "Good."[151]

---

[146] Ibid., nos. 698–700; Shaybānī, *Āthār*, 93, nos. 432–35.

[147] Mālik, *Muwaṭṭaʾ*, 3:152–54. In the *Muwaṭṭaʾ*, as well as in Abū Yūsuf's and Shaybānī's *Āthār*, the traditions that forbid *mutʿa* on the day of Khaybar, at the same time forbid eating the flesh of domesticated donkeys.

[148] After a husband has repudiated his wife a third or final time, the couple cannot remarry unless the wife has first married an intervening husband.

[149] Shāfiʿī, *Kitāb al-umm*, 5:79–80.

[150] See Spectorsky, *Chapters*, 115, §81, where ʿAbd Allāh b. Aḥmad b. Ḥanbal says: "I asked my father about a man who marries a woman while thinking to himself that he will divorce her. He said, 'I find that reprehensible. It is a *mutʿa* marriage.'"

[151] Ibn Abī Shayba, *Muṣannaf*, 3:288, no. 8.

2. Ibn ʿAbbās said: "Marriage with a free woman in addition to a slave [requires that a man] divorce the slave.[152]
3. On the question of a man already married to a free wife who marries in addition a slave wife, Ḥasan al-Baṣrī said: "He and the slave wife should not be separated."[153]
4. Ibn al-Musayyab said: "A man is permitted to marry a free woman in addition to a slave, but he cannot marry a slave in addition to a free woman.[154]

As we saw in Chapter 1, 4:3 and 4:25 permit a man who cannot afford to marry free wives to marry slaves. *Fiqh* texts all agree that he cannot marry his own slaves. If he wishes to marry one of his own slaves, he must first manumit her.[155] Otherwise, the disagreements among the jurists about whether a man can be married to a slave and a free wife at the same time is reflected in the traditions above. The first two are about whether a man can marry a free wife in addition to a slave. The first says that he can, the second that he cannot. The third and fourth reverse the question: can he marry a slave wife in addition to a free one? Again the answers are that he can and that he cannot. All our texts discuss one or several of these combinations. In the *Muwaṭṭa*ʾ, Mālik says that Ibn ʿUmar and Ibn ʿAbbās were asked whether a man married to a free wife could in addition marry a slave, and they found that reprehensible. To show his agreement with this view, Mālik quotes some of 4:25: *And whose is not able to afford to marry free, believing women, let them marry from the believing maids whom your right hands possess,* and then: *This is for him among you who fears to commit sin.*" Sin, he says, means fornication.[156] Presumably a man who already has a wife need not fear that he will commit fornication.

Shāfiʿī also says that a free man can marry a slave only if he cannot afford the marriage portion of a free woman and fears he will commit fornication if he remains unmarried. Both factors must be present. If he fears fornication and can afford to marry a free woman, he must marry a free woman; if he does not fear fornication and cannot afford to marry a free woman, he need not marry at all. However, Shāfiʿī says, if a man

[152] Ibid., 3:289, *bāb* 22, no. 2.
[153] Ibid., 3:288, no. 10.
[154] Ibid., no. 7.
[155] Neither a man nor a woman can own a spouse. If a free person marries a slave whom he or she owns, the marriage is invalid. If the slave is subsequently freed, then the couple can marry.
[156] Mālik, *Muwaṭṭa*ʾ, 3:146.

married to a slave wishes in addition to marry a free woman, he need not divorce the slave just because his financial situation has improved. Once it has, he cannot marry a second slave wife.[157] Shaybānī agrees with Shāfiʿī and reports on the authority of ʿAlī and others that a man cannot marry a slave in addition to a free woman, but he can marry a free woman in addition to a slave.[158] Ibn Ḥanbal disagrees and, agreeing with the second tradition above, does not allow the combination in any order. He says that if a man who has a slave wife wishes to marry a free woman, he must first divorce the slave.[159]

Discussion

In Chapter 1, I commented on the picture the Qurʾān painted of a pious Muslim woman. In particular, she is a member of a patriarchal household who is both cared for and controlled by a male guardian, ideally her father, until she reaches puberty and then by her husband. In this chapter, texts from the formative period add to the picture. The woman whose marriage contract reflects the concerns described above is both an Arab and a Muslim. She is not a recent convert to Islam, or lowly, or a slave. She is, as well, a woman whose family is proud of its *nasab*. She is in comfortable financial circumstances or at least comfortable enough to be contrasted with a woman who is very poor. She has a number of male relatives whose job it is to see to it that her status, and by extension their own, is maintained. She lives in a city or a town where she has neighbors who are expected to know something of her and her family and where she and her relatives have access to a *qāḍī* who can hear cases brought before him.

All jurists agree on the broad outlines of such a woman's marriage contract, but the foregoing description of their views shows *ikhtilāf* on a number of significant points. For example, on the extent of the authority of a woman's *walī*, Abū Ḥanīfa's view was that it is permissible for a woman to conclude her own marriage contract. Her ability to do this is circumscribed but real. As noted above, Shaybānī discusses the

[157] Shāfiʿī, *Kitāb al-umm*, 5:10.

[158] Shaybānī, *Kitāb al-ḥujja*, 3:255. Further, a free man can be married to as many as four female slaves at the same time. See Abū Yūsuf, *Āthār*, no. 599; and Shaybānī, *Āthār*, no. 392.

[159] See Spectorsky, *Chapters*, 62, §12, and 153, §27. Ibn Ḥanbal associates this opinion with Ibn ʿAbbās. See 62, note 2.

real aspect in his *Kitāb al-ḥujja*. If we look more closely at his discussion, we see that he points out that a woman can conclude marriage contracts for her male and female slaves. The Medinese, he continues, say she cannot do this, but must delegate a man to act on her behalf, to which he responds that if she has the authority to delegate a man to act as her *walī*, she can act as one herself. He adds that a woman has a stake (*naṣīb*) in her own marriage and should in any case be consulted about it. In addition to relating the story of Khansāʾ bt. Khudhām, he relates another about ʿĀʾisha. While her brother ʿAbd al-Raḥmān was out of town, ʿĀʾisha gave his daughter Ḥafṣa in marriage. When ʿAbd al-Raḥmān returned, he complained that his authority over his own daughter had been curtailed and refused to accept the marriage. ʿĀʾisha appealed to Ḥafṣa's husband, who said the validity of the marriage was up to ʿAbd al-Raḥmān. In the end, ʿAbd al-Raḥmān said he would not invalidate something ʿĀʾisha had decreed, so the marriage stood. Shaybānī points to ʿĀʾisha's belief (shared by Abū Ḥanīfa) that her independent action was valid.[160] But a woman's independent agency is circumscribed by Abū Ḥanīfa's insistence on the importance of concluding a marriage contract of equals. Mālik, Shāfiʿī, and Ibn Ḥanbal are adamant that a woman can never conclude a valid marriage contract, her own or anyone else's. Except for the general point that the Prophet agreed with Khansāʾ bt. Khudhām that her father could not give her in marriage without her permission, we cannot know exactly what aspect of her situation any jurist had in mind when he referred to her right to marry whomever she wished.

On the question of *kafāʾa*, Mālik differed from the Ḥanafīs, Shāfiʿī, and Ibn Ḥanbal and held firmly to the notion that all Muslims are each other's equals, while the other jurists included tribal and financial considerations in their assessment of whether the groom measured up to the bride. Mālik is also reported to have thought that if a woman wishes to marry a pious man poorer than herself, she should appeal to the *qāḍī* if her father is unwilling to conclude a marriage contract for her. However, at least in one case of extreme financial discrepancy between potential spouses, Mālik apparently did not approve of the marriage: in

[160] See Shaybānī, *Kitāb al-ḥujja*, 3:110–14. See also Stern, *Marriage in Early Islam*, 32–35 for a discussion of examples of marriages among the Companions taken from Ibn Ḥanbal's *Musnad* and Ibn Saʿd's *ṭabaqāt*, which do not provide a consistent picture of why some women seemed to have control over their own marriages, and others did not.

the *Mudawwana* his opinion is reported about a mother who still had custody of her young daughter and was divorced from the girl's father. She went to Mālik and informed him that her daughter was wealthy and desirable, particularly since she (i.e., the mother) had received a large marriage portion that the girl would inherit upon her death. The girl's father wished to give her in marriage to a paternal cousin who was destitute. "Do you think," the woman asked Mālik, "that I have the right to speak up?" Mālik replied: "Yes, I think that in this matter you have the right to make your opinion heard." Here, enormous disparity in wealth is clearly detrimental to the potential bride's well-being. "The right to have her opinion heard" means Mālik thinks she has every reason to bring the situation to the attention of the *qāḍī*.[161]

Mālik also differed from other jurists on whether a marriage contract needs to be witnessed to be valid. Although all agreed that a marriage should not be a secret, the question was how to make it public. Mālik insisted on communal knowledge and was willing to forego formal witnessing. Shaybānī and Shāfiʿī insisted on formal witnessing and were less concerned about communal knowledge. Ibn Ḥanbal seemed to prefer both or to assume that the two go together. Although only Shaybānī and Shāfiʿī referred directly to secrecy, both witnesses and communal knowledge of a marriage are designed to guard against it.

In a brief note on secret marriage, Goldziher pointed out that by the end of the first century A.H. Muslim jurists had not yet arrived at a consensus on the most significant components of a publicly established marriage.[162] This lack of consensus lasted into the second and third centuries as well. One of the reasons may be a lack of consensus on what exactly needed to be witnessed or publicized. In pre-Islamic Arabia, Goldziher noted, a man would wish to celebrate his marriage with a tribal equal and hide one with a lowly woman. In an Islamic context the point is to give a woman in marriage to an equal. Then there is also the question of proving that a couple are respectable. In a

[161] Saḥnūn, *Mudawwana*, 2:155. In this case, since the mother still has custody of her daughter, she is prepubescent. See *EI*, s.v. "Ḥaḍāna," for child custody arrangements. This particular set of circumstances is noted several centuries later in the *Mukhtaṣar* of Khalīl b. Isḥāq (d. 776/1374): "A mother has the right to speak [and apply to the court to interfere] in the case of a father's marrying his wealthy and sought-after daughter to a pauper." Khalil, *Mukhtaṣar*, 30. The translators refer back to the *Mudawwana* in a note (no. 83, n. 1) and add: "This is one of the rare instances in Muslim Law in which a mother may interfere in the disposal of her own children."

[162] Goldziher, "Über Geheimehen bei den Arabern," 32–34.

tradition in ʿAbd al-Razzāq's *Muṣannaf*, the Successor Ḥammād is asked about a man and a woman found together. The man says: "My wife!" The woman says: "My husband!" Asked about witnesses, they say: "They died," or "They are absent." The tradition ends with: "if they confess, they receive the *ḥadd* punishment for unlawful intercourse."[163] Mālik's point that widespread knowledge of a marriage provides adequate witnessing of it would prevent the kind of confrontation this tradition mentions and so would Ibn Ḥanbal's insistence on a combination of witnesses and publicity.

On the amounts of a woman's marriage portion, there was no agreement. Any amount a jurist mentioned depended on which traditions he followed, or on whether he chose to establish a minimum or maximum amount. The variety in numbers (e.g., 10, 400, 480, 500 dirhams), or Mālik's view that the minimum marriage portion should be three dirhams, or one quarter of a dinar—the minimum compensation for stolen goods—suggest many conflicting ideas about an appropriate marriage portion.[164] All agreed that a fair marriage portion is based on a woman's status and that when a marriage portion is due and an amount has not been fixed, she receives her fair marriage portion, but that does not provide clues about amounts.[165]

The question of whether a marriage portion can consist of some verses of the Qurʾān that a potential groom knows by heart is posed in a tradition in which the would-be groom cannot even find an iron ring to offer as a marriage portion. Although the Prophet marries him for some verses of the Qurʾān, no jurist expresses approval. Shaybānī insists that the marriage portion must have a real monetary value, and although Mālik relates a version of this tradition, he does not endorse it. Shāfiʿī supports a marriage portion of verses of the Qurʾān if the man is to teach them to his wife, but not if he merely knows them. Ibn Ḥanbal finds it reprehensible for a man to marry a woman on the basis

[163] ʿAbd al-Razzāq, *Muṣannaf*, 6:203, no. 10509.

[164] See Stern, *Marriage in Early Islam*, 46–56 for her discussion of the marriage portions of the wives and daughters of the Companions. She notes that there is no reliable information on what they were. See Schacht, *Introduction*, 38–39; and *Origins*, 107–8, for brief discussions of early views on marriage portions. Schacht points out that the differing amounts were based either on favoring one tradition over another or on different rough and ready analogies.

[165] Real amounts can be found in surviving marriage contracts rather than in *fiqh* texts. For a discussion of real marriage contracts, see Rapoport, "Matrimonial Gifts in Early Islamic Egypt."

of merely knowing some verses and says that teaching them is not part of the *ḥadīth* on this matter. Therefore a marriage portion cannot consist of verses of the Qurʾān.

In their treatment of questions that arose about *raḍāʿ*, all agreed that only nursing by an infant establishes a foster relationship. They disagreed on whether a certain number of suckling sessions were required. Shaybānī and Mālik said they were not; Shāfiʿī and Ibn Ḥanbal said they were. Among a number of other traditions, the crux of this disagreement was whether they accepted the tradition on the authority of ʿĀʾisha (that when the Prophet died, five suckling sessions were being recited as part of the Qurʾān), quoted both in Mālik's *Muwaṭṭaʾ* and also in *Kitāb al-umm*.

Above, we noted that Mālik quoted this tradition and then commented: "This is not the practice." However, Shāfiʿī quotes this tradition and uses it to insist that a minimum of five acts of suckling are needed to establish a foster relationship.[166] To add support to ʿĀʾisha's statement that during the Prophet's lifetime five suckling sessions established a foster relationship, Shāfiʿī points to the fact that the Prophet instructed Sahla to nurse Sālim five times. At the same time, he says that the story of Sahla nursing Sālim was particular to that situation.[167] Ibn Ḥanbal agrees with Shāfiʿī that fewer than five suckling sessions do not establish a foster relationship and rejects the traditions he knows of that support fewer than five acts of suckling.

These contrasts show that sometimes *ikhtilāf* is based on different emphases of a particular Qurʾān verse, sometimes on a choice of different traditions, sometimes on regional differences, and sometimes on a combination of these. Often it is not possible to tell what lies behind any particular choice. For his view of *kafāʾa*, for example, Mālik chose to emphasize 49:13; other jurists did not. For his choice of thirty rather than twenty-four months as the period of infant nursing, Abū Ḥanīfa chose to emphasize 46:15; other jurists did not. Shāfiʿī and Ibn Ḥanbal accepted the tradition on ʿĀʾisha's authority that when the Prophet

---

[166] See Burton, "The Interpretation of Q 4:23 and the Muslim Theories of *Naskh*," for his discussion of this *ḥadīth*, and his explanation that it represents one of the two instances of a form of *naskh* (abrogation) in which the text of the Qurʾānic ruling has been removed, but the ruling itself remains. The other instance of this form of *naskh* is the penalty of stoning for adultery (see below, Chapter 5).

[167] Shāfiʿī points to the tradition (which we quoted earlier from the *Muwaṭṭaʾ*) of the Prophet's wives saying this was a *rukhṣa* (dispensation) for Sahla. See *Kitāb al-umm*, 5:28.

died, five separate acts of suckling were being recited as part of the Qurʾān. Mālik and Shaybānī did not agree. Different traditions led to variety in marriage portion amounts.

As we consider these various solutions to different problems, it is important to remember the task the jurists set themselves: "[i]t is a presupposition of Muslim juristic thought that the law of God has not been given to human beings in the form of a ready-made code. Law is not sent down from heaven as a finished product. Rather it is something that human jurists must elaborate on the basis of textual sources. Preeminent among these are the Qurʾān and the Sunna of the Prophet. ..."[168] We said above that of the five qualifications, jurists were most concerned with the middle three—recommended, indifferent, and disliked or reprehensible. We saw that all jurists thought that a father should consult his *bikr* daughter before giving her in marriage. Even if he is not required to, the Prophet's *sunna* recommends that he do so. Indeed, it is reprehensible for him not to. It is preferable that a marriage be witnessed and publicized, but a secret marriage is valid, even though reprehensible. To illustrate the kind of admonitory vigilance suggested by these three qualifications and the discussions and decisions of early legal specialists, we can look more closely at Shāfiʿī's discussion of a father's authority over a daughter's marriage. Shāfiʿī starts with a hypothetical question: "If someone were to say (*in qāla qāʾilun*), 'What shows that he (i.e., a *bikr*'s father) is charged with consulting her, since she has no authority in conjunction with her father who is being charged with consulting her?' The answer would be that God said to his Prophet, *Consult them in the conduct of all affairs*." This quotation is from 3:159, which falls in the middle of a group of verses about the Battle of Uḥud. During the battle there was some disarray among the Muslim fighters. A group of archers meant to be protecting a flank of the Muslim army withdrew, and the Meccans took advantage of a break in the Muslim lines. It was rumored that the Prophet had been killed, but then the army rallied. However, some of the Muslims, thinking that they had already won, broke ranks to rush to get a share of the booty. Eventually, the Meccans departed, and the Muslims returned to Medina. The many accounts of the battle provide differing detail, but there is general agreement that some of the Muslims deserted and disobeyed their orders at crucial moments and that it is these men who are referred to in 3:159, where the Prophet is

[168] Weiss, *The Spirit of Islamic Law*, 22.

counseled both to forgive and consult them.[169] Shāfiʿī explains: "God did not give them (the Muslims) any authority over the Prophet; rather, He made it incumbent upon them to obey him. But, through consultation, they would find themselves in agreement with him; and, consultation would become a *sunna* for those who did not have the authority over others that the Prophet did; and the rationale (*istidlāl*) is that there might come from one of those consulted a good which was previously concealed from the one who asks advice. …"[170]

[169] See *EI*, s.v. "Uḥud."

[170] Shāfiʿī, *Kitāb al-umm*, 5:18. For "rationale" as a translation of *istidlāl*, see Lowry, *The Legal-Theoretical Content of the* Risāla, 52–53, 100–101.

CHAPTER THREE

DIVORCE IN THE FORMATIVE PERIOD

> Muʿādh b. Jabal related that the Prophet said: "O Muʿādh, God has not created anything on the face of the earth dearer to Him than manumission, and He has not created anything on the face of the earth more loathsome to Him than divorce. Thus when a man says to a slave of his that he is free if God wills, his slave is free, and his saying 'if God wills' does not affect his statement; but when he says to his wife, 'You are divorced if God wills,' his saying 'if God wills' does affect his statement, and he is not divorced."[1]

Since God never wishes a man to divorce a wife and always wishes him to manumit a slave,[2] a man's inclusion of the words, "*in shāʾ Allāh*" in each of these statements produces two different results. This tradition also highlights two other points. One is that there is a tendency often (but not always) discernable in *fiqh* discussions devoted to divorce, to avoid divorce and instead keep a marriage intact. Two is that the tradition assumes a divorce is brought about by a statement of repudiation that a man makes to his wife. "You are divorced" (*anti ṭāliq*)[3] is the norm, and if a man says it to his wife, she immediately begins her post-divorce waiting period, her *ʿidda*, of three menstrual periods or three months if she is too old or too young to menstruate. If she is pregnant, her *ʿidda* ends with her delivery. Once a woman has completed her *ʿidda*, a couple would no longer inherit from each other, and if they wish to remarry, there must be a new marriage contract. Before a woman's *ʿidda* ends, her husband may return to her and resume their marriage, but he can do this only twice. If a husband does return to his wife during her *ʿidda*, he has "used up" one or two divorces in his marriage with that woman. If he divorces her a third time, the divorce is

---

[1] ʿAbd al-Razzāq, *Muṣannaf*, 6:390, no. 11331. For this oath, see *EI*, s.vv. "In Shāʾ Allāh" and "ḳasam."

[2] See *EQ*, s.v. "Slaves and Slavery"; *EI*, s.v. "ʿAbd" (2. The Ḳorʾān. The Religious Ethic).

[3] *Ṭāliq*, "divorced," is an adjective that refers only to women and therefore does not form a feminine with *tāʾ marbūta*. See Wright, *A grammar of the Arabic Language*, 1:187.

irrevocable, and then the ex-husband cannot remarry his wife unless she has first been married to another man and had sexual intercourse in that marriage. Insistence on sexual intercourse in the intervening marriage is to avoid *taḥlīl* ("making lawful"), which in this context refers to a token marriage to another man, followed by an immediate divorce so the original couple can remarry.[4] There is a difference between an irrevocable (or triple) divorce and a definite divorce. A definite divorce results if a husband does not return to his wife during her *ʿidda*, for example after a first or second statement of divorce. A couple who have been definitely divorced can remarry on the basis of a new contract without the wife marrying someone else in between.

Ṭalāq al-Sunna

1. Ṭāwūs said: "*Ṭalāq al-sunna* means that a man divorces his wife in a period of purity without having had intercourse with her. Then he leaves her until she has menstruated three times."[5]
2. On the authority of Sālim b. ʿAbd Allāh [b. ʿUmar]: Ibn ʿUmar divorced his wife when she was menstruating. ʿUmar mentioned this to the Prophet who said: "Order him to return to her, then let him divorce her in a period of purity, or when she is pregnant."[6]

One cannot speak of an ideal divorce the way one does of an ideal marriage, but *ṭalāq al-sunna*—a divorce in accordance with the *sunna*, as described in the first tradition above—turns out to be one in which it is as easy as possible to reckon a woman's *ʿidda*.[7] All jurists point to Ibn ʿUmar's divorce, described in the second tradition as the standard, and all agree that *ṭalāq al-sunna* refers to a man divorcing his wife after she has completed a menstrual period and before again having intercourse with her. Thus Abū Yūsuf says: "Abū Ḥanīfa related to us … that Ibn ʿUmar divorced his wife while she was menstruating, but he was rebuked for that so he returned to her and divorced her in a period of purity."[8]

---

[4] This would be a *ḥīla* (plural, *ḥiyal*), a stratagem, for circumventing a legal regulation. For a discussion of these, see Schacht, *Introduction*, 79–81 and *EI*, s.v. "Ḥiyal."

[5] Ibn Abī Shayba, *Muṣannaf*, 4:5, no. 2.

[6] Ibid., 4:4, no. 8.

[7] Her *ʿidda* should last for three menstrual periods or three intervals of purity between periods. This depends on the meaning of the word *qurūʾ* (sing. *qurʾ*). In some traditions it refers to menstrual periods, but in others to the interval between two periods.

[8] Abū Yūsuf, *Āthār*, no. 589.

There is also the possibility that, in accordance with the *sunna*, a man can divorce his wife triply. He can divorce her again at the start of her second and third periods of purity, and thus by the end of her *ʿidda* a woman is triply divorced. Shaybānī notes that he and Abū Ḥanīfa think this procedure is lawful.[9] Mālik is adamant that it is not Medinese practice: in the *Mudawwana*, when Ibn al-Qāsim is asked Mālik's opinion of it, he reports that Mālik said he did not know anyone "in our town" who approved of that or gave a *fatwā* to that effect. However, Mālik admits that if a man does divorce his wife triply during her *ʿidda*, once in each period of purity, that is, in fact, a valid triple divorce.[10] Shāfiʿī says that the Prophet did not mention a number in his ruling on Ibn ʿUmar's divorce, and therefore *ṭalāq al-sunna* is about *when* to divorce, not *how many* divorces a man can pronounce.[11] Ibn Ḥanbal, when asked the meaning of *ṭalāq al-sunna*, agrees with Shāfiʿī and says: "That a man divorce his wife during a period of purity without having had intercourse with her, as the Prophet ordered Ibn ʿUmar to, and the question of single, double, or triple divorce is not part of it (i.e., of the definition of *ṭalāq al-sunna*)."[12] Here both Shāfiʿī and Ibn Ḥanbal interpret the tradition from the Prophet to address the question of when *ṭalāq al-sunna* takes place, not how many divorces are involved, and they take no position one way or the other on the question of triple divorce over the course of one *ʿidda*.

The opposite of *ṭalāq al-sunna* is *ṭalāq al-bidʿa*, or a divorce in accordance with an innovation.[13] It refers to a triple divorce pronounced in one session. All jurists disapprove of it, but at the same time they think it is valid. Shaybānī reports a tradition in which a man comes to Ibn ʿAbbās and says he has divorced his wife triply. Ibn ʿAbbās scolds him and says he has both disobeyed his Lord and forbidden himself his wife, unless she first marries another man. This combination of disapproval and declaring it lawful, Shaybānī says, is Abū Ḥanīfa's doctrine, as well as that of all scholars; there is no disagreement about it.[14] Shaybānī is correct: Mālik, Shāfiʿī, and Ibn Ḥanbal all note that triple divorce is not forbidden, but they do not approve of it.[15]

---

9 Shaybānī, *Āthār*, 99, nos. 462 and 463. See also *al-Jāmiʿ al-ṣaghīr*, 156.
10 Saḥnūn, *Mudawwana*, 2:419–20.
11 Shāfiʿī, *Kitāb al-umm*, 5:180.
12 Spectorsky, *Chapters*, 162, §63.
13 For a discussion of innovation, see *EI*, s.v. "Bidʿa."
14 Shaybānī, *Āthār*, 105, no. 486.
15 See Mālik, *Muwaṭṭaʾ*, 3:166–67; Shāfiʿī, *Kitāb al-umm*, 5:180; and Spectorsky, *Chapters*, 69, §67.

In the *Muwaṭṭa'*, Mālik reports a parallel story of a man who told Ibn ʿAbbās that he had divorced his wife one hundred times. Ibn ʿAbbās responded that the man had divorced his wife triply and mocked the *āyas* of the Qurʾān with the other ninety-seven.[16]

Divorce before Intercourse

1. Ṭāwūs and ʿAṭāʾ both said: "If a man divorces his wife triply before having intercourse with her, it counts as a single divorce."[17]
2. Shaʿbī said: "If, before he has had intercourse with her, her husband says to her, '*Anti ṭāliq, anti ṭāliq, anti ṭāliq*,' then she has become forbidden to him (*ḥarumat*)."[18]

If a man divorces his wife before the couple have had intercourse, she does not wait an *ʿidda* during which he can return to her, but she immediately becomes a "stranger" (*ajnabiyya*) to him. A man and a woman are described as "strangers" when they are not related to each other by marriage, consanguinity, or foster relationship. In this case, if he has divorced her singly and wishes to remarry her, a new contract and a new marriage portion must be negotiated. Jurists disagreed about what happened if he divorced her triply, depending on the exact wording of his divorce statement.

The first tradition above says that a single statement such as "You are triply divorced" does not count as more than a single divorce if a husband says it before having intercourse with his wife. In the second, three sequential declarations result in a triple divorce. Abū Ḥanīfa reverses the effect of each statement, so in *Āthār Abū Yūsuf*, there is a tradition from Abū Ḥanīfa on the authority of Ibrāhīm [al-Nakhaʿī] who said: "If a man says to a wife with whom he has not had intercourse 'You are divorced, you are divorced, you are divorced,' she was divorced by means of the first statement, and the next two are uttered regarding a person over whom he has no authority. However if he divorces her triply all at once (i.e., with the one statement "You are triply divorced"), she is not lawful for him until she has first been married to another husband."[19] Mālik, Shāfiʿī. and Ibn Ḥanbal all agree with

[16] See also Shaybānī, *Āthār*, 105, no. 486 for a similar story.
[17] Ibn Abī Shayba, *Muṣannaf*, 4:21, *bāb* 20, no. 1.
[18] The expression *ḥarumat*, "she has become forbidden," means that he cannot marry her. In this case he cannot marry her until she has first been married to someone else.
[19] Abū Yūsuf, *Āthār*, no. 605. This tradition is repeated in Shaybānī, *Āthār*, 101, no. 470.

Abū Ḥanīfa.[20] Shāfiʿī says that he himself chooses (*akhtāru*) that a husband who has not had intercourse with his wife behave the same way as one who has, that is, he should divorce her singly. That way, Shāfiʿī points out, if he has not had intercourse with her, a man can become his former wife's suitor and remarry her, and if he has had intercourse, he can return to his wife if he wishes to, during her *ʿidda*.[21]

ʿIdda

As we saw above, the length of time a woman must wait before remarrying after a divorce or the death of her husband is extensively covered in the Qurʾān. However, jurists debated additional issues both about the *ʿidda* of the divorcée and that of the widow. For the divorcée, one issue was the meaning of the word *qurʾ* (plural, *qurūʾ* or *aqrāʾ*). Another was how to reckon her *ʿidda* if she does not menstruate and begins waiting her *ʿidda* in terms of months but then starts to menstruate, or, conversely, begins waiting her *ʿidda* in terms of menstrual periods and then stops menstruating. Then there is the question of lodging and maintenance during the *ʿidda* of a woman who has been triply or definitely divorced, and finally, the question of a woman's comportment during her *ʿidda*.

Qurʾ, Aqrāʾ

1. Yaḥyā b. Saʿīd on the authority of ʿUrwa on the authority of ʿĀʾisha, who said: "*Al-aqrāʾ* are periods of purity."
2. Abū Bakr [b. Abī Shayba] said: "Ibn ʿUyayna related to us on the authority of Juwaybir on the authority of Ḍaḥḥāk [that] *al-aqrāʾ* are menstrual periods."[22]

In Chapter 1, the word *qurūʾ* in Qurʾān 2:228, translated as *three monthly courses*, can be understood to mean the interval between two menstrual periods, as it does in the first tradition above, or, it can mean a menstrual period, as it does in the second. The definition matters both in terms of inheritance and in cases where a husband wishes to return to his wife during her *ʿidda* after a non-final divorce. All texts devote

[20] See Shaybānī, *Muwaṭṭaʾ*, p. 236; Shāfiʿī, *Kitāb al-umm*, 5:180; Spectorsky, *Chapters*, 203–4 and index, s.v. "Divorce."
[21] Shāfiʿī, *Kitāb al-umm*, 5:180.
[22] Ibn Abī Shayba, *Muṣannaf*, 4:117, *bāb* 152, nos. 1, 2,

considerable attention to this word and adduce a number of traditions to support one or another meaning. In addition to the two above, two more in *Muwaṭṭaʾ Shaybānī* serve as good examples: Shaybānī reports that Mālik related on the authority of Sulaymān b. Yasār that a man in Syria divorced his wife and then died just as she started the third menstrual period of her *ʿidda*. She insisted that she still inherited from him; his sons said she did not. They brought the matter to the Caliph Muʿāwiya who, unable to find anyone knowledgeable about the problem in Syria, wrote to Zayd b. Thābit. Zayd responded that the minute the woman's third period began, the couple were free of any legal obligations to each other, and therefore she did not inherit from her deceased former husband. This story supports Mālik's understanding of the meaning of *qurʾ* in accordance with the first tradition above.[23]

However, the next story Shaybānī relates supports the second tradition and his own understanding of *qurʾ*, as well as that of Abū Ḥanīfa. Shaybānī says that Abū Ḥanīfa said that a woman waiting an *ʿidda* after a non-final divorce was on the verge of washing just after her third menstrual period when her husband came to her and said, "I return to you." She asked ʿUmar b. al-Khaṭṭāb about that in the presence of Ibn Masʿūd, to whom ʿUmar turned for his opinion. Ibn Masʿūd said that as long as the woman had not washed after the third menstrual period of her *ʿidda*, her husband had the right to return to her.[24] Shāfiʿī agrees with Mālik that *al-aqrāʾ* refers periods of purity and not to menstrual periods.[25] Ibn Ḥanbal does not commit himself to either meaning; he merely says a woman who menstruates waits an *ʿidda* of three *aqrāʾ*.[26]

An ʿIdda *of Three* Aqrāʾ *or Three Months*

> On the authority of Abū Ḥanīfa on the authority of Ḥammād on the authority of Ibrāhīm [who] said: "When a man divorces a woman singly or doubly, and then she menstruates once or twice but then ceases to expect further menstrual periods, she should restart an *ʿidda* of three months. But if she subsequently menstruates [before three months are

[23] Shaybānī, *Muwaṭṭaʾ*, 244–45. See also Mālik, *Muwaṭṭaʾ*, 3:203, for this same story, and 202 for a story in which ʿĀʾisha insists that *al-aqrāʾ* are the intervals of time between menstrual periods.

[24] See again Shaybānī, *Muwaṭṭaʾ*, 244–45. Shaybānī reports several more traditions to support his understanding of the term, see 245–46.

[25] See Shāfiʿī, *Kitāb al-umm*, 5:209–10. Shāfiʿī supports his view with a number of traditions identical to those found in Mālik's *Muwaṭṭaʾ*, as well as additional ones.

[26] See Spectorsky, *Chapters*, 86–87, §164 and §165, and also s.v. index, "*aqrāʾ*."

> up], then she waits an *ʿidda* on the basis of menstruation, since the *ʿidda* of months became invalid. Further, husband and wife inherit from each other, as long as she is in her *ʿidda*, and he has the right to return to her." He continued: "If a woman who has ceased expecting menstrual periods is divorced, she should wait an *ʿidda* of months. But if she waits a month, or two, or more, and then again menstruates, she should restart waiting her *ʿidda* in terms of menstrual periods. If the same process is repeated, she should start again in terms of months. She cannot wait an *ʿidda* reckoned in a combination of months and menstrual periods."[27]

This tradition provides Abū Ḥanīfa'a opinion of how to calculate a woman's *ʿidda* if she has started to wait three months and then begins to menstruate, or if she has started to wait three menstrual periods and then stops menstruating. His opinion is that however long it takes, a woman must wait an *ʿidda* either of three consecutive menstrual periods or three consecutive months. Shaybānī reaffirms Abū Ḥanīfa's opinion and points out that in the Qurʾān, four time limits are described for an *ʿidda*: the first, the term of a woman's pregnancy; the second, three menstrual periods; the third, three months for those too young to menstruate, and the fourth, three months for those too old to do so.[28] Mālik agrees with Abū Ḥanīfa and Shaybānī, as do Shāfiʿī and Ibn Ḥanbal.[29]

Lodging and Maintenance during the ʿIdda *of a Woman Triply or Definitely Divorced*

1. Shurayḥ said about the triply divorced woman: "She receives maintenance and lodging."[30]
2. Al-Ḥasan [al-Baṣ rī], ʿAṭāʾ, and Shaʿbī said about the triply divorced woman: "She receives lodging and not maintenance.[31]
3. Shaʿbī said: "Fāṭima bt. Qays said: 'My husband divorced me triply during the lifetime of the Prophet, and the Prophet said: "You receive neither lodging nor maintenance." ' "[32]

---

27 ʿAbd al-Razzāq, *Muṣannaf*, 6:340, #11099.

28 Shaybānī, *Muwaṭṭaʾ*, 247.

29 See Mālik, *Muwaṭṭaʾ*, 3:212–13; Shāfiʿī, *Kitāb al-umm*, 5:213; Spectorsky, *Chapters*, 133, §134; 203, §202. Shaybānī notes that Abū Ḥanīfa's and his own opinion holds, even if a woman's *ʿidda* is prolonged for eighteen months. This eventuality is the subject of several traditions in which one of the not-yet former spouses dies and the other inherits long after they had expected to be divorced. For two of these, see Spectorsky, *Chapters*, 85, n. 25.

30 ʿAbd al-Razzāq, *Muṣannaf*, 7:27, no. 12041.

31 Ibn Abī Shayba, *Muṣannaf*, 4:108, no. 6.

32 Ibid., 4:109, no. 2.

4. ʿUmar b. al-Khaṭṭāb said: "We do not forsake the book of our Lord for the words of a woman. The triply divorced woman receives lodging and maintenance."[33]

If a woman is waiting an *ʿidda* after a non-final divorce, her husband can return to her at any point during this time. Therefore, she remains in her marital home and receives both lodging and maintenance. In accordance with Qurʾān 65:6, a divorced woman who is pregnant receives lodging and maintenance until her delivery, regardless of whether she is waiting an *ʿidda* after a non-final or a final divorce. That leaves the question of the *ʿidda* of a woman who is triply or definitely divorced. The traditions above describe the controversy over whether she receives lodging and maintenance (in accordance with the first tradition), only lodging (the second tradition), or neither (the third). This tradition quotes Fāṭima bt. Qays, whose *ʿidda* is fully discussed in early texts. Those who disagree with her statement here, and support lodging and maintenance for the triply divorced woman, often discredit her by using the quotation from ʿUmar in the fourth tradition.

The Ḥanafī position is that the triply divorced woman receives both lodging and maintenance. In *Āthār Abī Yūsuf*, Abū Yūsuf quotes a version of the fourth tradition: "ʿUmar said, 'We do not forsake the book of God and adopt the doctrine of a woman when we do not know whether she told the truth or lied.' "[34]

Mālik and Shāfiʿī both agree with the second tradition that the triply divorced woman receives lodging but not maintenance. In the *Muwaṭṭaʾ*, Mālik says that Fāṭima bt. Qays's husband divorced her while he was in Syria and sent a representative to her with some wheat. Surprised at the inadequacy of the amount, she complained to the Prophet, who informed her that she did not receive maintenance during her *ʿidda*.[35] Further, Mālik relates that he heard Zuhrī say: "The triply divorced woman does not leave her house until she can lawfully

[33] Ibid., 4:108, no. 10.

[34] Abū Yūsuf, *Āthār*, no. 608. See also *Ikhtilāf Abī Ḥanīfa wa-Ibn Abī Laylā* in *Kitāb al-umm*, 7:158, where Abū Ḥanīfa quotes 65:6 with the unspoken assumption that the verse applies to all divorcées, pregnant or not. See also Shaybānī, *Muwaṭṭaʾ*, 240–42 for several stories of women who were made to remain in their houses until their *ʿidda*s had ended. Shaybānī says he and Abū Ḥanīfa support these.

[35] The Prophet then arranged for her to wait an *ʿidda* in the house of Umm Maktūm's son, who was blind. The implication is that this was a special arrangement occasioned by the fact that Fāṭima's husband's house was isolated or because she was abusive toward her husband's relatives, or they were abusive toward her. See Mālik, *Muwaṭṭaʾ*, 3:210 where Zurqānī's commentary mentions several possibilities.

remarry. She receives maintenance only if she is pregnant, in which case she receives it until she gives birth.' " Mālik adds: "This is our practice."[36] Shāfiʿī quotes Qurʾān 65:1 to point out that divorced women must not be expelled from their houses *unless they commit open immorality*. Maintenance, he says, is specifically mentioned for pregnant divorcées in Qurʾān 65:6 and therefore is not granted to those who are triply divorced and who are not pregnant.[37] Ibn Ḥanbal grants neither and says that 65:6 (*lodge them where you dwell*) applies only to revocably divorced women. Ibn Ḥanbal supports the third tradition above and says that the Prophet granted Fāṭima bt. Qays neither lodging nor maintenance and instructed her to wait her *ʿidda* in the house of Umm Maktūm's son, who was blind and therefore could not see her in an inappropriate manner. He disagrees with the fourth tradition and says: "I follow the *ḥadīth* of Fāṭima bt. Qays."[38]

There are many traditions about Fāṭima bt. Qays, whose husband Abū ʿAmr b. Ḥafṣ divorced her triply, either all at once or for the third time.[39] All state that she did not wait her *ʿidda* in her husband's house and that the Prophet arranged for her to wait it elsewhere. Some say the Prophet did this because triply divorced women are not entitled to lodging (as in the third tradition), others that special circumstances caused the Prophet to remove her, and others that whatever she had to say about her *ʿidda* was not to be trusted (as in the fourth tradition).[40]

ʿIdda *of the Widow*

1. ʿAṭāʾ said: "The widow waits an *ʿidda* of four months and ten days, even if her husband has not had intercourse with her, or if she is nursing or has weaned [her child]." Maʿmar said: "And someone who heard al-Ḥasan [al-Basrī] informed me that he said the same thing."[41]

---

[36] Mālik, *Muwaṭṭaʾ*, 3:210.

[37] Shāfiʿī, *Kitāb al-umm*, 5:235–37.

[38] Spectorsky, *Chapters*, 125, §110.

[39] In addition to the two quoted here, see Wensinck, *Concordance*, s.v. "Fāṭima bt. Qays" for those found in the Six Books. See also Stern, *Marriage in Early Islam*, 136–40 for discussion of those in Ibn Saʿd's *Ṭabaqāt* and Ibn Ḥanbal's *Musnad*.

[40] As here, ʿUmar b. al-Khaṭṭāb is the Companion usually quoted as dismissing her report. Ibn Ḥanbal, who holds that the triply divorced woman is not entitled to lodging or maintenance, says that the traditions from ʿUmar about Fāṭima bt. Qays are not sound. See Spectorsky, *Chapters*, 85–86, §160. For a full discussion of lodging and maintenance for a triply divorced woman, see Hawting, "The Role of Qurʾān and *Ḥadīth* in the Legal Controversy about the Rights of a Divorced Woman During her Waiting Period (*ʿIdda*)."

[41] ʿAbd al-Razzāq, *Muṣannaf*, 7:28, no. 12050.

2. Ibn ʿAbbās said: "God said: *She waits an ʿidda of four months and ten days*, and He did not say she waits it in her house. She waits an *ʿidda* wherever she wishes."[42]
3. Ibn ʿUmar said, "During her *ʿidda*, the widow does not leave her husband's house."[43]
4. Jābir b. ʿAbd Allāh said, "The widow does not receive maintenance; her inheritance suffices."[44]

The first tradition is a general statement about a widow's *ʿidda*; it suggests that regardless of the details of her marriage or her personal situation, propriety demands that she wait a full *ʿidda*. The second agrees with the first about the length of time her *ʿidda* must last and brings in another issue by saying she is free to wait it wherever she wishes. The third reflects disagreement about where she waits it. This disagreement is tied in with the fact, mentioned in the fourth tradition, that she is not entitled to maintenance since she inherits from her late husband.

The *ʿidda* of a pregnant widow is not specifically mentioned in the Qurʾān, which states only that a widow's *ʿidda* is four months and ten days (2:234), and that a pregnant woman's *ʿidda* ends with her delivery (65:4), but all jurists hold that a pregnant widow's *ʿidda* ends with her delivery, so they do not support the opinion attributed to ʿAṭāʾ and Ibn ʿAbbās (in the first and second traditions) that she should wait four months and ten days in any case.[45]

On the question of whether the widow may go out during the day, Shaybānī says he and Abū Ḥanīfa think that since she is not entitled to maintenance, she may go out during the day "to seek God's bounty," but she must not spend the night away from home.[46] Mālik's agreement with Shaybānī and Abū Ḥanīfa is illustrated by several stories in the *Muwaṭṭaʾ*. The first is that of Furayʿa bt. Sinān the sister of the Companion Abū Saʿīd al-Khudrī. When she was widowed, she asked the Prophet if she could return to her family since her husband had not left her in a house that he owned, and she was destitute. Initially the Prophet said she could but then changed his mind and said she must wait her *ʿidda* in the house she occupied when her husband died.

---

[42] Ibid., 7:29, no. 12051.
[43] Ibid., 7:31, no. 12062.
[44] Ibid., 7:37–38, no. 12085.
[45] See Mālik, *Muwaṭṭaʾ*, 3, 221–22; and Shāfiʿī, *Kitāb al-umm*, 5, 223–24. See also Abū Yūsuf, *Āthār*, no. 651 and no. 652; Shaybānī, *Muwaṭṭaʾ*, 234–35; and Schacht, *Origins*, 225–26.
[46] Shaybānī, *Āthār*, 111, nos. 512 and 513.

The second is about the widow of the Companion al-Sā'ib b. Khabbāb, who came to ʿAbd Allāh b. ʿUmar and said that her late husband had a tillage in Qanāt that she wished to cultivate. She asked whether she could spend the night there.[47] He did not allow her to, so she rose early to go cultivate her land and returned home at night to sleep. In a third story, ʿUmar b. al-Khaṭṭāb turned back several widows who had traveled in from the desert to start the pilgrimage before their *ʿidda*s had ended.[48] Ibn Ḥanbal too says that the widow can go out during the daytime, but must spend the night in her husband's house.[49]

Shāfiʿī tells the same story about the *ʿidda* of Furayʿa bt. Sinān that Mālik does, and he agrees that a widow should stay in her husband's house for the full four months and ten days. However, he explores a number of eventualities that might make it necessary for her to leave her home, or wait her *ʿidda* in a distant town where she happened to be when she learned of her husband's death, or move to a different place with her own relatives (rather than stay with her husband's) if it turned out her husband's relations were leaving the area before her *ʿidda* ended.[50]

Comportment during an ʿIdda

1. Saʿīd [b. al-Musayyib] said, "If a man has divorced his wife singly, he must seek her permission to enter [her house, or her room] and she wears whatever jewelry and clothing she wishes. However, if they have only one room, they should separate themselves from each other with a curtain, and he should greet her when he enters."[51]
2. Shuʿba on the authority of al-Ḥakam [that he said] about the triply divorced woman: "She should not apply kohl nor adorn herself." And this was more important to him than the fact that the widow [also should do neither of these things].[52]

In addition to receiving lodging and maintenance, a woman waiting an *ʿidda* after a non-final divorce is expected to behave in much the same way she would if still married, since her husband might return to her at any moment. However, her semi-married state is indicated in the first

[47] The Wādī Qanāt is to the east, on the outskirts of Madina.
[48] See Mālik, *Muwaṭṭa'*, 3:222–23.
[49] For example, see Spectorsky, *Chapters*, 86, §162, and §163.
[50] Shāfiʿī, *Kitāb al-umm*, 5:226–30. See Saḥnūn, *Mudawwana*, 2:475–76 for a discussion of the widow's status in her house when there are debts against her husband's estate.
[51] Ibn Abī Shayba, *Muṣannaf*, 4:142, no. 4.
[52] Ibid., 4:143, no. 5.

tradition above, which supports a certain physical distance between husband and wife. The triply divorced woman and the widow are lumped together in the second tradition, as well as in the discussions of the jurists. During their ʿ*idda*s both are expected to avoid personal adornment.

Shaybānī says, more directly than the first tradition, that he and Abū Ḥanīfa both agree that a woman waiting an ʿ*idda* after a non-final divorce adorns herself in the hope that her husband will return to her. Regarding the triply divorced woman and the widow, Shaybānī says they should not wear dyed clothing and should avoid kohl and scent except for medicinal purposes.[53] In general, Mālik agrees with Shaybānī and Abū Ḥanīfa both about a woman waiting an ʿ*idda* after a non-final divorce and about a triply divorced woman and a widow. So do Shāfiʿī and Ibn Ḥanbal, although all three emphasize slightly different details. For example, Mālik relates a tradition in which the Prophet's wife Umm Salama told a mourning widow with eye trouble to apply kohl at night but to rub it off during the daytime. Shāfiʿī says that the husband of a woman waiting an ʿ*idda* after a non-final divorce should treat her in every way as he would a triply divorced [ex-]wife. Ibn Ḥanbal says the husband of a woman awaiting a non-final divorce should not see her hair during this period.[54]

Return of a Husband to his Wife during her ʿIdda

1. Ibrahim said: "If a man claims that he has returned to his wife before the end of her ʿ*idda*, he must provide witnesses."[55]
2. Zuhrī said: "If a man claims he returned to his wife before the end of her ʿ*idda*, he is not believed, even if he provides witnesses [after the fact]."[56]

In Chapter 1 we saw that as a wife's ʿ*idda* after a non-final divorce draws to a close, in accordance with Qurʾān 65:2, her husband should call witnesses to the fact that he is either resuming the marriage or ending it. The first tradition above reinforces the Qurʾānic injunction, the second,

[53] See Shaybānī, *Āthār*, 106, no. 488; and also Abū Yūsuf, *Āthār*, no. 664, for the woman waiting an ʿ*idda* after a non-final divorce; and no. 646 for a triply divorced woman and a widow. I have translated *muʿaṣfar* as "dyed." Rescher defines it as dyed with a dye that is saffron-colored. See his *Vocabulaire du recueil de Bokhārī*, 60.

[54] See, for example, Abū Yūsuf, *Āthār*, no. 646; Mālik, *Muwaṭṭaʾ*, 3:230–37; Shaybānī, *Muwaṭṭaʾ*, 239–40; Shāfiʿī, *Kitāb al-umm*, 5:230–32, Spectorsky, *Chapters*, 140, §159.

[55] Ibn Abī Shayba, *Muṣannaf*, 4:175, *bāb* 248, no. 1.

[56] Ibid., no. 2.

suggests that he cannot claim after the fact that his return has been witnessed. Although all jurists agree with the first tradition, they do not agree with the second if facts on the ground indicate that a return has taken place.

Shaybānī, in accordance with the first tradition, says that during the *ʿidda* of a man's wife, if he wishes to take his wife on a trip, he cannot do so until his return to her has been witnessed. On the other hand, Shaybānī also says that if a woman gives birth less than two years after her husband divorced her, that shows that he returned to her, regardless of whether his return was witnessed.[57]

Mālik too seems willing to overlook the witnessing requirement because he is reported to have said that if a man returned to his wife during her *ʿidda* by having intercourse with her, and he was ignorant of the fact that he should have had his return witnessed, his return is valid. However, Mālik is also reported to have said that if the man knew of the witnessing requirement, then his return is not valid. Further, if the wife in questions says to her husband: "Do not have intercourse with me until your return to me has been witnessed," she has acted with propriety.[58]

Shāfiʿī says that to return to his wife, a man must have two reliable witnesses witness his return, as God ordered. Further, a man must make a statement of return. Shāfiʿī insists that just as there is no marriage or divorce without speech, so there is no return without it. Shāfiʿī offers various statements a husband can make. He can, for example, say such things as: "I return to her," or "I return her to me." He is not as lenient as Mālik: if, without saying anything, a husband merely returns to his wife and has intercourse with her, that, according to Shāfiʿī, is intercourse owing to an uncertainty (*shubha*). Such a man does not receive a *ḥadd*, but a *taʿzīr* punishment, and so does his wife if she was aware that he did not previously state his intention to return to her.[59]

---

[57] Shaybānī, *al-Jāmiʿ al-ṣaghīr*, 186–87.

[58] Saḥnūn, *Mudawwana*, 2:324. Saḥnūn also records a tradition from Ashhab on the authority of ʿAbd Allāh b. Dīnar that when Ibn ʿUmar divorced Ṣafiyya bt. Abī ʿUbayd, he had two men witness his divorce, and when he wished to return to her, he had two men witness his return before he [again] had intercourse with her. *Mudawwana*, 2:325.

[59] In this case, *shubha* refers to the fact that although it seemed as if the husband's return to his wife was lawful, since he failed to have his return witness, it was not. Shāfiʿī goes on to say that this invalid marriage requires both a new marriage portion and also an *ʿidda* before the husband can return to his wife on the basis of their original marriage. Shāfiʿī, *Kitāb al-umm*, 5:243–44.

Ibn Ḥanbal says only that a return must be witnessed: "In order to return to his wife, a man has two other men as witnesses when he says: 'I return to Fulāna bt. Fulān.'" He adds that a man must do this regardless of whether his wife is present.[60]

Condition of the Husband

Divorce in Death Illness (maraḍ al-mawt)

1. Regarding a man who divorced his wife while ill and then died, Ibn al-Zubayr said: "'Uthmān had the daughter of al-Aṣbagh al-Kalbiyya inherit, but as far as I am concerned, I do not think that a triply divorced woman (*mabtūta*) inherits."[61]
2. 'Ubayy b. Ka'b said: "If a man divorces his wife while ill, she inherits from him even if a year passes without his either recovering or dying."[62]
3. 'Umar b. al-Khaṭṭāb said: "If a man divorces his wife while ill, she inherits from him as long as she is in her *'idda*, but he does not inherit from her."[63]

By the 2nd/8th century, it was generally held that special rules applied to a terminally ill man that prevented him from disposing of more than the one-third of his estate that he was free to leave as a bequest.[64] For, in an effort to alter the distribution of the remaining two-thirds among his heirs, a terminally ill man might wish to divorce a wife (or wives) triply so that she immediately became a "stranger" to him and more of his estate could devolve on other relatives, or so that he could leave the divorced wife a discretionary bequest that would be larger than her widow's share of his estate. When we think about the divorce of an ill man, it is important to remember that only if he dies from the illness during which he pronounced a divorce, is the divorce invalid.

[60] Spectorsky, *Chapters*, 89, §175.
[61] Ibn Abī Shayba, *Muṣannaf*, 4:151, *bāb* 200, no. 3.
[62] Ibid., no. 2.
[63] 'Abd al-Razzāq, *Muṣannaf*, 7:64, no. 12201.
[64] Conversely, any transactions he undertook during an illness from which he recovered were valid. See *EI*, s.v. "*Mīrāth*" and *EQ*, s.v. "Inheritance." If a man divorces his wife while ill, then recovers and then dies of another illness, his divorce is valid. See Coulson, *Succession in the Muslim Family*, 277–79, for discussion of the legality of a terminally ill man's divorce. All illnesses are considered terminal until a person recovers. For a discussion of the early development of *maraḍ al-mawt*, see Hiroyuki Yanagihashi, "The Doctrinal Development of "*Maraḍ al-Mawt* in the Formative Period of Islamic Law," *Islamic Law and Society*, 5 (1998), 326–58.

The first tradition above refers to a story often used to illustrate condemnation of a divorce pronounced by an ill man. ʿAbd al-Raḥmān b. ʿAwf, husband of Tumāḍir bt. al-Aṣ bagh al-Kalbiyya, divorced her triply during his terminal illness. After he died, the Caliph ʿUthmān b. ʿAffān had her inherit from him despite the fact that her *ʿidda* had ended.[65] Ibn al-Zubayr himself, however, although he relates this tradition, thinks that a triply divorced woman does *not* inherit from her husband and that terminal illness does *not* affect this rule. In the second tradition, ʿUbayy b. Kaʿb emphasizes his agreement with ʿUthmān's position by referring to a situation in which the ill husband lingers long after his ex-wife's *ʿidda* has ended. In the third tradition, the Caliph ʿUmar disagrees and says that a wife divorced triply by a terminally ill husband inherits only during her *ʿidda*, not after it has ended.

Shaybānī reports his own and Abū Ḥanīfa's disagreement with ʿUthmān and their support of ʿUmar's view that the wife inherits only during her *ʿidda*.[66] Mālik adopts the position taken by ʿUthman in the first tradition above and by ʿUbayy b. Kaʿb in the second. In the *Mudawwana*, going one better than the second tradition above, Mālik is reported to have said that even if a woman has remarried after her husband died, as long as he divorced her while he was ill and subsequently died of that illness, she inherits from him.[67] Ibn Ḥanbal agrees with Mālik that a woman inherits from a husband who divorced her while terminally ill, both during and after her *ʿidda*, but not, he says, once she has remarried.[68] On the question of a terminally ill man divorcing his wife before the couple have had intercourse, the Ḥanafīs, Mālik, and Ibn Ḥanbal are agreed that she receives half her marriage portion and does not wait an *ʿidda*, as in the case of a healthy man's

[65] See Mālik, *Muwaṭṭaʾ*, 3:195, where Mālik tells this story (of which he approves) and also Zurqānī's commentary on it.

[66] Shaybānī, *Muwaṭṭaʾ*, 234. Shaybānī reports on Shurayḥ's authority that ʿUmar b. al-Khaṭṭāb wrote to him that a woman triply divorced by an ill husband inherits from him only if he dies during her *ʿidda*, but not after it has ended.

[67] In another version of Tumāḍir's divorce from ʿAbd al-Raḥmān b. ʿAwf, she asked him to divorce her, which he did, but as he was ill and subsequently died of that illness, ʿUthmān had her inherit from him after the end of her *ʿidda*. Other instances of ʿUthmān insisting on an [ex-]wife inheriting from an ill [ex-]husband who dies of his illness long after her *ʿidda* has ended are reported both in the *Muwaṭṭaʾ*, see 195–97, and Zurqānī's commentary. For these cases and a number of other details, see the discussion in Saḥnūn, *Mudawwana*, 3:34–40.

[68] See Spectorsky, *Chapters*, 178, §112. See 136, §140, where Ibn Ḥanbal refers to the Medinese position: "The Medinese say she inherits from him after the end of her *ʿidda*, even if she has remarried."

divorce before intercourse. However, Mālik says she also inherits from him. Abū Ḥanīfa, Shaybānī, and Ibn Ḥanbal say she does not.[69]

Shāfiʿī takes a very different view of a terminally ill husband's divorce. He says that God made the divorce of a sane man in his majority valid. Divorce, he continues, means that a man forbids himself a wife who was previously lawful for him, and whether he is ill or healthy at the time is not relevant. Following this logic further, Shāfiʿī points out that if a man divorces his wife before intercourse, or triply, she does not inherit from him, and if she is to die first, he will not inherit from her.[70] He quotes approvingly Ibn al-Zubayr's opinion in the first tradition above[71] and goes on to point out that triple divorce or divorce before intercourse means that the couple are no longer spouses and have immediately become "strangers." For one thing, the husband can no longer return to his wife; for another, they do not participate in preparing each other for burial if one of them dies. If, therefore, the husband dies of his illness, his wife does not inherit from him (even if she is waiting an *ʿidda*), because she is no longer his wife.[72]

Divorce of the Intoxicated Man

1. Abān b. ʿUthmān said ʿUthmān said: "Neither the insane nor the intoxicated man can divorce."[73]
2. Qatāda said: "His [the intoxicated man's] divorce is valid, and he is flogged appropriately."[74]

Conditions of the husband that may invalidate any divorce pronouncement he makes are intoxication, along with insanity, idiocy, and

---

[69] In Mālik, *Muwaṭṭaʾ*, 3:196–97, Mālik adds that in the case of divorce before intercourse, there is no difference in inheritance between the *bikr* and the *thayyib*. For Abū Ḥanīfa's and Shaybānī's view, see Shaybānī, *Āthār*, 102, no. 472; for Ibn Ḥanbal's, Spectorsky, *Chapters*, 83, §145.

[70] Shāfiʿī knows the story of ʿAbd al-Raḥmān b. ʿAuf and Tumādir, as well as several other traditions, all of which he considers weak. See Shāfiʿī, *Kitāb al-umm*, 5:254–55.

[71] Shāfiʿī provides an *isnād* for it, which he says is *muttaṣil* (i.e., unbroken, and hence sound and to be followed). *Kitāb al-umm*, 5, 254.

[72] Shāfiʿī, *Kitāb al-umm*, 5, 234–35. Shāfiʿī goes on to discuss terrifying illnesses that might invalidate divorce. He suggests that they are incapacitating illnesses, like pneumonia or pleurisy, and that death comes very quickly after a man sickens and becomes bedridden. The implication here is that in such dire circumstances, a divorce statement can only be motivated by a man's wish to alter his estate. See 5:235. For the difference between Shāfiʿī's (and the Shāfiʿīte position) and that of other jurists about the legal effects of actions a man takes when terminally ill, see Coulson, *Succession*, 276–77.

[73] Ibn Abī Shayba, *Muṣannaf*, 4:24, *bāb* 27, no. 2.

[74] That is, he is flogged in accordance with the *ḥadd* punishment for intoxication. ʿAbd al-Razzāq, *Muṣannaf*, 7:82, no. 12298.

delirium. There is no disagreement that an insane man's divorce statement is not valid, and, despite the opinion attributed to ʿUthmān in the first tradition above, there was general agreement that an intoxicated man's divorce statement is valid. Shaybānī reports several traditions on the authority of Abū Ḥanīfa about the divorce of a man who is intoxicated, delirious, or asleep. If a man is asleep, his divorce is not valid; if he is delirious, it is not valid until he recovers. Similarly, his divorce is not valid as long as he is irrational. If he is intoxicated, his divorce *is* valid.[75] Mālik also considered the divorce of the intoxicated man valid. In the *Muwaṭṭa*ʾ, he says that he has heard that "Saʿīd b. al-Musayyab and Sulaymān b. Yasār were asked about the divorce of the intoxicated man, and they said, 'If the intoxicated man divorces, that is valid, and if he kills, he is killed,' and that is our practice."[76]

In *Kitāb al-umm*, Shāfiʿī discusses differentiating between the divorce of an insane or an ill man and that of an intoxicated one. He discusses the intoxicated man in the framework of the duties of an adult Muslim.[77] Whoever is charged with the obligation of prayer and is subject to *ḥadd* punishments, Shāfiʿī says, can pronounce a valid divorce. The divorce of a man not of sound mind is not valid, nor is he charged with prayer or subject to *ḥadd* punishments. The same is true of the idiot and the man who is delusional, delirious, or otherwise ill in such a way that he loses his mind. If and when he recovers it, he can immediately pronounce a valid divorce and is again charged with the duties of an adult Muslim. But the intoxicated man, Shāfiʿī points out, is not in the same position as one granted remission by virtue of his illness, for whom, when he loses his mind, "the pen is lifted." The intoxicated man is a sinner, and the pen is not lifted for him.[78] Ibn Ḥanbal

---

[75] Shaybānī, *Āthār*, 108–9, see nos. 500–3.

[76] Mālik, *Muwaṭṭa*ʾ, 3:219. This story is repeated in the *Mudawwana*, along with several others that validate the divorce of the intoxicated man and invalidate that of the man who is delirious or ill. See Saḥnūn, *Mudawwana*, 3:29–30.

[77] See Shāfiʿī, *Kitāb al-umm*, 5:253–54. Shāfiʿī quotes Qurʾān 24:59 and 4:6 to point out that once a man has reached puberty, he becomes an adult with adult responsibilities. For a man, this is at fifteen years of age. Shāfiʿī notes here that the Prophet allowed Ibn ʿUmar to go to battle at the age of fifteen, but not at fourteen.

[78] For traditions about a person who is not to be judged for his actions or for whom "the pen is lifted," see Wensinck, *Concordance*, 8, s.v. *q*, *l*, *m*, (*qalam*). In an example in Nasāʾī's *Sunan* in *Kitāb al-ṭalāq*, ʿĀʾisha said that the Prophet said, "The pen is lifted for three people: the sleeping person until he awakes, the minor until he becomes an adult, and the insane person until he regains his mind or recovers." Nasāʾī, *Sunan*, 6:156. See also Bukhārī, *Ṣaḥīḥ*, 3:405.

knows the first tradition quoted above on the authority of ʿUthmān, but he agrees with Shāfiʿī and quotes him saying: "The pen is not lifted for the intoxicated man."[79]

Takhyīr *and* Tamlīk

A husband can transfer the option of initiating a divorce to his wife by giving her the choice (*takhyīr*) of separating from him. This option, as we saw in chapter 1, is associated with Qurʾān 33:28–29 and a moment of discord in the Prophet's household. Two kinds of statements are discussed by means of which a man temporarily transfers to his wife the right to divorce him. In one, he invites her to choose whether to be divorced or remain married to him (*takhyīr*); in the other, he tells her that her matter is in her hands, or that he is transferring to her the authority to initiate divorce (*tamlīk*). For *takhyīr*, jurists usually think of a man saying to his wife: "Choose!" For *tamlīk*, they think of him saying: "Your matter is in your hands."

1. Ibrāhīm [al-Nakhaʿī] said, concerning a man who gives his wife the choice: "Alī said, 'If she chooses herself, that becomes a single definite divorce. If she chooses her husband, a single divorce [and his return to her] has [automatically] taken place, and he has the right to her (i.e., to return to her during her *ʿidda* in a second divorce).' But ʿUmar b. al-Khaṭṭāb and ʿAbd Allāh b. Masʿūd said that if she chooses herself that means a single divorce, and he (i.e., her husband) has the right to [return] to her [during her *ʿidda*], but if she chooses her husband, nothing further happens." He continued: "Zayd b. Thābit said: 'If she chooses herself, that counts as a triple divorce.' "[80]
2. Masrūq said: "Giving a wife the choice (*takhyīr*) and putting her matter into her hands (*tamlīk*) are the same."[81]
3. Masrūq said: "A man came to ʿUmar and said: 'I put my wife's matter into her hands and she divorced herself triply.' Then ʿUmar said to ʿAbd Allāh [b. ʿAbbās]: 'What do you think?' ʿAbd Allāh replied: 'I think it is a single divorce and he has the most right to her.' ʿUmar said: 'That is my opinion as well.' "[82]

[79] Spectorsky, *Chapters*, 127, §119. Ibn Ḥanbal also refers to a tradition that says Muʿāwiya permitted the divorce of the intoxicated man, but refers to Shāfiʿī's position to support his own.

[80] ʿAbd al-Razzāq, *Muṣannaf*, 7:9, no. 11975. I have accepted the editor's footnoted emendations.

[81] Ibid., 7:8, no. 11969.

[82] Ibn Abī Shayba, *Muṣannaf*, 4:43, no. 1.

4. Shuʿba said: "I said to al-Ḥakam: 'She said, "I divorce myself triply." ' He [al-Ḥakam] said, 'If he put her matter into her hands, she is indeed triply divorced from him.' "[83]

The first tradition above mirrors the disagreements among jurists about the effect of a woman exercising the option her husband has given her. In the opinion attributed to ʿAlī, the choice itself results in a single divorce regardless of whether she chooses to separate from or stay with her husband. In that attributed to ʿUmar and Ibn Masʿūd, nothing happens if she chooses her husband; if she chooses divorce, her choice results in a single divorce. However, Zayd b. Thābit says that if she chooses herself, it results in a triple divorce. The second tradition says that *takhyīr* and *tamlīk* statements have the same effect. In the third, *tamlīk* gives a wife the right to divorce her husband singly, but in the fourth, the decision of whether to divorce singly or triply is hers.

Shaybānī goes over the options presented in the first tradition above, then says that he and Abū Ḥanīfa follow a *ḥadīth* on the authority of ʿĀʾisha who said: "The Prophet gave us the choice. Then we chose him, and that did not count against us as a divorce." Shaybānī disagrees with the second tradition and says that he and Abū Ḥanīfa both think that *takhyīr* and *tamlīk* differ whenever a wife opts for divorce: if her husband has said "Choose," and he meant by his statement to give his wife the option of divorcing him, if she chooses divorce, her choice results in a definite divorce, regardless of whether he had a single or a triple divorce in mind. However, if a husband says "Your matter is in your hands," and she chooses herself, then the nature of the divorce that results (i.e., single or triple) is in accordance with his intention in making the statement, and any ambiguity in what the husband meant is resolved by having him take an oath.[84]

Mālik supports the view attributed to ʿUmar and Ibn Masʿūd in the first tradition above, that if a woman chooses to stay with her husband, no divorce has taken place. However, he attributes this position to Zuhrī. "That is," Mālik says, "the best that I have heard." If she chooses herself, Mālik's position is the one attributed to Zayd b. Thābit in the first tradition: that her choice means a triple divorce, regardless of whether the

[83] Ibid., 4:44, no. 11.
[84] See Shaybānī, *Āthār*, 114–15, no. 530, and 116, no. 536. These are two of the traditions that Shaybānī devotes to *takhyīr* and *tamlīk*. I have simplified his discussion. For more ramifications of both *takhyīr* and *tamlīk*, see further in his *Āthār*, 115–16, nos. 531–534) and in *al-Jāmiʿ al-ṣaghīr*, 166–68.

husband insists that he did not mean to authorize her to divorce triply. This too Mālik describes as "the best that I have heard on this matter." In addition he says that if a man gives his wife the choice, and she says she accepts it only for a single divorce, her statement has no import, and she remains married to him.[85] On *tamlīk*, Mālik agrees with Abū Ḥanīfa and Shaybānī that it differs from *takhyīr*, but not quite in the same way that they hold it does. In accordance with the fourth tradition above, Mālik says that once a man has put his wife's matters into her own hands, it is up to her to decide how many divorces she wishes to effect. However, if the husband takes an oath that he meant to authorize her to divorce only singly, then he can return to her during her *ʿidda*.

Shāfiʿī discusses only *takhyīr*. He agrees with Mālik that the choice the Prophet gave his wives, and their choosing to remain with him, did not constitute a divorce, and he reports this on the authority of ʿĀʾisha. However, he notes that two traditions, also on the authority of ʿĀʾisha, support the view that the whole procedure meant that a single revocable divorce had occurred. If a wife chooses herself, Shāfiʿī says, Mālik's opinion that she has effected a triple divorce cannot be correct because that would mean a triple divorce all at once which the Prophet and the Companions disapproved of.[86]

Two opinions are reported from Ibn Ḥanbal. One is that if the wife chooses her husband no divorce has taken place; the other, that a single divorce has taken place.[87] On the difference between *takhyīr* and *tamlīk*, Ibn Ḥanbal says: "When a man says to his wife 'Your matter is in your hands,' then she decides what her status is to be." So here he seems to agree with the fourth tradition and with Mālik. He continues: "But when he says 'Choose!' and she chooses herself, that counts as a single divorce, and he has the right to return to her."[88]

Khulʿ

Khulʿ, a divorce initiated by a wife rather than her husband, as we saw in Chapter 1 is mentioned in Qurʾān 2:229–30. Jurists focused on

[85] Mālik, *Muwaṭṭaʾ*, 3:183.
[86] See Shāfiʿī, *Kitāb al-umm*, 5:139–40 and 7:172. Shāfiʿī does not provide an *isnād* for his own opinion on the authority of ʿĀʾisha, although he does for the opinion, also on her authority, that the whole procedure resulted in a single revocable divorce. See also Schacht, *Origins*, 215, for the development of these two views of *takhyīr*.
[87] See Spectorsky, *Chapters*, 126, §114, and 168, §83.
[88] Ibid., 200, §191.

several issues. Two of them are reflected in the following four traditions. One is whether *khulʿ* can really be defined as a divorce (and therefore counted as one of the three divorces allowed a couple before they are permanently divorced), or whether it is instead an annulment (*faskh*), different from divorce in that the wife buys her freedom or ransoms herself from her husband. The second, in connection with this latter, is debate about whether the husband can demand that his wife buy her freedom for more than he has given her as a marriage portion.

1. Dāwūd b. Abī ʿĀṣim [said] that Saʿīd b. al-Musayyab informed him that a [particular] woman was married to Thābit b. Qays b. Shamās, who had given her a garden as a marriage portion. He was extremely jealous, and he beat her and broke her hand. So she went to the Prophet and complained and said: 'I will return his garden to him.' The Prophet said, 'You will?' She said, 'Yes.' So the Prophet called her husband and said, 'She will return your garden to you.' He [i.e., Thābit] said: 'Is that lawful for me?' The Prophet said: 'Yes.' He said: 'Then I accept, O Messenger of God.' Then the Prophet said [to the two of them]: 'Go, and that counts as a single divorce.' "[89]
2. Ṭāwūs said: "Ibn ʿAbbās said, 'Ransoming is not divorce.' " Ṭāwūs also said, "I used to hear Ibn ʿAbbās recite from the Qurʾān concerning that question: '*Women who are divorced shall wait, keeping themselves apart, three (monthly) courses*' (2:228). Then he would recite: '*it is no sin for either of them if the woman ransom herself* (2:229)' Then he would say, 'God mentioned divorce before and after ransoming, and he mentioned ransoming between them.' I did not hear him mention divorce as part of ransoming; he (i.e., Ibn ʿAbbās) did not think ransoming was equivalent to divorce."[90]
3. Ibn Ṭāwūs on the authority of his father [Ṭāwūs], who said: "It is not lawful for him to take more from her than he [originally] gave her."[91]
4. Al-Ḍaḥḥāk said: "There is no harm in a woman ransoming herself from her husband for even more than he [originally] gave her."[92]

The first tradition is a fuller version of the story Ṭabarī related (see Chapter 1) as an occasion of revelation for Qurʾān 2:229 in order to explain that in a separation by *khulʿ*, the wife initiates it. In all versions of this story the husband named is always Thābit b. Qays, and his wife always returns to him the garden he had given her as a marriage

[89] ʿAbd al-Razzāq, *Muṣannaf*, 6:482, no. 11757.
[90] Ibid., 6:485–86, no. 11765.
[91] Ibn Abī Shayba, *Muṣannaf*, 4:92, *bāb* 116, no. 4.
[92] Ibid., 4:94, no. 6.

portion.[93] The particular version of the story above also includes the Prophet's authority for the fact that *khulʿ* results in a divorce. However, in the second tradition, Ibn ʿAbbās's understanding of 2:229 leads him to think that *khulʿ* means a wife ransoms herself from her husband which is not the same as a divorce. The third tradition says that a husband must not take from his wife more than he gave her as a marriage portion; the fourth, that there is no harm in his doing so.

Shaybānī, in his version of the *Muwaṭṭa,ʾ* starts the chapter on *khulʿ* with a tradition on the authority of Mālik that a female slave of Ṣafiyya bt. Abī ʿUbayd ransomed herself from her husband for everything she had, and Ibn ʿUmar did not disapprove of that. Shaybānī says that is lawful, although "we find it reprehensible," even if the marital discord stems from her behavior. If it stems from his behavior, Shaybānī continues, we do not like him to take either more or less than he originally gave her (*mā nuḥibbu lahu an yaʾkhudha akthara mimmā ʿaṭāhā*). This, Shaybānī says, is also Abū Ḥanīfa's doctrine.[94] Further, Shaybānī says *khulʿ* produces a single definite divorce, unless the husband mentioned or intended triple divorce.[95] Like Shaybānī, Mālik thinks that *khulʿ* produces a definite divorce: in the *Muwaṭṭaʾ*, he says "A woman who has ransomed herself can return to her husband only on the basis of a new marriage."[96] Further, he says that a woman can ransom herself for more than her husband originally gave her. He supports this view with the same tradition Shaybānī quotes about Ṣafiyya bt. Abī ʿUbayd's female slave. Unlike Shaybānī, Mālik does not find this reprehensible. He says, "This is what we have heard, and it is our practice."[97] Shāfiʿī agrees that separation by means of *khulʿ* results in a definite divorce, but stresses that the husband must actually divorce his wife for the compensation she gives him. At that point she waits an *ʿidda* during which he cannot return to her. He agrees with Shaybānī and Mālik that a husband can

---

[93] The wife's name is usually Ḥabība bt. Sahl. Many traditions recount, with varying details, the story of this couple. For a listing of those in the Six Books, see Wensinck, *Concordance*, 8, s.v. "Thābit b. Qays b. Shamās al-Khazrajī."

[94] Shaybānī, *Muwaṭṭaʾ*, 230. For Shaybānī's view, see also *al-Jāmiʿ al-ṣaghīr*, 178.

[95] Shaybānī, *Muwaṭṭaʾ*, 230. Again, a definite divorce means a couple can remarry in a new contract that includes a new marriage portion. A triple divorce would require a woman to marry another man before remarrying the one from whom she had been triply divorced.

[96] Mālik, *Muwaṭṭaʾ*, 3:186.

[97] Ibid., : Ṣafiyya bt. Abī ʿUbayd was married to ʿAbd Allāh b. ʿUmar, and Mālik adds here that ʿAbd Allāh b. ʿUmar did not object to his wife's slave divesting herself of everything she had in order to be rid of her husband.

take more from his wife than he originally gave her and says this is because no amount is mentioned in the Qur'ān.[98]

Ibn Ḥanbal disagrees with his predecessors on two counts: one, he says that *khul'* is tantamount to an annulment rather than a divorce. He quotes 2:229–30 and then rejects the same statement by Ibn 'Abbās that is in the second tradition above. Two, he supports the third tradition above, about a man's compensation for *khul'*, and says, "He should not take from her more than he gave her."[99]

Khul' *and Arbitration*

1. A man asked 'Aṭā': "Can the two arbitrators (*al-ḥakamāni*) separate a couple?" He replied: "Not unless the couple have given them permission to do so."
2. Ḥasan al-Baṣrī said: "The two can adjudicate a joining [of the spouses], not a separation."
3. Al-Sha'bī said: "If the two arbitrators wish to, they separate, and if they wish to, they join [a couple]."[100]

We saw in Chapter 1 that Qur'ān 4:35 mentions arbitration for a couple who were not getting along and that Ṭabarī noted differences of opinion about what the arbitrators were charged with. The three traditions above reflect disagreement over the interpretation of the role 4:35 gives the two arbitrators.[101] They are always welcome to reconcile or join (*al-ijtimā'*) a couple. The question is whether and to what extent they have the authority to separate them. In the first tradition they can do so only if the couple have authorized them to. In the second the arbitrators' job is to keep the couple together, and in the third they are authorized to use their own judgment.

Mālik agrees with the third tradition and says that the two arbitrators, one chosen from the husband's family and one from the wife's, have the authority to either separate or reconcile the couple. "'And that', Mālik said, 'is the best that I have heard from the scholars; whatever the two arbitrators decide regarding a husband and wife,

[98] See Shāfi'ī, *Kitāb al-umm*, 5:196–97.

[99] Spectorsky, *Chapters*, 250, §355.

[100] 'Abd al-Razzāq, *Muṣannaf*, 6:511–12, nos. 11880, 11881, 11884.

[101] Ṭabarī includes a tradition about 'Alī b. Abī Ṭālib (also found in 'Abd al-Razzāq's *Muṣannaf*, 6:512, no. 11883) granting the two arbitrators the right to separate or reconcile the couple and insisting that the couple abide by their decision. See Fierro, "Ill-treated Women Seeking Divorce," for a discussion that suggests linking this tradition to the arbitration at Siffin.

separation or joining (*al-ijtimāʿ*), is valid.' "[102] Further, Mālik is reported to have said that the arbitrators are sent by the *qāḍī*, but that they exercise their judgment independently and have the authority to separate the couple without further reference to him. Further, if they deem it appropriate, they take some of her wealth and thus create a separation by means of *khulʿ*.[103]

Shāfiʿī starts by discussing the problem of the refractory wife, the one guilty of *nushūz*.[104] In case of *nushūz* on the wife's part, he says, God permitted that she be chastised and, if that did not work, that her husband shun her (*banish them to beds apart*) and, as a last resort, that he beat her. In case of *nushūz* on the husband's part (*and if you fear a breach between them* [4:35]), Shāfiʿī said that God permitted reconciliation (*ṣulḥ*). Shāfiʿī seems to support the second tradition when he goes on to say that if both fear they cannot keep within the limits imposed by God (4:35), and they bring the matter to the attention of the *qāḍī*, he appoints two arbitrators, one from each of their families, whose job it is to see if they can reconcile the couple. However, he also supports the first tradition by saying that the *qāḍī* cannot order them to separate the couple without the express permission of the husband. In addition he adds that the arbitrators cannot take any of the wife's wealth without her express permission.[105]

Ḥanafī texts from the formative period do not discuss the two arbitrators, and Ibn Ḥanbal does not mention them in his responses.

Liʿān

A man who wishes to deny paternity of a child with whom his wife is pregnant can, in accordance with Qur'ān 24:6–9, accuse her of adultery. If at any time during the *liʿān* procedure he admits that he has lied, he is punished for slander (*qadhf*).[106] If he persists in his accusation, he

[102] Mālik, *Muwaṭṭa'*, 3:214.

[103] See Saḥnūn, *Mudawwana*, 2:367–69. A husband is always free to divorce his wife, but he may not wish to, particularly as he would thereby lose any access he might have to her wealth or property.

[104] For a discussion of the lexical meaning of *nushūz* (refractory behavior), as well as discussion of the issue among pre-modern and modern jurists, see Rispler-Chaim, "*Nushūz* between Medieval and Contemporary Islamic Law: The Human Rights Aspect."

[105] Shāfiʿī, *Kitāb al-umm*, 5:194–95.

[106] See *EI*, s.v. "Ḳadhf" and Schacht, *Introduction*, 179. Technically, the one who slanders receives a *ḥadd* punishment only if the person slandered is *muḥṣan*, or has the

has successfully denied paternity, and the child is related only to its mother. The wife is expected to deny the accusation. After a *liʿān* procedure, the couple is definitely divorced, although there was disagreement about whether they could remarry after *liʿān*.

1. [Sufyān] al-Thawrī said: "If he (i.e., the husband) admits he is lying before he has completed the *liʿān* procedure, he is flogged [for slandering his wife] and she remains his wife."[107]
2. On the authority of Ibn al-Musayyab, "If a husband who has instituted the *liʿān* procedure against his wife repents and confesses after the *liʿān* procedure has been completed, he is flogged, the child is his, and his wife is definitely divorced from him, although he may seek her hand with other suitors. That [is the case] when he admits he has lied.[108]
3. Zuhrī said: "If he confesses that he has lied, they can never remarry."[109]
4. ʿAlī said: "The couple who has participated in the *liʿān* procedure cannot remarry."[110]

All jurists agree with the first tradition, that if the husband does not follow through on the liʿān procedure, the couple remain married, and the husband is punished for slandering his wife. The tradition assumes that the procedure began in front of a *qāḍī* and that the husband interrupted himself at some point, before he had sworn four times and then a fifth, invoking the curse of God upon himself if he were lying about his wife. Jurists disagreed about whether once the *liʿān* procedure was completed and the couple definitely divorced, they could ever remarry. The second tradition says they can: if the husband admits that he has lied about his wife, he may become a suitor of his ex-wife, on an equal footing with any others. The third says the couple cannot remarry even if the husband admits he has lied, and the fourth mentions no extenuating circumstances, but simply says that the couple cannot remarry.

In *Athār Abū Yūsuf*, Abū Ḥanīfa's opinion is that if a man institutes *liʿān* proceedings in front of the *qāḍī*, the procedure itself results in a definite divorce, the child belongs to its mother, and she receives

quality of *iḥṣān*. Here, it is understood that a person with this quality, one of moral uprightness, has never committed unlawful intercourse and therefore can only be falsely accused of doing so. For a discussion of the meaning of the term *iḥṣān* in *fiqh* discussions, see *EI*, s.v. "Muḥṣan."

[107] ʿAbd al-Razzāq, *Muṣannaf*, 7:110, no. 12425; see also 113, no. 12440.

[108] Ibid., 7:111–12, no. 12430.

[109] Ibid., 7:113, no. 12438.

[110] Ibid., 7:112–13, no. 12436.

lodging and maintenance as long as she is waiting her *ʿidda*. If a man does not follow through in his accusation against his wife, he is punished for slander (*qadhf*), but if they subsequently divorce, he can remarry his wife. He is also punished for slander, and the child is considered his, if he first acknowledges paternity of a child with whom his wife is pregnant, but then denies it by instituting *liʿān* proceedings after he has divorced her. Abū Ḥanīfa also makes the point that only free Muslim spouses can participate in *liʿān*.[111] Shaybānī says that the *liʿān* procedure itself does not result in a divorce. The *qāḍī* must separate the couple, and if he does, that counts as a definite divorce. If the husband subsequently confesses that he was lying when he accused his wife of adultery, he may seek her hand.[112]

In the *Muwaṭṭaʾ*, Mālik begins the chapter on *liʿān* with an occasion of revelation to explain Qurʾān 24:6–9.[113] Mālik relates on the authority of Zuhrī that the Companion Sahl b. Saʿd al-Sāʿidī informed him that ʿUwaymir al-ʿAjalānī first went to ʿĀṣim b. ʿAdī and asked him to ask the Prophet what a man should do who finds his wife *in flagrante delicto*. Should he, ʿUwaymir wonders, kill the man so that he is in turn killed?[114] ʿĀṣim goes to question the Prophet, who is displeased at this line of questioning. ʿĀṣim relays the Prophet's displeasure to ʿUwaymir, who then decides to go question the Prophet himself. By the time he reaches the Prophet, 24:6–9 have been revealed, and the Prophet instructs ʿUwaymir to fetch his wife and return. ʿUwaymir does so, and the Prophet institutes *liʿān* proceedings between them. ʿUwaymir then says that if he were to remain married to his wife, that would suggest that he had lied about her, so he divorced her triply, before the Prophet ordered him to.[115] After relating this *ḥadīth*, Mālik says, "Zuhrī said: 'Thereafter, that has been the *sunna* regarding a husband and wife who participate in the *liʿān* procedure.'"[116] Mālik disagrees with the opinion

---

[111] See Abū Yūsuf, *Athār*, nos. 702–6.

[112] Shaybānī, *al-Jāmiʿ al-ṣaghīr*, 198. Shaybānī also points out that Abū Yūsuf did not think they could remarry. See also Shaybānī, *Āthār*, 114, no. 526.

[113] Mālik's *ḥadīth* is similar to the one found in al-Wāḥidī (see Chapter 1), where an anonymous man asks the Prophet what to do.

[114] Zurqānī comments here that the victim's relatives would avenge his death. Mālik, *Muwaṭṭaʾ*, 3:187.

[115] Another issue taken up is some *fiqh* texts was whether the *liʿān* procedure itself resulted in divorce, or the husband subsequent to it divorced his wife, or the *qāḍī* divorced the couple.

[116] Mālik, *Muwaṭṭaʾ*, 3, 186–88. See *EI* (first edition) or *Shorter EI*, s.v. "Ṭalāq" for Schacht's concise summary of this group of exigetical traditions, as well as his clear

Abū Yūsuf reports from Abū Ḥanīfa that the *liʿān* procedure itself results in divorce.[117] He goes on to say that if the man confesses to having lied about his wife, he receives the *ḥadd* punishment for slander, the child is his, his wife does not return to him, and they can never remarry. This, Mālik reports, is "our *sunna* in which there is no doubt and about which there is no disagreement." Further, Mālik says, a man can institute *liʿān* proceedings against a pregnant wife whom he has triply divorced. He can do this if it is reasonable to assume that he might be the father of her unborn child. He cannot, however, first accept that the child is his and then deny it. If he does so, he slanders a "stranger" and is subject to the *ḥadd* punishment.[118] Mālik disagrees with Abū Ḥanīfa that *liʿān* can take place only between free Muslim spouses. He points to 24:6 (*As for those who accuse their wives*) and says that since a Muslim man, whether free or slave, can marry a Muslim slave or a free Jewish or Christian woman, he can institute the *liʿān* procedure against her, and she can respond. "This," he says, "is our practice."[119]

Shāfiʿī agrees with the points Mālik makes in the *Muwaṭṭaʾ*, but he elaborates them at greater length. He adds that the couple should swear in a mosque if they are Muslims, in a church if they are Christians, or wherever the *qāḍī* holds his sessions if they are polytheists. Further, he adds, if a deaf and dumb wife who is fully rational can understand the *liʿān* procedure and participate in it, her husband can initiate it.[120] Ibn Ḥanbal agrees with Shāfiʿī about the *liʿān* procedure and the deaf and dumb wife, but disagrees with both Mālik and Shāfiʿī about a triply divorced couple. When asked about a man who divorces his wife triply, then slanders her, and then she gives birth, he says: "There cannot be *liʿān* between them. Allāh said: *Those who accuse their wives* … and this woman is not a wife."[121]

---

description of the development of the doctrine of *liʿān*. This material has not been included in the second edition of the *EI*. See also Wensinck, *Concordance*, 8, s.v. "ʿUwaymir b. Abyaḍ" for a listing of the *ḥadīth* collections that include this *ḥadīth* with variant wordings. In *Kitāb al-umm*, Shāfiʿī includes several versions of it; see 5, 289–90.

[117] Subsequently, all schools agreed that the *qāḍī* separates the couple after the *liʿān* procedure. See *Shorter EI*, s.v. "Ṭalāq."

[118] Mālik, *Muwaṭṭaʾ*, 3:191–92.

[119] Mālik, *Muwaṭṭaʾ*, 3:192.

[120] Shāfiʿī, *Kitāb al-umm*, 5:286–88.

[121] See Spectorsky, *Chapters*, 46 and 81, §135.

Problematic Statements: Divorce Using Indirect or Ambiguous Expressions

Instead of using a word with the root letters of *ṭ, l, q*, a man can divorce his wife by uttering a variety of indirect or ambiguous statements. The number of these is enormous, and there is often no discernible reason for a jurist's decision about the effect of any one of them. The basic principle, however, is that an ambiguous statement must be resolved, and the speaker's intention (*niyya*) clarified.[122] There are a great many of these expressions and discussion revolved around how many divorces they resulted in, or whether they in fact resulted in any divorce at all. Three of the most commonly discussed were a husband saying to his wife: "*Anti khalīya*," "*Anti barīya*," or "*Anti bāʾina*."[123] These are often discussed together. The expression "*Anti ṭāliq al-battata*"[124] is sometimes discussed with them, as in the first tradition below, but at other times it is discussed on its own, as in the second. The first tradition below encapsulates the disagreement about the effect of these expressions. Each one can mean either that a man has divorced his wife singly or triply or that the number of divorces he has pronounced depends on his intention, which must be ascertained. When *ṭalāq al-batta* is treated separately, it is often in traditions about the Companion Rukāna b. ʿAbd Yazīd, who divorced his wife *al-batta*, and then, uncertain about what he had done, went to ask the Prophet what the expression signified. The second tradition, on the authority of his grandson, tells this story.

1. ʿUmar [said] concerning *al-khalīya, al-barīya, al-battata*, and *al-bāʾina* that they are single [divorces] and he (i.e., a woman's husband) has the right to return to his wife. He (i.e., ʿUmar) said that ʿAlī said that they were [all] triple divorces, and Shurayḥ said that [a man's] intention [must be ascertained], and if he meant triple, then [what the husband said produced] a triple divorce. But if he meant only a single divorce, then it is single. Sufyān [al-Thawrī] said that he is made to swear an oath.
2. From the grandson of Rukāna [b. ʿAbd Yazīd] ... Rukāna divorced his wife *al-battata* and then went to the Prophet and asked him about that.

---

[122] For intent, see *EI*, s.v. "Niyya."

[123] For *khalīya*, see Lane, s.v. *kh-l-w*; for *barīya*, see Lane, s.v. *b, r,* ʾ. Both mean to be or become free. *Barīya* is usually written without ḥamza in early texts dealing with divorce formulas. For *bāʾina*, see Lane, s.v. *b, y, n,* which means "to be or become separated."

[124] For *al-battata*, see Lane, s.v. *b-t-t*, which means "to cut off," "sever," or "separate."

> The Prophet asked him: "What did you mean by that?" He replied: "By God, I meant only a single divorce." The Prophet said: "Then return to her on the basis of it (i.e., the single divorce)."[125]

In his version of the *Muwaṭṭa'*, Shaybānī says that he and Abū Ḥanīfa believe that divorce statements that include the words *khalīya*, *barīya*, or *bā'ina* result in triple divorces if the husband uttering them means them to. If he does not, they result in a single, definite divorce regardless of whether the couple have had intercourse.[126] Again, the practical difference between a definite and a triple divorce is that if the divorce is triple, the couple cannot remarry unless the woman, who is now an ex-wife, has first married another man and had intercourse in that marriage.

Mālik says of "*Anti khalīya*," "*Anti barīya*," and "*Anti bā'ina*," that they are all statements resulting in triple divorce whenever a man has had intercourse with his wife. If he has not had intercourse with her, he is asked to swear about whether he intended a triple or a single divorce. If he intended a single divorce, then he becomes a suitor like any other if he wishes to remarry his wife. If he intended triple divorce, then he cannot remarry her unless she has been married to and divorced from another man. Mālik treats *al-batta* separately and says, on the authority of Zuhrī, that it is a triple divorce.[127] Further, if a man says to his wife, "You are forbidden to me (*Anti ʿalayya ḥarām*)," that too is a triple divorce. However, if he says: "You have free rein," his intention must to be ascertained.[128]

Shāfiʿī disagrees with Mālik. He includes the statements "*Anti khalīya*," or "*Anti barīya*," or "*Anti bā'ina*" with a number of others, such as "Go!" "Get married!" "I have no need of you," and "Your affairs lie in the dwelling of your family." With all these, Shāfiʿī says, a man's intention must be ascertained. If he did not mean to divorce his wife, then he has not done so, if he did mean to divorce her, he has. If he meant a single divorce, it is, and if he meant it to be triple, it is. This also holds true, Shāfiʿī says, for *ṭalāq al-batta*.[129]

Ibn Ḥanbal says that *khalīya*, *barīya*, and *bā'ina* divorce statements all result in triple divorce in one session. He mentions several other

[125] Ibn Abī Shayba, *Muṣannaf*, 4:50, *bāb* 63, no. 1.
[126] Shaybānī, *Muwaṭṭa'*, 243. See also Shaybānī, *Āthār*, 107, no. 406.
[127] Mālik, *Muwaṭṭa'*, 3:168. See also, Saḥnūn, *Mudawwana*, 2:395–404. See Schacht, *Origins*, 146–47 and 195–98, for a summary of the early history of various views on the meaning of divorce with *batta*.
[128] Mālik, *Muwaṭṭa'*, 3:168.
[129] See Shāfiʿī, *Kitāb al-umm*, 5:259–62.

statements, such as "I have no wife," or "I make you a gift to your family," which result in single divorces (the latter statement, only if the woman's family accepts her). "You are divorced like this house" results in a single divorce unless by saying it the speaker intended it to be triple.[130] His view of divorce with *batta* is not entirely clear, although he tends to classify it with *khalīya*, *barīya*, and *bā'ina*.[131] Other statements such as "Get out!" "Go!" and "You are free," Ibn Ḥanbal says, require finding out a man's intentions. Here he agrees with Shāfiʿī. In the case of "You have free rein," he says that it results in a triple divorce; in this he disagrees with Mālik, who says the husband's intention has to be ascertained.

Again, it is not clear why some of these expressions produced triple and others single divorces, or why the meaning of some depend more on a man's intention than others.[132] The above are only a small sampling of the different expressions jurists discussed.[133]

Oaths

Divorce by means of the Oath of Ẓihār

1. Ibn al-Musayyab [held] that if a man swore an oath of *ẓihār* with regard to his wife, then had sexual intercourse with her before he expiated his oath, the Prophet ordered him to perform only one act of expiation.[134]
2. Maʿmar reported on the authority of Zuhrī that if a man breaks his oath of *ẓihār* by having intercourse with his wife before he has expiated it, he must expiate it twice.[135]
3. Ṭāwūs said: "If he takes ill, he completes what remains [of the time period of fasting], he does not start all over again."[136]

[130] See Spectorsky, *Chapters*, 31.
[131] See Spectorsky, *Chapters*, s.v. index, "*Batta*."
[132] For a fuller discussion of the role of a man's intention in determining the effect of various divorce statements, see Powers, *Intent in Islamic Law*, especially Chapter 5, 130–44.
[133] Two divorces at once are mentioned less often than single or triple divorce, because use of the dual would make a man's intention clear. For a discussion of fractions of divorce, see Russell and Suhrawardy, *A Manual of the Law of Marriage*, 174–77. For an almost exhaustive treatment of all possible problematic statements that might or might not result in divorce, see Ibn Qudāma, *Mughnī*, 8:263–479. These include conditional statements, such as "You are divorced if you speak to a certain person," or "You are divorced if I do not speak to you for one month."
[134] ʿAbd al-Razzāq, *Muṣannaf*, 6:431, no. 11527.
[135] Ibid., 6:432, no. 11530.
[136] Ibid., 6:429, no. 11520.

4. Saʿīd b. al-Jubayr said: "[To expiate his oath of ẓihār, a man must fast] two consecutive months, as God said. If he breaks his fast between them, he must start over again."[137]

In Chapter 1, we saw that in the Qurʾān the oath of *ẓihār* was both discouraged and regulated. If a man swore that his wife was to him as the back of his mother, he had to expiate his oath before he could resume sexual relations with her. The above traditions touch on two of the details jurists took up regarding both the oath and its expiation. The first is whether a man must expiate his oath twice if he breaks it before expiating it by having intercourse with his wife. The answers (in the first and second traditions above) are that he does not need to and that he must. The second detail was whether a man who interrupts his expiation of fasting needs to start all over again, or whether he can complete the requisite amount of time when he is able. Again there are two answers.

There is no disagreement among the Ḥanafīs, Mālik, Shāfiʿī, and Ibn Ḥanbal on these two issues. In accordance with the first tradition, only one act of expiation is required if a man breaks his oath of *ẓihār*. If his expiation is fasting, because the Qurʾān says *let him fast for two successive months* (58:4), they agree with the fourth tradition that he cannot stop for a certain period and then take up where he left off.[138]

A number of other issues relevant to the oath of *ẓihār* are taken up at some length in all *fiqh* texts, such as how much food is required to *feed sixty needy ones* (Qurʾān, 58:4) and whether, if a couple are divorced and then remarry before a man has expiated his oath, he must still expiate it before having intercourse with his wife in the couple's second marriage.[139]

The Oath of īlāʾ

1. Ibn Ṭāwūs on the authority of his father that he (i.e., Ṭāwūs) said: "*Īlāʾ* means that a man swears he will never have intercourse with his wife, or [he will not have intercourse with her] for a shorter time period, as long as he swears for more than four months."[140]

---

[137] Ibid., 6:428, no. 11514.

[138] See Shaybānī, *Āthār*, 119, no. 551; Mālik, *Muwaṭṭaʾ*, 176–78; Shāfiʿī, *Kitāb al-umm*, 277–78; Spectorsky, *Chapters*, 131–32, §132,

[139] For a description of these details, see Spectorsky, *Chapters*, 39–42 and references there.

[140] ʿAbd al-Razzāq, *Muṣannaf*, 6:447, no. 11606.

2. Al-Nuʿmān b. Bashīr swore an oath of *īlāʾ* regarding his wife, and then Ibn Masʿūd said, "When four months have passed, she is divorced from him a single divorce."[141]
3. Qatāda said: "ʿAlī and Ibn Masʿūd said, 'She waits an *ʿidda* after the four [months have passed], the *ʿidda* of a divorcée.'" Qatāda said: "Ibn ʿAbbās said: 'Do not prolong things for her. When the four months are over, it is lawful for her to remarry.'"[142]

A man who swears he will not have intercourse with his wife for a specific period of time has sworn an oath of *īlāʿ*. According to the Qurʾān (2:226–27), the time period associated with *īlāʾ* is four months. The first tradition deals with the amount of time a man must swear not to have sexual relations with his wife for his oath to "qualify" as one of *īlāʾ*. The period of time—if it is not forever—must be more than four months. The second tradition indicates that at the end of a four-month period, a *mūlī* is automatically singly divorced from his wife. The third shows disagreement about whether the wife waits an *ʿidda*, in addition to the four-month period of *īlāʾ*, if her husband decides on divorce. Unlike *ẓihār*, revoking an oath of *īlāʾ* does not require expiation, but simply that a husband resume sexual relations with his wife.

However, it is possible for *ẓihār* to turn into *īlāʾ* if a man swears an oath of *ẓihār* against his wife and then refrains from having intercourse with her for four months.[143] Shaybānī reports that if a man combines the two oaths by saying to his wife: "You are to me like the back of my mother if I have intercourse with you," and he then abstains from intercourse with her for four months, she is divorced from him because the four-month period of an oath of *īlāʾ* has passed. If, however, he has intercourse with her within the four-month period, he must perform the expiation for *ẓihār*.[144] Mālik is concerned that a husband harms a wife against whom he has pronounced an oath of *ẓihār* if he neither expiates it, so that he can resume having intercourse with her, nor divorces her. Therefore, if it is clear that he has the capacity to expiate his oath (by fasting or feeding sixty poor people), after four months his marriage is suspended like that of a *mūlī*, and at that point he can either expiate his oath

[141] Ibn Abī Shayba, *Muṣannaf*, 4:96, no. 2. See also 97, no. 13. Other traditions say he is definitely divorced from her, so that a new marriage would be required for him to return to her after the end of her *ʿidda*. See, for example, 4:96, nos. 4, 6–11.

[142] ʿAbd al-Razzāq, *Muṣannaf*, 6:445, no. 11646.

[143] On the other hand, in a tradition expressing disapproval of the combination, Shaʿbī says: "*Īlāʾ* is not *ẓihār* and *żihār* is not *īlāʾ*." ʿAbd al-Razzāq, *Muṣannaf*, 6:440, no. 11574. For a tradition expressing approval of it, see idem, 6:440, no. 11576.

[144] Shaybānī says this is also Abū Ḥanīfa's opinion. Shaybānī, *Āthār*, 119, no. 552.

or his wife can be divorced from him.[145] Shāfiʿī agrees with Mālik's concern that a man not harm his wife and says that at the end of four months a man is given the opportunity to expiate his oath of *ẓihār* on the spot or divorce his wife.[146] Ibn Ḥanbal agrees with Mālik and Shāfiʿī and adds the point that if a husband does not expiate his oath of *ẓihār* after four months, the *qāḍī* divorces the couple. Ibn Ḥanbal states what the others seem to take for granted in discussions of *īlā*, which is that a wife must bring her situation to the attention of the *qāḍī*. If neither she nor her husband say or do anything, her situation as the recipient of the oath of *īlāʾ* or, for that matter of *ẓihār*, could theoretically last indefinitely.[147]

"Every woman I marry is divorced"

This oath is often, but not always, countered by the statement: "There can be no divorce before marriage." In the first tradition below, the statement is attributed to the Prophet; it is also often attributed to a Companion or a Successor. In the second tradition, Ibn ʿAbbās quotes the Qurʾān to make the point that divorce cannot precede marriage. In the third, Saʿīd b. al-Musayyab puts the matter more colorfully. However, in the fourth tradition such an oath is considered binding, and the woman in question becomes a divorcée right after she has been married.

1. The Prophet said: "There can be no divorce before marriage."[148]
2. Ibn ʿAbbās said: "God said, *O you who believe, if you wed believing women and divorce them before you have touched them. ...*Therefore, there cannot be divorce until there has been marriage."[149]
3. Saʿīd b. al-Musayyab, Mujāhid, and ʿAṭāʾ were asked about a man who says: "On the day I marry a certain woman (*fulāna*), she is divorced." They said: "His statement has no effect." Saʿīd added: "Does a flood come before rain?"
4. Shaʿbī was asked about a man who says to his wife: "Every woman I marry in addition to you is divorced." He [Shaʿbī] said, "Every woman he marries in addition to that one is indeed divorced."[150]

Shaybānī reports in some detail on Abū Ḥanīfa's position. In *Āthār Shaybānī*, he relates on the authority of Abū Ḥanīfa that the Successor al-Aswad b. Yazīd had been told about a certain woman and said:

---

[145] See Saḥnūn, *Mudawwana*, 3:60–61.
[146] Shāfiʿī, *Kitāb al-umm*, 5:280.
[147] Spectorsky, *Chapters*, 186, §139.
[148] Ibn Abī Shayba, *Muṣannaf*, 4:14, no. 1.
[149] Qurʾān 33:49. Ibn Abī Shayba, *Muṣannaf*, 4:16, *bāb* 15, no. 3.
[150] Ibn Abī Shayba, *Muṣannaf*, 4:16, *bāb* 16, no. 4.

"If I marry her, she is divorced," but later on he did not think his statement had any effect. The scholars of the Hijāz were asked, and they too did not think his statement had any effect, so he married and had intercourse with her. But then he mentioned that to Ibn Masʿūd, who ordered him to tell her she had the most right to herself (i.e., that she was divorced from him). Shaybānī says: "We adopt the position of Ibn Masʿūd. Further, she receives half the marriage portion for which he married her (since, in theory, divorce took place before intercourse), as well as a fair marriage portion, since he has in fact had intercourse with her. This is also Abū Ḥanīfa's doctrine."[151]

Mālik differentiates between a man saying that every woman he marries is divorced and a less general statement in which he names a particular woman, a tribe to which she might belong, or a locale she might come from. A general statement is without legal effect (as in the fourth tradition above),[152] but any detail in a man's statement means that he breaks his oath the minute he marries, and his wife is divorced (as in the third tradition above).[153]

Both Shāfiʿī and Ibn Ḥanbal are adamant about the basic fact that a man cannot divorce a woman before he has married her, and they therefore do not think variations in the details of a statement a man might utter (such as his mentioning a particular woman or tribe or locale) make any difference at all. Ibn Ḥanbal, for example, quotes a tradition in which the Prophet says: "No oath should be taken by a man concerning the disposition of something that is not in his possession; no slave should be manumitted before actually being taken into physical custody, and no woman divorced before she is actually married."[154]

"You are divorced, God willing" (in shāʾ Allāh).

1. Regarding a man who says to his wife: "You are divorced *in shāʾ Allāh*," Ḥammād said: "His saying *in shāʾ Allāh* is valid." Al-Ḥakam said the same thing.[155]

[151] Shaybānī, *Āthār*, 110. Shaybānī here gives the woman in question half her marriage portion on the basis of divorce before intercourse and in addition a full marriage portion because her [ex-] husband has had intercourse with her. See also Abū Yūsuf, *Āthār*, no. 623; and Shaybānī, *Muwaṭṭaʾ*, 230.

[152] See Mālik, *Muwaṭṭaʾ*, 3:214.

[153] Ibid., 3:215. For more variants on these statements, see Saḥnūn, *Mudawwana*, 3:18–19.

[154] Spectorsky, *Chapters*, 124, §109. See also index, s.v. "Divorce before marriage" and Shāfiʿī, *Kitāb al-umm*, 5:251–52.

[155] Ibn Abī Shayba, *Muṣannaf*, 4:38, *bāb* 46, no. 3.

2. Ḥasan al-Baṣrī said: "If a man says to his wife that she is divorced *in shāʾ Allāh*, she is divorced and his saying *in shāʾ Allāh* has no effect.[156]

The tradition at the beginning of this chapter makes it clear that there is no question about God's displeasure with divorce. However, there was disagreement about the effect of using—or misusing—*in shāʾ Allāh* in a divorce statement. The two traditions above take opposing views. The first agrees with the one at the beginning of the chapter and thus adding *in shāʾ Allāh* means that divorce does not take place. In the second, adding it has no effect, and divorce does take place. Abū Ḥanīfa and Shāfiʿī agree with the first tradition. In his *Āthār*, Shaybānī adds, on the authority of Abū Ḥanīfa, that a *triple* divorce is invalidated if *in shāʾ Allāh* is part of the divorce statement.[157] Mālik and Ibn Ḥanbal agree with the second tradition. Ibn Ḥanbal pairs it with manumission (like the tradition at the beginning of the chapter but with the opposite effect) and says: "I do not allow it. As a rule a woman is divorced if *in shāʾ Allāh* is added to the divorce statement, and the same is true in cases of manumission. That is because divorce is not an oath in which *istithnāʾ* is relevant."[158]

Discussion

The chapters in *fiqh* texts devoted to divorce include a myriad of details and vastly more casuistic discussion than those on marriage. While the above survey has included a number of these details, I have left many out. Within all the subtle arguments is an occasional admonitory statement urging that a man act with restraint. So, for example, in his discussion of divorce before intercourse, Shāfiʿī says that he "prefers" (literally: "chooses" [*akhtāru*]) that a man pronounce only a single rather than a triple divorce, so that it is possible for him to return to his wife during her *ʿidda*, or, if he divorces her before having intercourse with her, he can remarry her without it being necessary for her to consummate an intervening marriage with another man. Shaybānī says of

---

[156] Ibid., 4:38, *bāb* 36, no. 5.

[157] See Abū Yūsuf, *Āthār*, nos. 620 and 628; Shāfiʿī, *Kitāb al-umm*, 5:187; Shaybānī, *Āthār*, 110–11. A third possibility is that divorce does not take place because it *is* permissible, and by invoking God's will, a man has abdicated forming an intention and thus divorce does not take place. See Spectorsky, *Chapters*, index, s.v. "*Istithnāʾ*."

[158] See *EI*, s.v. "Ḳasam" for extra-judicial oaths. See also Saḥnūn, *Mudawwana*, 3:16, for a more extensive explanation of Mālik's view of *in shāʾ Allāh* in divorce statements; and Spectorsky, *Chapters*, 163, §67 for Ibn Ḥanbal's. See also Schacht, *Introduction*, 117, 159.

a man who separates from his wife by means of *khulʿ* and takes back more than he gave her as a marriage portion, "We do not like it." It is, nonetheless, lawful.

The "model" divorce, *ṭalāq al-sunna*, is based on a combination of Qurʾān 65:1 (*When you (men) put away women, put them away for their (legal) period [liʿiddatihinna] and reckon the period*) and of the tradition of the Prophet's insisting that Ibn ʿUmar not divorce his wife while she was menstruating, but instead divorce her in a period of purity before he had resumed having intercourse with her. All jurists agreed on this basic description, but disagreed on whether *ṭalāq al-sunna* could be a triple as well as a single divorce. Shaybānī and Abū Ḥanīfa said it could be, and if a man wanted to be triply divorced from his wife, they said he could divorce her initially and then twice more during her *ʿidda* at the start of each period of purity, thereby becoming triply divorced from her by the end of one *ʿidda*. Shāfiʿī and Ibn Ḥanbal were both unwilling to go beyond the traditions they knew about this matter and so were neutral, but Mālik was opposed to a triple divorce over the course of one *ʿidda*, despite the fact that if it occurred, it was lawful.

On the other hand, contingent statements of divorce elicited casuistic discussion where neither admonitory advice nor logic seems to predominate. The statement "Every woman I marry is divorced" points to a regional difference between the Ḥanafī and Medinese positions. For the Kufans, once al-Aswad b. Yazid learned from Ibn Masʿūd that having said "Every woman I marry is divorced," he was obliged to divorce his wife and owed her a marriage portion and a half (half her marriage portion for divorce before intercourse and her full marriage portion for intercourse during the marriage). Mālik's position that the statement has no effect bears out Shaybānī's reference to "the scholars of the Hijaz," but then Mālik adds the refinement that any specificity in a statement of divorce before marriage (such as naming a woman's tribe or the town in which she lives) makes it valid, so his position very little different from that of the Ḥanafīs.

Similarly, neither admonitory advice nor logic seems to apply in the discussions of indirect or ambiguous expressions of divorce that require asking a man about his intentions. It turns out, for no discernible reason, that some statements (e.g., "I have no wife") produce a single divorce, while others (e.g., "You have free rein") require explanation. In the case of *ṭalāq al-batta*, for Shaybānī and Abū Ḥanīfa it results in a single, definite divorce, but for Mālik it is triple, and for Shāfiʿī and Ibn Ḥanbal, a man must be asked what he intended by making a statement with *batta*.

At times both traditionists and jurists ask and answer questions about how best to carry out the Qur'ān's dictates. For *ẓihār* and *īlā'*, for example, the traditions and the jurists' discussions both point to concern for the details of the procedures a man should follow in order to expiate his oath and resume sexual relations with his wife. On *li'ān*, the Qur'ān does not specify what happens if the wife maintains she is innocent throughout the procedure. In the occasion of revelation we saw in Chapter 1, Wāḥidī reported that when the wife maintained her innocence, her husband divorced her. This report agrees with the opinion attributed to Mālik, Shāfi'ī, and Ibn Ḥanbal, who all think that the *li'ān* procedure must be followed by divorce, but Abū Ḥanīfa and Shaybānī disagreed and said that the procedure itself resulted in divorce. Another issue was whether the couple could ever remarry. The answer was that they could only if the husband failed to follow through in his accusation. When that happened, even though he was punished for slander and the couple were definitely divorced, he could seek his ex-wife's hand along with other suitors.

Takhyīr is connected to verses 33:28–29 of the Qur'ān. There was general agreement that these verses describe the fact that the Prophet gave his wives the choice of leaving or staying with him and that 'Ā'isha led the way in immediately choosing to remain married. Different interpretations arose about whether the choice itself produced a divorce, whether if a woman exercised her option, she could decide on a single or a triple divorce, or whether the single or triple divorce was automatic. *Tamlīk* (not mentioned in the Qur'ān) is either synonymous with *takhyīr* or depends on the husband's intention.

Khul' elicited much discussion. Only Ibn Ḥanbal, following a tradition from Ibn 'Abbās, said that a wife's ransoming herself resulted in an annulment. The other jurists thought it resulted in a divorce, but disagreed about whether it was single and definite, or a triple divorce. Although not stated directly, it is assumed that after separation by *khul'*, the couple could not return to each other since the woman was no longer in possession of her marriage portion. The only question was whether, if they wished to remarry, the wife had to have an intervening marriage.

On the problem of where the triply divorced woman waited her *'idda* and whether she received maintenance during it, Abū Ḥanīfa, Mālik, and Shāfi'ī thought that Qur'ān 65:6 (*lodge them where you dwell*) applied to all divorcées, but Ibn Ḥanbal thought it applied only to revocably divorced women.

CHAPTER FOUR

FROM THE FORMATIVE TO THE CLASSICAL PERIODS

We said above that the classical period was marked by the formation of the schools of law. In its broadest definition, a school of law, a *madhhab*, consists of a group of scholars committed to studying the development of doctrine based on the interpretation of the texts attributed to the school's eponymous founder. "The most striking characteristic of the classical legal tradition was its literary form of commentaries. For medieval Muslims legal scholarship was an ongoing debate about the correct understanding of God's Will according to which all humans should live."[1] By the 4th/10th century, the start of the classical period (as defined in the introduction), a formal system of *madhhab* learning was gradually replacing the informal activity of the scholars who had acted as the elders of the community in the formative period. *Madhhab* learning took place in mosques and *madrasa*s where jurists studied and taught full time and trained the next generation of scholars, many of whom became *qāḍī*s or *muftī*s.[2] These jurists were the authors of the *fiqh* works that were built on the texts attributed to the founders of the school, as well as on the previous commentaries and interpretations that reinforced the doctrines, which had evolved over time as authoritative for their particular *madhhab*.[3] For *fiqh*, that did not mean there came to be only one answer to every legal question. There may be several possible answers, but they are based on the cumulative thinking of

[1] Buskins, "A Medieval Islamic Law?" 472.

[2] For bibliography on the evolution and development of the *madhhab*, see *EI*, s.v. "Madhhab." For the development of the *madrasa* as an institution of *madhhab* learning, see *EI*, s.v. "Madrasa" (1. The Institution in the Arab, Persian, and Turkish Lands).

[3] This process of reinforcing the work of the founders of the *madhhabs* is *taqlīd*, *EI*, s.v. Belonging to a *madhhab* gave a scholar an intellectual and legal identity and made him an *ʿālim*, a member of the *ʿulamāʾ*. See Humphries, *Islamic History: A Framework for Inquiry*, 96, where he says of the *madhhab*, "[i]t assured continuity and stability both in education and doctrine, and through affiliaton with a *madhhab* a scholar became connected with a wide-ranging professional and social network." More generally, see his Chapter 8, "The *ʿUlamāʾ* in Islamic Society." For the relationship of master-teacher and student, see Makdisi, "*Ṣuḥba* et *Riyāsa* dans L'Enseignement Médiéval."

the school. What does this mean in terms of actual doctrine? In this chapter I have used a selection of classical texts to look at examples of continuous development and then at change between the formative and classical periods. To do this I have used a *mukhtaṣar* by a scholar from each school and then a longer work of *fiqh* (referred to in the introduction as a *mabsūṭ*), again one by a scholar from each school, which covers the same points in more detail.

For the Ḥanafīs, I have used the *Mukhtaṣar* of Abu'l-Ḥusayn al-Qudūrī (d. 428/1037), who was the leading Ḥanafī scholar in Baghdad during his lifetime.[4] A fuller description of Ḥanafī law is provided by Burhān al-Dīn al-Marghīnānī (d. 593/1197) in his *al-Hidāya, sharḥ bidāyat al-mubtadī,* which is a commentary on Qudūrī's *Mukhtaṣar* and Shaybānī's *al-Jāmiʿal-ṣaghīr*. Marghīnānī traveled widely to study *fiqh* and *ḥadīth* before returning to teach in Marghīnān. His *Hidāya* has been widely studied, and there is an extensive commentary tradition on it.[5]

For the Mālikīs, I have relied on the *Risāla* of Ibn Abī Zayd al-Qayrawānī (d. 389/998), which is a summary of Mālikī law, and on *al-Kāfī fi'l-fiqh,* a manual of Mālikī law by the Andalusian jurist Ibn ʿAbd al-Barr (d. 463/1070). Ibn Abī Zayd studied with a number of Mālikī scholars in the East when he made the pilgrimage, as well as with leading scholars in Qayrawān, including Saʿdūn al-Khawlānī (d. 324 or 325/935 or 936), who had studied with Muḥammad b. Saḥnūn (d. 256/870), the son of Saḥnūn b, Saʿīd al-Tānūkhī, compiler of the *Mudawwana.* Ibn Abī Zayd did not compose his *Risāla* as a reference work for jurists, but rather to provide a clear distillation of

[4] See *EI*, s.v. "al-Ḳudūrī, Abu'l Ḥusayn." His *Mukhtaṣar*, also often referred to simply as *al-Kitāb*, has been commented on many times. The edition I have used includes the commentary *al-Lubāb fī sharḥ al-kitāb*, by ʿAbd al-Ghānī al-Ghanīmī al-Maydānī (who studied with the eminent Syrian jurist Ibn ʿĀbidīn [d. 1258/1842] [see *EI*, s.v.]) and was published under this title (see bibliography). I have also consulted the translation of Qudūrī's *Mukhtaṣ ar* by G.-H. Bousquet and L. Bercher (see bibliography). One of Qudūrī's most famous pupils was the polymath al-Khatīb al-Baghdādī, who said of him, "He was distinguished in *fiqh* owing to his great intelligence, and he wound up as the leader of the followers of Abū Ḥanīfa in Iraq. His standing among them was great and his fame spread." *Tārīkh Baghdād*, 4:377.

[5] See *EI*, s.v. "al-Marghīnānī, Burhān al-Dīn" for a table of commentaries and synopses of the *Hidāya*. Marghīnānī first wrote *Bidāyat al-mubtadī*, a legal compendium based on Qudūrī's *Mukhtaṣar* and Shaybānī's *al-Jāmiʿal-ṣaghīr*, which he later abridged into the *Hidāya*. The 19th-century English translation, *The Hedaya*, by Charles Hamilton (see bibliography) should not be used without reference to the Arabic text.

Mālikī law for all Muslims to understand and follow.[6] Ibn ʿAbd al-Barr was born and grew up in Cordova, which at that time was a center of book production and scholarship. He never made the pilgrimage or traveled to the East, but spent his entire life in al-Andalus, where he traveled widely to study with its leading scholars. He became a *qāḍī* both in Lisbon and Santarem and was a prolific author of both of *uṣūl* and *fiqh* works.[7]

For the Shāfiʿīs I have relied on two works by the renowned legal scholar Abū Isḥāq al-Shīrāzī (d. 476/1083), his *Tanbīh fī fiqh al-īmām al-Shāfiʿī*, a summary of Shāfiʿī *fiqh*, and his more extensive *Kitāb al-muhadhdhab*.[8] Shīrāzī studied first in Firuzabad, where he was born, then in Shiraz and Basra, and finally in Baghdad with the *qāḍī* Abu'l-Tayyib al-Ṭabarī (d. 450/1058), whose teaching post he took over after Ṭabarī's death. From 459/1066 until his death, Shīrāzī taught at the Madrasa Niẓāmiyya, which the Seljuk wazīr Niẓām al-Mulk had endowed for him.[9]

For Ḥanbalī *fiqh*, I have used the *Mukhtaṣar* by Abu'l-Qāsim al-Khiraqī (d. 334/945) and the exhaustive commentary on it *al-Mughnī*, by Muwaffaq al-Dīn b. Qudāma (d. 620/1223).[10] Khiraqī studied with Ibn Ḥanbal's two sons, ʿAbd Allāh and Ṣāliḥ, in Baghdad and then moved to Damascus shortly before his death. His *mukhtaṣar* is the first summary statement of Ḥanbalī *fiqh*.[11] Ibn Qudāma studied both in Damascus and Baghdad. His *Mughnī*, although ostensibly a commentary on Khiraqī's *Mukhtaṣar*, functions as a primary source for Ḥanbalī jurisprudence but also as a secondary source, for in the process of commenting on Khiraqī's *mukhtaṣar*, he also provides a history of the

---

[6] See *EI*, s.v. "Ibn Abī Zayd al-ḳayrawānī"; *GAS*, 1:478–81; H. R. Idris, "Deux juristes Kairouanais de l'époque zīrīde: Ibn Abī Zayd et al-Qābisī," *AIEO Alger*, 1954, 121–98.

[7] In addition, he is the author of a collection of biographies of the Companions, *al-Istiʿāb fī maʿrifat al-aṣḥāb*. See *EI*, s.v. "Ibn ʿAbd al-Barr"; Ibn Farhūn, *al-Dībāj*, 440–42, and a full description of Ibn ʿAbd al-Barr's life and work in Vol. 1 by the editors of his *al-Tamhīd li mā fī'l-Muwaṭṭa' min al-maʿānī wa'l-asānīd* (Rabat, 1977–89).

[8] For Shīrāzī, see EI, s.v. "al-Shīrāzī, Abū Isḥāḳ Ibrāhīm b. ʿAlī." I have also used the French translation of sections of the *Tanbīh* by G.-H. Bousquet (see bibliography).

[9] *EI*, s.v. "Shīrāzī, Abū Isḥāq Ibrāhīm b. ʿAlī." Shīrāzī describes his teachers in his own *Ṭabaqāt al-fuqahā'*.

[10] For Khiraqī, see *GAS*, 1:512–13. For Ibn Qudāma, see *EI*, s.v. Ibn ḳudāma al-Maḳdisī, Muwaffaḳ al-Dīn.

[11] *EI*, s.v. "al-Khiraqī, ʿUmar b. al-Ḥusayn"; *GAS*, 1:512–13; Laoust, "Le Ḥanbalisme sous le Caliphat de Baghdad," 85.

evolution of any particular ruling among all Sunnī jurists, along with many of the traditions used to prove or disprove it.[12]

I have chosen these texts for their clarity and accessibility, as well as for the importance of each author within the tradition of his school. All these men were leading scholars and teachers during their lifetimes, and their pupils carried on and commented on their work.[13] That said, their texts differ from each other not only because they represent different school traditions, but also in length and complexity. Ibn Abī Zayd and Khiraqī compiled brief statements or directives on appropriate procedure, with little explanation or discussion of alternatives. The texts by Qudūrī and Shīrāzī are more discursive. Qudūrī includes the views of Abū Ḥanīfa, Abū Yūsuf, and Shaybānī and sometimes discusses them, while Shīrāzī frequently notes that several opinions prevail in the Shāfiʿī school, sometimes indicating which one is preponderant or which one he himself considers best, but other times not. The longer works of *fiqh* also vary in length and complexity. Marghīnānī and Shīrāzī often mention opinions of other schools and refer to traditions. Ibn ʿAbd al-Barr mentions only Mālikī opinions, sometimes naming earlier Mālikī scholars. Ibn Qudāma, as noted above, is all-inclusive.

Several points are worth noting before I describe the actual content of these works. First, scholars of the classical period drew upon many more traditions than the few I quote throughout this volume, as well as upon texts and opinions attributed to the founders that have been lost or have changed over time. This means that their descriptions of what earlier scholars thought or said do not necessarily replicate what I have described and that the opinions of earlier scholars cannot always be correlated with what later authors attribute to them. Second, one of the generalizations made about *fiqh* in the classical period is that all Sunni schools based their doctrines on the Qurʾān, the *sunna* of the Prophet expressed in traditions, *ijmāʿ*, and *qiyās*. How to utilize these sources is explored in works of *uṣūl*.[14] The authors of compilations of *furūʿ* (who were usually also authors of works of *uṣūl*) work within this

---

[12] *EI*, s.v. "Ibn Ḳudāma al-Makdisī, Muwaffaḳ al-Dīn." Ibn Qudāma also wrote a summary of his *Mughnī, al-ʿUmda*, which was translated by Laoust (*Le Précis de Droit d'Ibn Qudāma*), who prefaced his translation with an introduction on Hanbalism in Damascus in the 6th/12th century and Ibn Qudāma's contribution to it.

[13] This generalization is less true of Khiraqī, perhaps because there was no established head of the Ḥanbalī school in Baghdad until the end of the 4th/10th century. See Melchert, *Formation of the Sunni Schools*, 148–55.

[14] See again Calder in *EI*, s.v. "Sharīʿa."

framework, but they do not necessarily articulate it. They may or may not refer to a relevant Qurʾān verse, and when they refer to a tradition, they do so the way earlier scholars did, often not citing an *isnād* but simply referring to the *matn* to prove a particular point. Most of the time they engage with earlier discussions. This does not necessarily mean adhering to the opinions of the founders, although it may. It may also mean adding material to the ongoing discussion, material that originated in casuistry, the influx of new cases, or some combination of both. It is not always possible to tell why they examine a particular issue.[15] As a consequence of incorporating the new material, the applicability of earlier rulings may be altered by being limited, enlarged, or sometimes declared no longer relevant. Finally, there are a variety of reasons for misrepresentation of the opinions of earlier scholars. It can result from textual instability, from polemics among different schools, as a consequence of discussion within the same school, from a tendency to identify a scholar's doctrines with the traditions he reports, or from a desire to retroject authority for any new doctrine back to earlier experts.[16]

To demonstrate continuous development and change between the formative and classical periods, I have chosen several problems discussed in Chapters 2 and 3. However, instead of taking traditions from the *Muṣannafs* of ʿAbd al-Razzāq and Ibn Abī Shayba, I preface my discussion of each issue with traditions found in the Six Books and Ibn Ḥanbal's *Musnad*.[17] As was true of ʿAbd al-Razzāq and Ibn Abī Shayba, the authors of these collections worked with the same legal material the jurists did.[18] For the most part I follow the format of Chapters 2 and 3.

[15] For a clear discussion of this question, see Johansen, "Casuistry: Between Legal Concept and Social Practice."

[16] See Schacht, "Sur la transmission de la doctrine dans les écoles juridiques de l'Islam." Schacht provides examples of later misrepresentation of early Ḥanafī and Mālikī positions in the *Mabsūṭ* of the Ḥanafī jurist Muḥammad b. Aḥmad al-Sarakhsī (d. 483/1090). Schacht also points to the ease with which the phrase "in accordance with an analogy to Abū Ḥanīfa's doctrine" (*fī qiyās qawl Abī Ḥanīfa*) can be changed to "in accordance with Abū Ḥanīfa's doctrine" (*fī qawl Abī Ḥanīfa*) by leaving out the word *qiyās*. Schacht does not mention textual instability, but that should always be kept in mind for the pre-modern period.

[17] Many of these traditions are also found in the collections of ʿAbd al-Razzāq and Ibn Abī Shayba, who are often found in later *isnāds*. Ibn Ḥanbal studied traditions with ʿAbd al-Razzāq, and Ibn Abī Shayba was a teacher of Bukhārī', Muslim, and Abū Dāwūd.

[18] The traditionists' concern with *isnāds* affected their choice of *matns* differently from the jurists. In the case of divorce, Scott Lucas has shown that for the authors of

I summarize the Ḥanafī, Mālikī, Shāfiʿī, and Ḥanbalī views of a particular issue, but I do not always use all eight works for each issue. Sometimes those from the same school merely repeat each other; at other times one author will mention details that another does not. The contrast between Khiraqī and Ibn Qudāma is particularly notable. Ibn Qudāma goes into virtually all possible ramifications of every issue, but sometimes Khiraqī's brief statements seemed adequate for demonstrating my point. On the other hand, Ibn Qudāma's comprehensiveness means he takes up a number of issues Khiraqī does not.

Continuous Development from the Formative to the Classical Period

Marriage

A Woman's Guardian

1. The Prophet said: "There can be no marriage contract without a *walī*."[19]
2. The Prophet said: "No woman can give another in marriage. Nor can she give herself in marriage. Only an adulteress gives herself in marriage."[20]
3. Khansāʾ bt. Khudhām al-Anṣārīya [said] that her father gave her in marriage after she had become a *thayyib*, and she disliked that, so she went to the Prophet, who revoked her marriage.[21]

We saw in Chapter 2 that the Ḥanafīs were of the opinion that a woman could conclude her own marriage contract. The fact that this is a view not shared by jurists of other schools is reflected in the first two traditions above. The third suggests that the Prophet's willingness to allow Khansāʾ bt. Khudhām to choose her own husband means that a woman can (at least under certain circumstances) marry without a *walī*'s permission and seems to support the Ḥanafī opinion.

Later Ḥanafīs continue to say that a woman can conclude her own marriage contract, but within limits about which Abū Ḥanīfa, Abū Yūsuf, and Shaybānī did not all agreed. Qudūrī says, "According to Abū

---

the Six Books, this meant the elimination of a number of details found in the collections of ʿAbd al-Razzāq and Ibn Abī Shayba. See Lucas, "Divorce, *Ḥadīth*-Scholar Style."

[19] Ibn Māja, *Sunan*, 1:605, no. 1881.

[20] Ibid., 1:606, no. 1882.

[21] Bukhārī, *Ṣaḥīḥ*, 3:372, no. 5138.

Ḥanīfa, the marriage contract of a free, adult, legally competent woman can be concluded with her agreement even if a *walī* does not conclude it on her behalf, and regardless of whether she is a virgin or a *thayyib*." He then notes, "Abū Yūsuf and Muḥammad (i.e., Shaybānī) said it could be concluded only by a *walī*."[22] Commenting on this difference among the early Ḥanafīs, Marghīnānī says that according to the *ẓāhir al-riwāya*,[23] Abū Yūsuf agreed with Abū Ḥanīfa, that it is also related that Abū Yūsuf required a *walī*, and that Shaybānī said such a contract was suspended until her *walī* approved it. Thus any shortcoming in the contract would be eliminated by requiring his approval.

The reasoning given by Marghīnānī for permitting a woman to conclude her own contract is that she is fully competent to act on her own behalf. For example, she can manage her own property and choose a husband. However, "the reason a *walī* is needed for a marriage contract is so that impudence will not be laid at a woman's door. In addition, according to the *ẓāhir al-riwāya*, there is no difference between her marriage to an equal or a non-equal in terms of whether the contract is valid. However, the *walī* can invalidate her marriage contract to a non-equal."[24]

Although we saw in Chapter 2 that Mālik is said to have made an exception in the case of a lowly woman, later Mālikīs do not leave room for any woman to conclude her own contract. Ibn Abī Zayd says, "A woman can marry only with the consent either of her *walī*, or a responsible relative like a man of her tribe, or the *qāḍī*."[25] Ibn ʿAbd al-Barr reinforces this by saying, "A woman cannot act as a *walī* for her own marriage contract or for anyone else's," and he then adds the later Mālikī position that there are no exceptions: "[This is the case] regardless of whether she is a noble or a lowly woman, and regardless of whether her *walī* did or did not give her permission to act on her own behalf." Under no circumstances is such a marriage valid: "If she does conclude a marriage contract, it is always invalid, both before and after

---

[22] Qudūrī, *Mukhtaṣar*, 3:8.

[23] In Ḥanafī texts, *ẓāhir al-riwāya* refers to the accepted doctrine of the Ḥanafī school. It is, theoretically, based on six of the works attributed to Shaybānī. One of these is *al-Jāmiʿ al-ṣaghīr* (see Chapters 2 and 3). The other five are *al-Mabsūṭ*, *al-Ziyādāt*, *al-Jāmiʿ al-kabīr*, *al-Siyar al-kabīr*, and *al-Siyar al-ṣaghīr*. See Hallaq, *Authority*, 48, n. 98. For a description of these works, see *GAS*, 1:422–30.

[24] That is, there is no difference between an equal and a non-equal in terms of whether the contract is valid or suspended. Marghīnānī, *Hidāya*, 2:475–76.

[25] Ibn Abī Zayd, *Risala*, 174 (*First Steps*, 4, no. 9).

the marriage has been consummated."[26] The Shāfiʿī view, represented by Shīrāzī, is the same as the Mālikī, but he also includes the fact that a woman cannot conclude a marriage contract for a female slave of hers: "A woman's marriage contract is valid only if concluded by a male *walī*. If she is a slave, her master gives her in marriage. If she is owned by a woman, whatever male guardian is in charge of giving her owner in marriage, gives her in marriage with her owner's permission."[27]

Khiraqī's statement for the Ḥanbalīs is the same as the first tradition above: "There can be no marriage without a *walī*." Ibn Qudāma begins his commentary on this statement of Khiraqī's by discussing the Ḥanafī view: "Abū Ḥanīfa said that she had the right to give herself and someone else in marriage, as well as to appoint a representative to give [her] in marriage. [Abū Ḥanīfa said that this was the case for the following reasons:] because God said, *And place not difficulties in the way of their marrying their husbands* (Qurʾān 2:232), and thereby He connected marriage with them (i.e., women) and forbade preventing them from it. [Abū Ḥanīfa also said,] because it is a woman's unadulterated right and women are among those people who can conclude a contract directly (i.e., unlike slaves who must have an owner's permission), a marriage contract concluded by a woman is valid, just as her selling a female slave of hers is valid. ..." Having explained this, Ibn Qudāma disagrees and stresses that the Ḥanbalī opinion is supported by the tradition on ʿĀʾisha's authority, "There can be no marriage without a *walī*." Ibn Qudāma takes up the point mentioned by Ibn ʿAbd al-Barr (see above) that it does not matter whether her *walī* gave her permission to act on her own behalf.[28] He says that because her opinion about a potential marriage should be taken into account, it has been inferred that she can, once she has received her *walī*'s permission, conclude her own marriage contract. This, he says, is Shaybānī's opinion. Here Ibn Qudāma explains that even though the tradition in which the Prophet said, "The contract of any woman who marries without her *walī*'s permission is void, void, void" could possibly be understood this way (i.e., that once the *walī* has given permission, she is free to act

[26] Ibn ʿAbd al-Barr, *al-Kāfī fi'l-fiqh*, 2:527.
[27] Shīrāzī, *Tanbīh*, 404.
[28] Unless Ibn Qudāma specifically says so (which he does not in this case), we cannot tell whether he is reacting specifically to a text of Ibn ʿAbd al-Barr or to another text, or to the Mālikī view, in general.

independently), the correct position is contained in the first tradition he quoted, "There can be no marriage without a *walī*."[29]

In these details that the later scholars added to earlier descriptions of the role of a woman's *walī* in concluding her marriage contract, there is a discernible tendency on the part of Ḥanafī and Mālikī jurists to further restrict her capacity to conclude her own contract, so that their positions on this question become virtually indistinguishable from those of the Shāfiʿīs and Ḥanbalīs.

Raḍāʿ

1. The Prophet said: "Nursing requires hunger."
2. The Prophet said: "Nursing forbids what lineage does."[30]

In Chapter 2 we saw discussion among the scholars of the formative period as to whether a minimum number of suckling sessions are required to establish a foster relationship and whether such a relationship can be established if the individual being nursed is an adult. The first tradition above succinctly restates the point that only nursing during infancy establishes foster relationship. Infants nurse because they are hungry; adults, only because they are attempting to create a foster relationship. The second restates the position that relationships established through nursing parallel those of consanguinity. All classical texts agree that only nursing during infancy establishes foster relationship, regardless of how many suckling sessions occur. In addition, they include further details about foster relationships and marriage that qualify the Prophet's statement in the second tradition above. In both cases, possibilities that were entertained in the formative period are effectively ruled out.

Qudūrī in his *Mukhtaṣar* describes some of the complexities involved in figuring out whether two people are or are not related through nursing. For example, as the first tradition above shows, since nursing after infancy does not create foster relationship, if a wet nurse

---

[29] Ibn Qudāma, *Mughni*, 7:337–38. He concludes by saying that to prevent a woman from concluding her own contract is "to prevent her from handling directly a matter which would make obvious her impudence, levity, and inclination for men" (a view he shares with Marghīnānī). Note that Ibn Qudāma's description of what Shaybānī said does not exactly match Marghīnānī's.

[30] See, Wensinck, *Handbook*, s.v. "Nursing," for the many instances of this and the previous Prophetic tradition in the Six Books.

nurses a boy after the appropriate moment at which he should have been weaned, and at the same time she nurses an infant girl, the two do not become foster-siblings. Although both consanguinity and nursing relationships create a barrier to marriage, there are some exceptions. Thus a man can marry the mother of his foster-sister, but not the mother of one of his half-sisters or of a half-sister of his own son. Qudūrī also points out that a man can marry his foster-brother's sisters, just as he can his paternal brother's maternal stepsisters.[31] Like other jurists who treat this topic, Qudūrī mentions many complications, not necessarily realistic, such as the relationship between two infants nursed by the same animal, or whether swallowing the milk of a dead woman establishes the same relationships as that of a living woman. Ibn Abī Zayd also modifies the notion that nursing relationships and consanguinity are equivalent. He points out that when a woman becomes a male infant's foster-mother, both her daughters and those of her husband (born previously or subsequently) become his sisters. However, just as Qudūrī concluded, they do not become the sisters of his brother (nursed by a different woman), who is therefore free to marry any of them.[32]

Above, we saw that the Ḥanafī and Ḥanbalī opinion was that intercourse, whether forbidden or lawful, also resulted in foster relationship, while the Mālikī and Shāfiʿī opinion was that it did not. However, Shīrāzī points to a situation in which intercourse can make a marriage retroactively invalid. If a man unknowingly has intercourse with his wife's mother or daughter, or if his father or his son has intercourse with his wife, his marriage is annulled, because any of those instances are reasons for permanent prohibition the way nursing is. Shīrāzī points out the difference between this situation and fornication (which according to the Mālikī and Shāfiʿī view does not establish affinity): it is that the intercourse takes place within a marriage, which, even though it stands to be annulled, has the consequences of a legal marriage (e.g., marriage portion and *ʿidda*), since it was not annulled before intercourse.[33]

Khiraqī restates the Ḥanbalī position that unlawful sexual intercourse establishes the same relationships that lawful sexual intercourse

[31] Qudūrī, *Mukhtaṣar*, 3:31–33.
[32] Ibn Abī Zayd, *Risāla*, 192 (*First Steps*, 38, nos. 126, 127).
[33] Shīrāzī, *Tanbīh*, 409–17; *Muhadhdhab*, 2:42–43.

does; so, he adds, does intercourse owing to uncertainty (*shubha*).[34] Ibn Qudāma summarizes the differences of opinion among the schools by noting that the Mālikī and Shāfiʿī positions are supported by a tradition from the Prophet, "The forbidden does not forbid the lawful." Then, however, he points to Qurʾān 4:22 (*and marry not those women whom your fathers married*), which, he says, should be interpreted as including both lawful and unlawful intercourse, as well as various lustful acts. He quotes a second tradition from the Prophet, "God does not look at a man who has seen the private parts of both a woman and her daughter," and as a further way of discrediting "The forbidden does not forbid the lawful," he disparages the *isnād*.[35]

Marriage Portion

1. The Prophet said: "The women who are most blessed are those who have the fewest possessions."[36]
2. A member of the Banū Fazāra married a woman for a pair of sandals, and the Prophet permitted that.[37]
3. ʿUmar b. al-Khaṭṭāb said: "Do not be excessive in women's marriage portions. … A man can increase a woman's marriage portion to such an extent that he harbors animosity toward her."[38]

These three traditions indicating that marriage portions should not be extravagant or excessive are sentiments that the classical jurists may have shared, but did not dwell upon. When later texts mention amounts for marriage portions, they repeat those mentioned by the founders. Qudūrī repeats the earlier Ḥanafī number of 10 dirhams as the smallest sum a woman can receive as a marriage portion, Ibn Abī Zayd says it is the Mālikī minimum of 3 dirhams, and Shīrāzī, like Shāfiʿī, says a marriage portion should not exceed 500 dirhams.[39] Khiraqī, like Ibn Ḥanbal, does not name a sum. Khiraqī does say, however, that when a father gives his daughter in marriage, whatever marriage portion he chooses for her, it must be something that can be halved.[40] All say that if a

[34] al-Khirāqī, *Mukhtaṣar*, 139. In this case, uncertainty about how and whether the two partners are related to each other.
[35] Ibn Qudāma, *Mughnī*, 7:482–83. See Schacht, "Adultery as an Impediment to Marriage."
[36] Ibn Ḥanbal, *Musnad*, 6:145.
[37] Ibid., 3:445.
[38] Ibn Māja, *Sunan*, 1:608.
[39] See Ibn Abī Zayd, *Risāla*, 172 (*First Steps*, 3, no. 3); Shīrāzī, *Muhadhdhab*, 2:432; Qudūrī, *Mukhtaṣar*, 3:14.
[40] Khiraqī, *Mukhtaṣar*, 145.

marriage contract is concluded for anything illegal, such as wine or pork, the bride is still owed her fair marriage portion, whatever it may be. Further, once a marriage has been consummated, if there is dispute about the details of her marriage portion that cannot be resolved, all agree that what is ultimately due is her fair marriage portion, whatever that is. If the marriage portion consists of something that becomes destroyed or damaged, such as a house that collapses or a slave who escapes, and this happens before the couple have intercourse, the marriage contract is defective, and the marriage portion must be replaced. The same is true if the marriage portion is a particular article that is repossessed by its previous owner. If, however, these things happen after the couple have intercourse, the wife is owed her fair marriage portion.

On this topic, whatever details classical jurists add embellish, but do not alter the material of earlier texts.

Witnesses to a Marriage Contract

1. The Prophet said, "There can be no marriage contract without witnesses."
2. The Prophet said, "Only lewd women marry without witnesses."[41]

The first tradition is one of many that reinforce the need for witnesses to a marriage contract. The second points to the fact that if a marriage contract is not witnessed, the bride's reputation cannot be safeguarded. In Chapter 2 we saw several different opinions about witnesses to a marriage contract. Mālik was reported to have considered a marriage valid regardless of whether it had been witnessed, so long as it was made public after the fact. The Ḥanafīs allowed one man and two women as witnesses, Shāfiʿī and Ibn Ḥanbal mentioned two men as witnesses, and Shāfiʿī added that the two witnesses must be trustworthy.[42]

Later Mālikī discussion is more explicit about the importance of public knowledge of a marriage. Ibn Abī Zayd says, "There can be no marriage without a *walī*, a marriage portion, and two trustworthy witnesses. If the required witnesses were not present at the time of the contract, the husband should not have intercourse with his wife until

[41] Tirmidhī, *Sunan*, 2:384, nos. 1110, 1109.
[42] For trust worthiness, see *EI*, s.v. "ʿAdl."

the contract has been witnessed."[43] Ibn ʿAbd al-Bārr alludes to past Mālikī discussion by emphasizing that a secret marriage is not allowed: like a contract of sale, a marriage contract can be concluded without witnesses, but the marriage must be publicly announced before the couple have intercourse. If it is not, then the contract is defective. However, if it is initially secret and then announced and publicized, it is not defective. He goes on to say that Mālik said that if two men witness a marriage and then hide it, that is a secret marriage. "But some of our companions (i.e., fellow Mālikī jurists) say that if two trustworthy men witness a marriage, it has ceased to be a secret, and this is the view of the vast majority (*jumhūr*) of jurists."[44]

Following the opinion of Abū Ḥanīfa and Shaybānī, Qudūrī says, "A marriage contract can be concluded only in the presence of two witnesses who are sane, adult Muslims, either two men, or one man and two women, regardless of whether they are trustworthy, or have been punished for an accusation of slander."[45] Enlarging on this, Marghīnānī points to the Prophet's saying, "There can be no marriage without witnesses." "This," he says, "is evidence against Mālik's stipulation that a marriage is valid without witnesses, so long as it is publicly announced."[46]

Shīrāzī expands on Shāfiʿī's insistence that there be two male witnesses to a marriage contract. He starts by saying that the jurist Abū Thawr said that a marriage contract without witnesses was valid, because it was a contract like a sale.[47] Shīrāzī disagrees because ʿĀʾisha related from the Prophet that he said, "Every marriage contract not concluded in the presence of four things is invalid: a groom, the bride's *walī*, and two witnesses." Shīrāzī adds that a marriage contract is not like a sale contract, the goal of which is money. The goal of marriage is enjoyment and children, and the foundation of both of

---

[43] Ibn Abī Zayd, *Risāla*, 172 (*First Steps*, 2, nos. 1, 2).

[44] Ibn ʿAbd al-Bārr, *al-Kāfī*, 2:520. Khalīl b. Isḥāq says the contract should be witnessed by two just witnesses, but that if it is not, it will not be annulled and there will be no penalty, as long as the marriage is publicized. Russell and Suhrawardy, nos. 5 and 6.

[45] Qudūrī, *Mukhtaṣar*, 3:3. For slander, see *EI*, s.v. "*Ḳadhf*."

[46] Marghīnānī, *Hidāya*, 2:460.

[47] We just saw that this is also the Mālikī view. Abū Thawr (d. 240/854), an Iraqī jurist, is sometimes described as the founder of a short-lived school of law and sometimes as an adherent of Shāfiʿī's. See *EI*, s.v. "Abū Thawr" and Sezgin, *GAS*, 1:491, where he is included among the Shāfiʿīs.

these is prudence (*iḥtiyāṭ*).[48] Therefore, there must be two male witnesses to a marriage contract, and one man and two women do not make it valid. He says, "Ibn Masʿūd reported that the Prophet said, 'There can be no marriage without a *walī* and two trustworthy witnesses.' If one does not know whether the witnesses are truly trustworthy or only appear to be," Shīrāzī continues, "there are two opinions: one, that the contract is not valid, the second, that it is. The second is the opinion of the *madhhab*, because if we took the inner quality of trustworthiness (*ʿadāla*) into account, the marriages of common people could take place only in the presence of a judge (*ḥākim*), because they do not know what the conditions of trustworthiness are, and there is hardship (*shaqqa*) in that. Thus, the outward appearance of trustworthiness suffices." But he goes on to say that if it happens that the two witnesses turn out to be sinners, the marriage is, in fact, invalid. He compares this situation with one in which a judge uses *ijtihād* to arrive at a ruling and then finds a revealed text that contravenes his decision. In this case, or in case there is *ijmāʿ* on the issue (e.g., *ijmāʿ* of which the judge had been unaware), his decision is revoked. Otherwise, it stands.[49]

Commenting on Khiraqī's statement that a contract must be concluded in the presence of two Muslim witnesses, Ibn Qudāma reports that the prevailing opinion from Ibn Ḥanbal is that a valid marriage contract requires two male witnesses. If they are sinners, he says, there are two opinions: the marriage is valid, or it is not. In either case, he says, the contract is valid if the witnesses *appear* to be trustworthy. Here he agrees with Shīrāzī on the witnesses and shares his concern for common people, but he disagrees with him that if, after the fact, the witnesses are discovered to be sinners, the marriage contract is invalidated: it remains valid because at the time it took place, they appeared to be trustworthy. Thus, if a man and a woman affirm that they married with a *walī* and two trustworthy witnesses, one accepts what they say, and their marriage is valid on the basis of their affirmation (*iqrārihimā*).[50]

---

[48] See Schacht, *Introduction*, 123 for brief reference to concern for bringing underlying motive and legal validity into accord.

[49] Shīrāzī, *Muhadhdhab*, 2:40.

[50] Khiraqī, *Mukhtaṣar*, 134; Ibn Qudāma, *Mughnī*, 7:340–41. For "affirmation," see *EI*, s.v. "Iḳrār."

Discussion

On the question of whether a woman can conclude her own marriage contract, we see that the Ḥanafī position evolved to include so many conditions that a woman has little or no leeway to conclude her own contract. Further, Marghīnānī adds that the presence of a *walī* prevents her from displaying unseemly interest in men. The Mālikīs insist that a *walī* conclude a woman's marriage contract and no longer make an exception for a lowly woman. Thus the Mālikī view has become the same as the Shāfiʿī and Ḥanbalī. Ibn Qudāma uses a well-known tradition to restate the Ḥanbalī position and concludes by echoing Marghīnānī's point that a *walī* restrains a woman from unseemly behavior.

On forbidden degrees, there is much detail on the different ways foster-relationship is established, and it turns out that despite traditions to the contrary, consanguinity and foster-relationship are not exactly the same. Although Shāfiʿī held that the forbidden did not forbid the allowed, Shīrāzī says that a man cannot remain married to the mother of a woman with whom he has had intercourse even though he had intercourse in a marriage that was initially deemed legal.

On the question of witnesses to a marriage contract, the later Mālikī position qualifies the earlier one that a valid contract does not require formal witnessing as long as the marriage is widely known. Ibn Abī Zayd says that two witnesses *are* an integral part of the contract, whereas Ibn ʿAbd al-Barr, like the earlier Mālikīs, emphasizes witnessing as a way to prevent a secret marriage. Otherwise, later scholars emphasize different aspects of earlier discussion. The Ḥanafīs insist on witnesses, two men or one man and two women, and Marghīnānī specifically says that since the Prophet said, "There can be no marriage without witnesses," the Mālikīs are wrong to say that publicity alone is adequate. Shīrāzī says that the two male witnesses should be trustworthy, but points out that in consideration of the needs of the common people, the preponderant opinion of the *madhhab* is that they need only appear to be trustworthy. However, if they do, in fact, turn out to be sinners, then a marriage they witnessed is invalid. Ibn Qudāma also shows concern for the common people, but his concern leads him to disagree with Shīrāzī and say that since the common people cannot distinguish between trustworthy and untrustworthy witnesses, a marriage stands if the witnesses appeared to be trustworthy at the time the contract was concluded.

Divorce

Ṭalāq al-sunna

> Āmir al-Shaʿbī said: "I said to Fāṭima bt. Qays, 'Tell me about your divorce.' She replied, 'My husband divorced me triply while he was away in the Yemen, and the Prophet said that that was valid.'"[51]

We noted in Chapter 3 that *Ṭalāq al-sunna* is a divorce in which a man who wishes to divorce his wife does so at the start of a period of purity when he has not had intercourse with her. He may also divorce her twice more at the start of each successive period of purity so that by the end of her *ʿidda*, she is triply divorced. Shaybānī said that was lawful, and Mālik is reported to have agreed that it was, but to have strongly disapproved of it. Shāfiʿī and Ibn Ḥanbal did not come down on one side or another. In *ṭalāq al-bidʿa*, a man pronounces a triple repudiation in one statement or in one period of purity. No one expressed approval of *talāq al-bidʿa*, although all said it was valid, and the tradition above reinforces that validity. Later jurists do not alter this basic picture, but the Ḥanafīs add to it.

In his discussion of divorce, Qudūrī makes a distinction within *ṭalāq al-sunna*. First, he describes "the best divorce" (*aḥsanu'l-ṭalāq*) as one in which a man divorces his wife singly in a period of purity without having had intercourse with her and then leaves her until her *ʿidda* ends. In *ṭalāq al-sunna*, he divorces her triply over the course of one *ʿidda*. Other details Qudūrī adds are that a man can divorce at any time a wife who is either too young or too old to menstruate and a pregnant woman after having had intercourse with her. The case of the pregnant woman brings out disagreements over the conditions for multiple divorces. Abū Ḥanīfa and Abū Yūsuf said that a man can divorce a pregnant woman twice more in each successive month and have that triple repudiation be an example of *ṭalāq al-sunna*, but Shaybānī said that in the case of a pregnant woman, *ṭalāq al-sunna* meant a single repudiation only.[52] Marghīnānī, discussing this view of Shaybānī's, points to the fact that since pregnancy is one long period of purity, a man cannot pronounce a second and third repudiation in subsequent periods of purity.[53]

---

[51] Ibn Māja, *Sunan*, 1:652, *Ṭalāq* 4, no. 2024.

[52] Qudūrī, *Mukhtaṣar*, 3:37–39. *Ṭalāq al-bidʿa*, Qudūrī reaffirms, is valid, and if a man pronounces a triple divorce in one statement or in one period of purity, he is certainly triply divorced, but he has sinned.

[53] Marghīnānī, *Hidāya*, 2:534.

Ibn Abī Zayd follows Mālik's view that during a woman's *ʿidda*, a man should not follow one pronouncement of repudiation with another, even though it is lawful.[54] Shīrāzī repeats Shāfiʿī's advice that it is best for a man to divorce his wife only once, even though it is lawful for him to divorce her triply over the course of one *ʿidda*, and it is better for him not to divorce her triply all at once, even though that too is lawful. Khiraqī agrees and adds that by repudiating a wife triply all at once, a man deprives himself of the option of returning to her.[55]

All jurists retain the possibilities allowed by the earlier definitions, but express increasing emphasis on preferring only single divorce.

*Returning to a Wife after Non-final Divorce (*al-rajʿa*)*

> ʿImrān b. al-Ḥuṣayn was asked about a man who divorces his wife and then has intercourse with her without witnesses either for his divorce or his return. He replied, "You thereby divorce without a *sunna* and return without a *sunna*. Have your divorce and your return to her witnessed!"[56]

In Chapter 1 we saw that Qurʾān 65:2 said that two trustworthy witnesses should witness a man's return to his wife after a single or double divorce. Then in Chapter 3 we saw that in addition to this verse and two examples of traditions that say witnesses are needed for a return, both Shaybānī and Mālik said that it was also possible for a man to return to his wife without witnesses. Shaybānī pointed out that a man should have witnesses attest to his return to his wife, but that it was also possible for him simply to return to her without formal witnessing, and Mālik said that a man's return to his wife should be witnessed if he knows of the requirement. Shāfiʿī and Ibn Ḥanbal, however, said that a return should definitely be witnessed. Later texts all emphasize that, in accordance with Qurʾān 65:2, a husband lawfully returns to his wife by stating in the presence of two witnesses that he is returning to her, and the above tradition reinforces the verse. Nonetheless, in classical texts the Ḥanafīs and Mālikīs maintain their earlier positions that although witnesses are desirable, they are not required, and Shīrāzī for the Shāfiʿīs and Khiraqī and Ibn Qudāma for the Ḥanbalīs admit the possibility of a return without witnesses.

[54] Ibn Abī Zayd, *Risāla*, 182 (*First Steps*, 22, no. 68).
[55] Shīrāzī, *Tanbīh*, 445. Khiraqī, *Mukhtaṣar*, 152.
[56] Ibn Māja, *Sunan*, 1:652, *Ṭalāq* 5, no. 2025.

In his description of a return, Qudūrī says that a man can return to his wife by announcing that he is returning to her, having intercourse with her, kissing her, or gazing at or touching her with lust. It is recommended that he call two men to witness his return, but if he does not do so, his return is still valid.[57] Marghīnānī explains this view in more detail: if a return is thought of as the resumption of a marriage that was ended by the husband's statement of repudiation, then it would need to be witnessed. However, he says that since the wife's *ʿidda* has not ended, a return also can be thought of as the continuation of a marriage that has not come to an end, and continuation can be shown by acts as well as words. Calling two men to witness his return, Marghīnānī says, is recommended for a husband, but if he does not do so, his return is still valid.[58]

Ibn ʿAbd al-Barr too says that after a non-final divorce, it is recommended that a husband have two trustworthy men witness his return, in accordance with the Qurʾān. But if a husband says to his wife, "I am returning to you," without his statement being witnessed, it counts as a return and can be witnessed after the fact.[59] Ibn ʿAbd al-Barr repeats the opinion we saw attributed to Mālik (see Chapter 3) that if a woman refuses to have intercourse with her husband before he calls witnesses to his return to her, she has acted appropriately. If, intending to return to his wife, he has intercourse with her before he has had a statement of return witnessed, it is possible to consider that act of intercourse a return if he meant it to be, and the fact that he has thereby returned to her can be witnessed after the fact.[60]

Shīrāzī says that a man must not simply return to his wife by having intercourse with her without first having stated that he is returning to her, but he points to two opinions on whether a man's return statement must be witnessed. One is that it must be, since it involves his making a particular woman's private parts lawful for himself and that cannot

[57] Qudūrī, *Mukhtaṣar*, 3:54.

[58] Marghīnānī, *Hidāya*, 2:582–83.

[59] A statement of return without intercourse counts as a return, unless the husband is a *mūlī* (one who has sworn an oath of *īlāʾ*), or one who cannot maintain his wife. The *mūlī* must actually have intercourse with his wife, and the husband who cannot maintain his wife must show that his circumstances have improved. Ibn ʿAbd al-Barr, *al-Kāfī*, 2:618. See below for the Mālikī view that the *qāḍī* can separate a couple if the husband fails to provide for his wife.

[60] Ibn ʿAbd al-Barr, *al-Kāfī*, 2:617–18. Ibn ʿAbd al-Barr also notes disagreement among some of the Mālikīs about whether intercourse can be considered a return if a man did not intend it to be.

take place without witnessing; thus a return must be witnessed like a marriage contract. The other is that it is permissible not to have his return statement witnessed because a return does not involve a *walī* (i.e., it is not a new marriage contract), and therefore it does not require witnessing, as is the case in a contract of sale.[61]

Khiraqī says that a return after non-final divorce consists of a man saying to two Muslim men, "Bear witness to the fact that I am returning to my wife." However, he says that it has also been related from Ibn Ḥanbal that a return did not need to be witnessed.[62] Ibn Qudāma explains these contradictory statements attributed to Ibn Ḥanbal. He says that, understood literally, the Qurʾān says that a return must be witnessed, but there can be two opinions on the question. One is that a return should be witnessed because it means that a man is about to deem a particular woman's private parts lawful for himself. Thus, like a marriage contract and unlike a contract of sale, witnesses are required. The other is that unlike a marriage contract, a return does not require acceptance (*qabūl*) on the part of the wife, and no *walī* is required.[63] Therefore, no witnesses are required, just as none are required for any of the other rights a husband has over his wife. However, he says that witnessing is recommended.[64]

The views of the jurists on this particular question seem to contradict the Qurʾān, but they are understandable in the context of the development of *uṣūl al-fiqh*. I said in the introduction that classical authors of *furūʿ* were also authors of *uṣūl*. Here either as scholars or authors of works of *uṣūl* they are all aware of the ongoing effort (their own and those of other scholars) to fully understand the nature of God's commands in the Qurʾān. Understood literally, *call to witness two just men among you*, in Qurʾān 65:2, is an imperative. However, as we have just seen, there are times when God's commands are understood as recommendations rather than imperatives, and in the classical period the command to call two trustworthy men to witness a man's return to his wife is understood as a recommendation.[65]

[61] See Shīrāzī, *Tanbīh*, 458–60 and *Muhadhdhab*, 2:103.

[62] Khiraqī, *Mukhtaṣar*, 158.

[63] A marriage contract is concluded by an offer (*ījāb*) on the part of the groom or his representative, and acceptance (*qabūl*) on her behalf by the bride's *walī*. See *EI*, s.v.v. "Nikāḥ"; "Īdjāb"; "ʿAḳd."

[64] Ibn Qudāma, *Mughnī*, 8:481–82.

[65] For a discussion of the divine command in the *uṣūl* writings of Ibn Qudāma, see Wakin, "The Divine Command in Ibn Qudāmah." See also Kemali, *Principles of Islamic*

ʿIdda

> ʿĀmir (al-Shaʿbī] said: "Fāṭima bt. Qays related to me that her husband divorced her triply, and the Prophet ordered her to wait her *ʿidda* in Umm Maktūm's house."[66]

According to the Ḥanafīs, the triply divorced woman received both lodging and maintenance. Mālik and Shāfiʿī said she received only lodging, and Ibn Ḥanbal said she received neither. We saw in Chapter 3 that these three opinions were based on a combination of the interpretation of Qurʾān 65:1 and 6 and an understanding of the traditions about the *ʿidda* of a contemporary of the Prophet's, Fāṭima bt. Qays, who was reported to have received neither maintenance nor lodging after her husband divorced her triply. The above tradition points to a fact generally agreed upon that the Prophet instructed Fāṭima to wait her *ʿidda* in the house of Umm Maktūm whose son was blind and therefore unable to see her in an inappropriate manner. Either it proves the point that the triply divorced woman receives neither maintenance nor lodging, or it can be understood as a story about a special case.[67] In the classical period, jurists provide various explanations in support of their *madhhab*'s position, but only Ibn Qudāma refers specifically to the many traditions about Fāṭima bt. Qays.

For the Ḥanafīs, Qudūrī simply states that all divorcées receive both lodging and maintenance during an *ʿidda*. Marghīnānī explains that lodging and maintenance is due a woman in her *ʿidda* for two reasons: one, because the main purpose of marriage is offspring, and two, because maintenance is compensation for keeping someone in custody. Since the main purpose of marriage is offspring, the triply divorced woman is in custody in order to safeguard any potential offspring. Therefore, she should be maintained the way a pregnant divorcée is. As support for the Ḥanafī view, Marghīnānī quotes the tradition from ʿUmar about Fāṭima bt. Qays: "We do not forsake the Book of our Lord for the words of a woman without knowing whether she lied or told

---

Jurisprudence, 34–35, where he draws attention to the application of speculative reasoning to the Qurʾānic statements that both a return after divorce and a contract of sale should be witnessed.

[66] Ibn Ḥanbal, *Musnad*, 6:411–12. In some versions of this tradition, the woman is Umm Sharīk rather than Umm Maktūm.

[67] For example, see again *Muwaṭṭaʾ*, 3:210, for Zurqānī's commentary on Mālik's treatment of Fāṭima bt. Qays's *ʿidda*.

the truth, remembered or forgot. I heard the Prophet say, 'The triply divorced woman receives maintenance and lodging, as long as she is waiting her *ʿidda*.'"[68]

Ibn ʿAbd al-Barr for the Mālikīs and Shīrāzī for the Shāfiʿīs repeat that the triply divorced woman receives only lodging and no maintenance. Ibn ʿAbd al-Barr adds that she is permitted to go out during the daytime if she needs to and she cannot get anyone else to go out in her stead. If she spends the night away from home, she has sinned and must not do so again for the remainder of her *ʿidda*. Shīrāzī says also that she can go out if she needs to, for example to buy cotton or to sell yarn, but only in the daytime.[69]

The Ḥanbalī position is that a triply divorced woman receives neither lodging nor maintenance. Thus Khiraqī says, "If a man divorces his wife irrevocably, she receives neither lodging nor maintenance unless she is pregnant." Ibn Qudāma describes the opinions of the other schools along with the Companions and Successors who support those opinions and then says that the preponderant view of the Ḥanbalī school is that a triply divorced woman who is not pregnant receives neither maintenance nor lodging. He goes on to marshal arguments for the Ḥanbalī view by saying, "We have in our favor what Fāṭima bt. Qays said," and then he recounts the story we saw above in the *Muwaṭṭaʾ* (Chapter 3), that while he was away, her husband divorced her triply and sent her an amount of wheat she found inadequate. But Ibn Qudāma's version of what happened next goes beyond Mālik's. Ibn Qudāma says that when she complained to the Prophet, the Prophet responded, "He (i.e., your husband) owes you neither maintenance nor lodging" and then ordered her to wait her *ʿidda* in Umm Sharīk's house.[70] Ibn Qudāma emphasizes the weight that should be given to Ibn Ḥanbal's support for the traditions about Fāṭima bt. Qays that are related from the Prophet rather than from Companions and Successors. In particular he points to a tradition in which the

[68] Marghīnānī, *Hidāya*, 2:652. Marghīnānī lists other Companions who agreed with ʿUmar about lodging and maintenance for the triply divorced woman. See again Wensinck, Concordance, s.v. "Fāṭima bt. Qays," for traditions about her *ʿidda* in the Six Books.

[69] Ibn ʿAbd al-Barr, *al-Kāfī*, 2:623–24; and Shīrāzi, *Tanbīh*, 489.

[70] In the *Muwaṭṭaʾ*, the Prophet says only that she receives lodging but not maintenance. See again Mālik, *Muwaṭṭaʾ*, 3:210; and also Spectorsky, *Chapters*, 57–58.

Prophet specifically says to her that her husband owes her neither lodging nor maintenance.[71]

Discussion

Jurists of the classical period do not differ from earlier ones on the nature of *ṭalāq al-sunna*. They restate earlier positions, and, particularly in Qudūrī's case, add some details. It is also the case that on the question of lodging and maintenance for a triply divorced woman during her *ʿidda*, later scholars reiterate the founders' positions on the issue of Fāṭima bt. Qays's status during her *ʿidda* after Abū ʿAmr b. Ḥafṣ had divorced her triply. Ibn ʿAbd al-Barr and Shīrāzī who both say she receives lodging, both say she may go out during the day if she needs to, and Shīrāzī provides a glimpse of the fact that she may be earning her maintenance by spinning when he says she might need to go out to buy cotton or sell yarn.

In the classical period the answer to whether a man's return to his wife after a non-final divorce must be witnessed becomes uniform in response to legal-theoretical reasoning on the nature of God's commands. Shīrāzī for the Shāfiʿīs and Ibn Qudāma for the Ḥanbalīs now agree with the Ḥanafī and Mālikī positions that two witnesses are recommended but not required.

Change Over Time

Equality between husband and wife (*kafāʾa*) and divorce initiated by a wife (*khulʿ*) are two issues where continued development also introduces marked changes between the way they are treated in formative texts and the way they are treated in classical texts. Here we see the later jurists taking social reality and practice into account.

Kafāʾa

Two questions involving *kafāʾa* will illustrate how emphases can change significantly over time to accommodate social realities. The first is the importance of *kafāʾa* in a valid marriage contract; the second, its role in determining the appropriate marriage portion.

[71] See Ibn Qudāma, *Mughnī*, 9:288–90.

Kafāʿa *and the Marriage Contract*

1. The Prophet said: "A woman is married for four things: her wealth, her lineage, her beauty, and her piety. Choose a wife who possesses the quality of piety, lest you be damned."[72]
2. The Prophet said: "A woman is married for three things: her piety, her wealth, and her beauty. Choose piety lest you be damned."[73]
3. Abū Hurayra said: "Abū Hind treated the Prophet by cupping his vertex, and afterwards, the Prophet said, 'O Banū Bayāḍa, give your daughters in marriage to Abū Hind, and let him marry them. And, if there is anything for which you wish good treatment, treat it with cupping.' "[74]

In the first tradition above, although lineage (*nasab*), wealth, and beauty are also mentioned, the Prophet points to piety as the most important quality in a potential wife. The second tradition is a variant of the first, but leaves out lineage. The third tradition combines lineage and profession but deprecates their importance. Abū Hind was not actually a member of the Banū Bayāḍa tribe, but a *mawlā* of theirs and therefore, theoretically, not of an appropriate rank to marry a free Arab woman. Further, cupping was a despised profession, along with others that involved the body or dirt, such as sweeping, tanning, weaving, or being a bath attendant.[75] Here, the Prophet urges that a man who was both a *mawlā* and a practitioner of a lowly profession be considered an Arab woman's equal. Other traditions show support for cuppers, such as one in which the Prophet's wife Umm Salama asked permission to be cupped, and the Prophet permitted it. On the other hand, still others compare the wages of a cupper to those of a prostitute.[76] Thus all three traditions strike an inclusive tone, but it

[72] Abū Dāwūd, *Sunan*, 6:30; Ibn Māja, *Sunan*, 1:597, no. 1858; Bukhārī, *Ṣaḥīḥ*, 3:360, no. 5090. The Arabic of the last sentence translated above is *faẓhar bi-dhāt al-dīn ṭaribat yadāka*. See Lane, s.v. *ṭ-r-b* for the expression *ṭaribat yadāka*. The translation above is taken from O. Houdas's French translation of Bukhārī's *Ṣaḥīḥ*. Another possible translation of this sentence is "whoever acquires the quality of piety becomes more pious." A third possibility is "but take hold of piety, and you will be satisfied with what you have."

[73] Tirmidhī, *Sunan*, 2:275, no. 1092.

[74] Abū Dāwūd, *Sunan*, 6 (of 5 and 6 printed in vol. 3):91. See also Ibn Ḥanbal, *Musnad*, 2:342 and 423, where Abū Hurayra says only, "The Prophet said, 'If there is anything for which you want good treatment, treat it by cupping.' "

[75] For cupping, see *EI*, s.v. "Faṣṣād, Ḥadjdjām." For other professions considered suitable only for slaves or those on the lowest rungs of society, see Brunschvig, "Metiers vils en Islam."

[76] For the tradition on Umm Salama's cupping, see Ibn Māja, *Sunan*, 2:1151–2, no. 3480. In this tradition, she is treated by Abū Ṭayba, a cupper who served the Prophet

is not borne out by the discussions of the classical jurists, who all emphasize differences in lineage and wealth, along with those of profession. In earlier texts Mālik's opinion, based on 49:13, that lineage makes no difference had stood out. Shāfiʿī discussed a suitable groom only in terms of lineage, and the Ḥanafīs and Ibn Ḥanbal were concerned with lineage and wealth. In the classical period, there is even more emphasis on lineage, and the Mālikī and Shāfiʿī texts move toward the Ḥanafī and Ḥanbalī.

In classical texts the Ḥanafīs show the most interest in *kafāʾa*. Qudūrī expresses the concern of earlier Ḥanafīs for equality of lineage, religion, wealth, and profession. He particularly notes that what wealth means is that the groom's financial circumstances should enable him to pay his wife's marriage portion as well as maintain her. According to Abū Ḥanīfa, Qudūrī explains, if a woman marries for a marriage portion that is less than her fair one, her *walī*s can block the marriage until her marriage portion is increased so that it is a fair one, or until the groom himself separates from the bride. They can also separate the couple if the groom is not her equal.[77] We saw this concern above, in the case of a woman concluding her own marriage contract. In effect then, it was *kafāʾa* that imposed the limits on a woman's freedom to conclude her own marriage contract: she can conclude a contract exactly like the one a responsible *walī* would conclude for her on her behalf.

Enlarging on the different components of *kafāʾa*, Marghīnānī quotes the Prophet to underline the importance of lineage: "Quraysh are each other's equals, sept for sept (*baṭn bi'l-baṭn*); Arabs are each other's equals tribe for tribe, and *mawālī* are each other's equals, man for man."[78] He continues his commentary by saying that Abū Ḥanīfa and Abū Yūsuf said piety is a significant aspect of *kafāʾa* because a woman is shamed if her husband is a sinner (*fāsiq*) more than she is by the lowliness of his lineage.[79] But Shaybānī said that piety is of concern for

and was highly thought of. See again *EI*, s.v. "Faṣṣād, Ḥidjdjām." For a tradition denigrating cuppers, see, for example, Ibn Ḥanbal, *Musnad*, 3:464.

[77] Qudūrī, *Mukhtaṣar*, 3:12–14.

[78] Marghīnānī, *Hidāya*, 2:485. He distinguishes among different generations of *mawālī* by saying that those who are third-generation Muslims are more the equals of each other than those who are second-generation, or who are the first converts in their families.

[79] Someone who is *fāsiq* has sinned to the point that he does not possess the requisite qualities to be a trustworthy witness. See *EI*, s.v. "Fāsiq."

the world to come rather than this one, and worldly rulings are not based on it. Therefore it is not a consideration unless a husband is publicly humiliated. Marghīnānī then says that a man who cannot afford a marriage portion and maintenance for a prospective bride cannot be her equal. Her marriage portion is in exchange for possession of her private parts and thus must be paid in full, and maintenance sustains enduring matrimony. He goes on to reiterate that Abū Ḥanīfa and Abū Yūsuf insisted on wealth adequate both for the marriage portion and for the wife's maintenance, whereas Shaybānī was less concerned with wealth because it comes and goes. As for profession, Marghīnānī says that Abū Yūsuf considered it significant only if it were a lowly one, but in addition, there are two views on the matter from all three of them: one, that profession is important because people respect honorable professions and despise lowly ones; the other, that profession is not important because a man can change from a lowly to a high one.[80]

When we examine Shāfiʿī and Ḥanbalī texts, it turns out that with slight variation, they share the same concerns as the Ḥanafīs. Shīrāzī says that *kafāʾa* includes lineage, piety, profession, and freedom. An Arab woman is not to be given in marriage to a non-Arab, nor a woman of the Quraysh tribe to a man who is not also a member of that tribe. Like Marghīnānī, Shīrāzī makes a further distinction between the rest of the Quraysh and the family of the Prophet and says that a Hashimite woman should be given in marriage only to a Hashimite man. Further, a pious woman should not be given in marriage to a sinner (*fāsiq*), nor the daughter of a merchant or a wealthy man to a weaver or a cupper, nor a free woman to a slave. If her *walī* gives a woman in marriage to someone who is not her equal, without her consent and also without the consent of her other *walī*s, then the marriage is invalid. But, says Shīrāzī, it is also said that there are two opinions on the matter. One is that the marriage is invalid, the other is that the wife is given the option of separating from her husband.[81] On the question of the importance of wealth, Shīrāzī says that "our companions" (i.e., fellow Shāfiʿī jurists) hold two opinions. One is that it is taken into account because the Prophet said, "Rank is wealth, munificence, and piety," and the maintenance a woman receives differs depending on a husband's wealth. The other is that wealth is not a factor because it comes and goes.[82]

---

[80] Marghīnānī, *Hidāya*, 2:485–86.
[81] Shīrāzī, *Tanbīh*, 406–7.
[82] See Shīrāzī, *Muhadhdhab*, 2:39.

Ibn Qudāma reports conflicting opinions from Ibn Ḥanbal on the importance of *kafāʾa*. "It has been related from him [Ibn Ḥanbal] that he said it [*kafāʾa*] is a condition for the validity of a marriage contract and that if a *mawlā* marries an Arab woman, the couple are separated. It has also been related from him that if a man drinks alcohol, he is not an Arab woman's equal, and that if he is a weaver,[83] the couple are separated in accordance with ʿUmar's saying, 'We forbid the private parts of noble women to anyone except their equals.' The second opinion from Ibn Ḥanbal was that *kafāʾa* is not actually a condition for a valid marriage contract, and this is the opinion of the majority of scholars in accordance with the Qurʾān, *Lo! the noblest of you in the sight of Allah is the best in conduct* (49:13)." Ibn Qudāma goes on to mention that Abū Dāwūd relates the tradition of Abū Hind cupping the Prophet (the third tradition above), but that Ibn Ḥanbal considered this a weak tradition of which he strongly disapproved. In fact, this is borne out by what we saw in Chapter 2—Ibn Ḥanbal was very clearly in accord with the sentiments expressed by ʿUmar. Ibn Qudāma does not deny Ibn Ḥanbal's position, but, swayed by the egalitarian sentiment in 49:13, he makes an effort to steer a middle course. He says that since *kafāʾa* is not a *condition* for the validity of a marriage contract, what has been related concerning it must be further interpreted: although it is not intrinsic to the validity of the contract, the potential wife and all her *walī*s have a stake in her marriage, and whoever among them is not satisfied with the contract has the right to invalidate it. He discusses the various components of *kafāʾa* (such as freedom, profession, and wealth) and summarizes the views of the other three schools, but then returns to the importance of lineage on the grounds that unlike freedom, profession, and wealth, it is inherent and devolves on a potential couple's children.[84]

Mālik saw no objection to a marriage between an Arab woman and a *mawlā*, and he did not show great concern for disparity in wealth per se, so it is not surprising that in *al-Kāfī*, Ibn ʿAbd al-Barr does not discuss *kafāʾa* directly. However, in his discussion of a *tafwīḍ* marriage, he says that once the marriage has been consummated, the bride is owed her fair marriage portion based on wealth, beauty, rank (*manṣib*), and circumstances.[85]

---

[83] For the inclusion of weaving among the lowly professions, see again, Brunschvig, "Métiers vils en Islam"; and *EI*, s.v. "Ḥaʾik."

[84] Ibn Qudāma, *Mughnī*, 7:371–74.

[85] Ibn ʿAbd al-Barr, *al-Kāfī*, 2:552.

Kafāʾa *and a Marriage Portion*

We saw above that there was no agreement about the amount of a bride's marriage portion or about her "fair" marriage portion. Some texts mentioned specific amounts; others said it could be whatever the parties agreed upon; others connected it with a bride's status. Also we saw that classical texts are not necessarily more specific about amounts, but continue to insist that it be "fair."

To arrive at a woman's fair marriage portion, Qudūrī says that one takes into consideration her sisters, paternal (i.e., agnatic) aunts, and paternal cousins, but not her mother or her maternal aunt, unless they happen to be from her tribe. Also one takes into account the bride's age, beauty, chastity, wealth, intelligence, piety, locale, and era.[86] Enlarging on this, Marghīnānī adds that Ibn Masʿūd said that a woman receives the marriage portion of the women of her family, no more, no less. The women of her family, Marghīnānī continues, are her paternal female relatives rather than her maternal ones, because the value of anything is based on its genus.[87]

Shīrāzī agrees that to establish a fair marriage portion for a woman, she should be compared with those of her agnatic female relatives who live in her town and who are like her in age, wealth, beauty, and chastity. In the absence of agnatic female relatives, a woman's marriage portion should be comparable to that received by her closest female relatives. In the total absence of any female relatives, she is compared with the women in her town. If there are none, then to women who most resemble her.[88]

Ibn Qudāma provides even more detailed guidelines for taking status into account. He first notes that several opinions are reported on Ibn Ḥanbal's authority about how to arrive at a woman's fair marriage portion. One says that it is figured on the basis of what her agnate female relatives receive; another, that it is on the basis of what her maternal female relatives receive, and another, that it is on the basis of what both her paternal and maternal female relatives receive. The correct opinion, he says, is that she is compared with her agnatic female relatives, because a woman's nobility (*sharaf*) comes from her *nasab*, which is not determined by her mother and her maternal aunts. Indeed,

[86] Qudūrī, *Mukhtaṣar*, 3:22–23.
[87] Marghīnānī, *Hidāya*, 2:502.
[88] Shīrāzī, *Tanbīh*, 434–35.

her mother may be a *mawlā,* and she a noble woman, or her mother may be noble, while she is not. Therefore, a bride should be compared only with her agnatic female relatives, and specifically with those who are like her in piety, intelligence, beauty, wealth, and chastity. Further, they should be residents of her town, because values are different in different towns. Only if she has no agnatic female relatives should she be compared with those on her maternal side. If she has no female relatives at all, then she is to be compared with other women in her town, but if there are none, with women of a neighboring town. Ibn Qudāma adds that if there are also no women with whom she may be compared in a neighboring town, then her marriage portion is commensurate with her moral excellence (*faḍīla*).[89]

Ibn ʿAbd al-Barr says, "According to Mālik, no account is taken of a woman's relatives." As we saw above, he himself says her fair marriage portion is calculated on the basis of her own wealth, beauty, rank, and circumstances.[90] However, the 8th/14th-century Mālikī jurist Khalīl b. Isḥāq describes a fair marriage portion much the way the other three schools do and indicates that lineage *is* important. He says a marriage portion is based on a woman's piety, beauty, wealth, and locale, but also on the amount received by any of her consanguine or germane sisters. It is not based on the amount received by her mother or her father's maternal half-sisters. These women are not of the same rank as the woman in question, because they may have different fathers and a different lineage.[91]

Discussion

In classical discussions of *kafāʾa*, earlier concerns for piety, lineage, wealth, and profession are repeated, but new emphases among these reflects an evolving Muslim society. Lineage remains of paramount importance, despite the disclaimers found in the traditions quoted above, and any direct description of *kafāʾa* harks back to early discussion

---

89 Ibn Qudāma, *Mughnī,* 8:59–60.

90 Ibn ʿAbd al-Barr, *al-Kāfī,* 2:552. Later, the Mālikī jurist Ibn Juzayy (d. 756–58/1355–57) bears out the Mālikī lack of interest in lineage and says that a fair marriage portion is arrived at by consideration of a woman's piety, wealth, and beauty. See his Qawānīn, 228.

91 See Russell and Suhrawardy, *A Manual of the Law of Marriage,* 77, nos. 209, 210. Reference to "her father's sister" must be to a uterine sister, as a full sister would have the same lineage as a bride's father.

about the superiority of the Arab Muslims over all others and the distinction of the Quraysh among the Arabs. However, contemporary realities are reflected in the Ḥanafī, Shāfiʿī, and Ḥanbalī insistence that only a woman's agnatic female relatives are taken into account. Ibn Qudāma in particular reveals the possibility that a woman's paternal and maternal relatives may be of different lineages and social classes. The generalized notion of social rank in which lineage is the biggest factor subsumes the importance of wealth and profession, even as these are acknowledged to be variable over a lifetime.

Khulʿ

The question of divorce initiated by a wife elicited considerable attention from later scholars, especially in regard to the particulars of a bad marriage.

1. The Prophet said: "A woman who asks her husband for a divorce when she is not in a situation where she is being harmed will find the fragrance of The Garden forbidden to her."[92]
2. ʿĀʾisha said that Ḥabība bt. Sahl was married to Thābit b. Qays who beat her and broke her shoulder bone. After the morning prayer, Ḥabība went to the Prophet, who summoned Thābit and said, "Take some of her property and part from her." Thābit asked, "Is that permissible?" The Prophet replied, "Yes." Thābit said, "I gave her a marriage portion of two gardens, which are in her possession." The Prophet said, "Take them and separate from her," and Thābit complied.[93]

The first of these traditions is more general than the ones quoted in Chapter 3. It expresses disapproval of the process unless the wife has a compelling reason for wanting to be free of her husband. The second is another version of the story of Ḥabība bt. Sahl and Thābit b. Qays. In the tradition quoted in Chapter 3, he broke her hand; here he breaks her shoulder. There it was one garden, here two. Both traditions point to the fact that she has reason to wish to extricate herself from her marriage.[94] We saw in Chapter 3 that separation of a couple by means of *khulʿ* generated disagreement among the founders about whether it

[92] Ibn Māja, *Sunan*, 1:666, no. 2055.
[93] Abū Dāwūd, *Sunan*, 3:222.
[94] See Wensinck, *Concordance*, 8, s.v. "Ḥabība bt. Sahl al-Anṣārīya" for the many different versions in the Six Books of the end of her marriage to Thābit. In some accounts she comes to the Prophet and says only that she cannot bear Thābit.

produces a definite divorce or is instead an annulment.[95] Shaybānī reported his and Abū Ḥanīfa's opinion that *khulʿ* is a definite divorce. Mālik and Shāfiʿī also held this opinion, but Ibn Ḥanbal agreed with the interpretation of Qurʾān 2:229, associated with Ibn ʿAbbās, that *khulʿ* is not to be equated with a divorce, but means instead that the wife ransoms herself from her husband, which results in an annulment. These views do not change and are repeated in later texts. The subjects that are of most concern to the later authors are the role of the arbitrators, the question of compensation, and the need to deal with the problem of *nushūz*.

The early Ḥanafīs and Ibn Ḥanbal did not address the question of two arbitrators as part of the process of *khulʿ*; Mālik said that the job of the arbitrators was either to separate or reconcile the couple. Shāfiʿī's discussion of their role was the most detailed. They should either reconcile the couple or arrange a settlement in which the husband divorces his wife in return for a compensation, usually the return of her marriage portion (as in the case of Ḥabība bt. Sahl and Thābit b. Qays).

Qudūrī continues the earlier Ḥanafī discussion and makes no mention of the arbitrators.[96] He is concerned with the problem of compensation and discusses it in more detail. First of all he says that anything that can lawfully be a marriage portion can become compensation for a *khulʿ* divorce. Although it is reprehensible for a man to take back more than he gave his wife as a marriage portion, it is completely lawful. If a wife dupes her husband by offering him a compensation that he accepts and that then turns out to be a forbidden substance, once he has agreed to accept it, he has no recourse. However, if a specific compensation had previously been named and agreed upon, he can demand it. Qudūrī also observes that *khulʿ* results in a definite divorce, but only if the husband receives a compensation from his wife.[97]

---

[95] An annulment would not count as one of the divorces allowed a couple. After a third divorce, they cannot remarry unless the wife has had an intervening marriage with another husband.

[96] Two eminent Ḥanafī scholars who refer briefly to an agent for each spouse are Muḥammad b. Aḥmad al-Sarakhsī (d. 483/1090) and ʿAlāʾ al-Dīn al-Kāsānī (d. 587/1189). Sarakhsī mentions the empowerment of two agents, one from the wife and the other from the husband, who can carry out whatever mission they have been given. If they have been instructed to negotiate a separation of the couple, they can do so, but they cannot decide on their own whether reconciliation or separation would be best. Sarakhsī, *Mabsūṭ*, see 6:193. Kāsānī also discusses two agents. See *Badāʾiʿ*, 3:144–53. For agency in Islamic law, see *EI*, s.v. "Wakāla."

[97] If a wife retains her marriage portion, then her husband can return to her during her *ʿidda*, and their separation is not really an example of *khulʿ*. Qudūrī, *Mukhtaṣar*, 3:64–67.

For the Mālikīs, Ibn Abī Zayd says that a wife can free herself from her husband for more or less than her marriage portion, as long as he has not harmed her in an effort to extract it from her. If he has, she gets back what she gave him, but they are, nonetheless, separated by means of *khulʿ*.[98] Ibn ʿAbd al-Barr too says that as long as a husband has not harmed his wife (i.e., to pressure her into buying her freedom), it is lawful for her to ransom herself from him, and this produces a definite divorce. However, if it turns out that he has injured her or forced her to buy her freedom, then whatever she gave him is returned to her. At that point there are two opinions about whether the divorce is definite. One holds that it is, because, although the wife has not compensated her husband for it, she initiated it and therefore it is a *khulʿ* divorce (which is definite); the other holds that the divorce is not definite, because, since the husband has not taken back any payment he made to her, he has the right to return to her during her *ʿidda*. Ibn ʿAbd al-Barr says that he and other scholars consider this latter the soundest opinion (this was also Qudūrī's opinion). In either case, if, on the basis of a new contract and a new marriage portion, the couple remarry, they can divorce only twice more (i.e., a second divorce would be final).[99]

Ibn ʿAbd al-Barr also discusses the role of arbitrators: when relations break down between husband and wife, and it is not clear who is at fault, they may bring the matter to the attention of the *qāḍī*. He can appoint one arbitrator from the husband's relatives and another from the wife's. The arbitrators must be trustworthy, possess sound judgment, and be versed in *fiqh*. They make an attempt to establish who is at fault and to reconcile the couple, but if they are unable to do so, they have the right to separate them. If the husband is at fault, they separate the couple without compensating him for divorcing her; if the wife is at fault, they take whatever they think best from her to compensate the husband. Regardless of compensation, if the arbitrators separate the couple, the result is a single definite divorce. However, the husband can ask that the divorce be triple.

At the end of his description, Ibn ʿAbd al-Barr notes approvingly that in a situation that required sending two arbitrators, Yaḥyā b. Yaḥyā

---

[98] Ibn Abī Zayd, *Risāla*, 192 (*First Steps*, 36, nos. 118, 119).

[99] Ibn ʿAbd al-Barr assumes that the divorce by means of *khulʿ* is the first of three, and that even though the couple have remarried, that divorce carries over into their new marriage. Thus if they wish to remarry after two divorces, the wife will first have to have intercourse in a marriage with another man.

used to give a *fatwā* in favor of the house of a trusted man and that, he says has become our practice.[100] The trusted man's charge is to ascertain which spouse is at fault and, if possible, to reconcile the couple.[101] This addition of a man whose job it is to try to reconcile the couple before the arbitrators negotiate a *khul*ʿ settlement also becomes part of the classical Shāfiʿī and Ḥanbalī discussions.

In his description of *khul*ʿ, Shīrāzī deals first with *nushūz* (refractoriness), which may be exhibited either by a wife or a husband. If the wife is refractory, her husband may take the steps laid out for him in Qurʾān 4:34. If a husband is refractory, which Shīrāzī describes as his having become ill or old and therefore paying inadequate attention to his wife, she may take the steps laid out for her in Qurʾān 4:128. However, if the spouses accuse each other, the *qāḍī* should house them near a reliable person who will try to ascertain which spouse is at fault and stop his or her oppressive behavior. If that effort fails, and the couple reach the point of insults and blows, then the *qāḍī* sends two trustworthy, free Muslims as arbitrators to ascertain whether reconciliation is possible or separation required.

In one opinion, Shīrāzī continues, each arbitrator is an agent of the spouse he represents and is therefore bound to carry out whatever he has been charged with, such as divorce for compensation on the husband's side, or expenditure of the compensation on the wife's. In another opinion, the one that Shīrāzī says is best, the arbitrators are sent by the *qāḍī,* who entrusts them to achieve reconciliation or separation, regardless of the wishes of the couple, because God did not mention their consent. It is recommended that the arbitrators be relatives of the spouses, one a relative of the husband's, the other of the wife's. They

[100] Ibn ʿAbd al-Barr, *al-Kāfī*, 2:297. For the notion of "practice" (*ʿamal*) in legal texts, see *EI*, s.v. "ʿAmal" (3.). For a brief but useful discussion of Mālikī *ʿamal*, see Toledano, *Judicial Practice and Family Law in Morocco*, 9–24.

[101] Ibn ʿAbd al-Barr, al-Kāfī, 2:293–97. For the "fatwā in favor of the house of a trusted man," see *EI*, s.v. "Yaḥyā b. Yaḥyā al-Laythī." [In addition to his role in the dissemination of Mālik's *Muwaṭṭaʾ* in al-Andalus,] "he was also the introducer of customs and doctrines that took root in al-Andalus, such as abandoning the Ḳurʾānic precept of two arbiters sent to the house of a husband and wife to solve their marital problems, and substituting for it the practice of sending the couple to the house of a trusted man (*dār amīn*)." For a discussion of this practice in al-Andalus, see Fierro, "Ill-treated Women Seeking Divorce." See Fierro, 344, for different views among Mālikī jurists about whether lodging a couple in the house of a "trusted man" replaced the arbitration mentioned in the Qurʾān (4:35) or was a step that preceded it.

must be trustworthy, and if they are *qāḍī*s, they must also be jurists (*faqīhayni*).[102]

As for *khul*ʿ itself, Shīrāzī says that both spouses must be sane and adult, and there are only two conditions in which it is not reprehensible. One is if the couple fears that they cannot keep within the limits established by God (see Qurʾān 2:229), and the other is when a man swears that he will be triply divorced from his wife if he does something that he is, in fact, bound to do. In this case he can part from his wife by means of *khul*ʿ, do whatever it is he is bound to, then remarry his wife without breaking his oath.[103]

Khiraqī, like Shīrāzī, separates *khul*ʿ and *nushūz*. *Khul*ʿ he treats more narrowly than the other jurists by mentioning particular issues that come up when a wife begins the process of buying her freedom (or ransoming herself) from her husband. But he deals first with *nushūz*: if the wife is guilty of it, her husband can follow the steps prescribed for him in Qurʾān 4:34 by first admonishing her, then absenting himself from her bed, and then, if neither of the earlier measures is effective, beating her. However, Khiraqī says, "If enmity occurs between the spouses, and it is feared that that will impel them to refractoriness, the *qāḍī*, with their assent, sends one trustworthy arbitrator chosen from his relatives and one chosen from hers, both of whom are empowered to reconcile or separate the couple as they see fit. Whatever they decide is binding."[104] Commenting on Khiraqī's treatment of *nushūz*, Ibn Qudāma says that when a rift has occurred between husband and wife, the *qāḍī* looks into the matter, and if it becomes clear to him that the problem is due to the wife's behavior (her *nushūz*), the situation is handled in accordance with Qurʾān 4:34. But if it is due to the husband's,

[102] The word Shīrāzī uses, which I have changed to "*qāḍī*," is "*ḥākim*." See Tyan, *Histoire de l'organisation judicaire*, 111–12 for the term *ḥākim*, which, he says, is often synonymous with *qāḍī*. Strictly speaking, *qāḍī* refers to the judges in the capital city where the ruler resides, and *ḥākim* refers to judges in provincial towns. However, the terms are sometimes used interchangeably. Here, Shīrāzī must be referring to provincial judges, who are not necessarily also scholars, or to local representatives of the governor, who, in the absence of a *qāḍī*, are in charge of settling legal problems. For judicial organization, see Chapter 3 of Tyan, especially 119–55.

[103] Shīrāzī, *Tanbīh*, 440–41 and *Muhadhdhab*, 2:69–70. For the use of this kind of oath and *khul*ʿ divorce in Mamluk society, see Rapoport, *Marriage, Money and Divorce*, especially Chapter 5, "Repudiation and public power," 91–96. Rapoport notes that Ḥanbalī judges ruled that *khul*ʿ separations were annulments, and therefore a couple could part by means of *khul*ʿ as many times as they wished (95). This is a legal stratagem or *ḥīla* (see *EI*, s.v. "Ḥīla.").

[104] al-Khiraqī, *Mukhtaṣar*, 150.

the *qāḍī* lodges the couple with a trustworthy person who prevents him from harming or attacking her. Similarly, if each claims the other is at fault, the *qāḍī* lodges them in proximity to someone who will oversee their behavior and enjoin them to be just to each other. Only if the efforts of the trustworthy person fail does the *qāḍī* send the two arbitrators, in accordance with Qurʾān 4:35 (*appoint an arbiter from his folk and an arbiter from her folk*...).

Ibn Qudāma says that two opinions are reported from Ibn Ḥanbal on what the job of the two arbitrators is. In one, they are agents of the spouses and can separate the couple only if both spouses have previously given them permission to do so. This, Ibn Qudāma says, is Shāfiʿī's and Abū Ḥanīfa's opinion, because the husband has the right to his wife's private parts, and the wife has the right to her husband's wealth, and both are adults capable of knowing their own minds. The second opinion is that the two arbitrators do what they think best. This is Mālik's opinion, which, Ibn Qudāma says, accords with Qurʾān 4:35 (and is therefore the better opinion). In that verse God called them arbitrators, and He did not mention the satisfaction of the two spouses.[105]

Discussion

A change in the way *khulʿ* is treated between the earlier and classical texts is the inclusion of another step in the process that precedes the activity of the two arbitrators: when relations between a couple break down, they are placed in proximity to a reliable man whose task it is to oversee their behavior and try to modify it in such a way that the couple can be kept together. The arbitrators mentioned in Qurʾān 4:35 are called upon to act only after this reconciliation effort fails. This process is not part of Ḥanafī discussion, but is covered in Mālikī, Shāfiʿī, and Ḥanbalī texts.

Various things are taken for granted when this process is mentioned. The first is that the husband does not wish to repudiate his wife and that she does not wish to part from him by means of a *khulʿ* divorce. Leaving aside any emotional investment the couple may have in their marriage, economic concerns certainly figure in efforts at reconciliation. If a husband divorces his wife, he owes the deferred portion of her

---

[105] Ibn Qudāma, *Mughnī*, 8:166–68.

marriage portion (if there is one), or if he has already given it to her in full, he loses access to it. The wife, on the other hand, has to buy her way out of the marriage by relinquishing her marriage portion or possibly even more than she initially received. The second is that a particular case of marital discord has been brought to the attention of the *qāḍī*, or a representative of the local administrative authority, by one or both spouses or by their relatives. The third is that only if the assessment of the reliable man and his personal appeals to one or both spouses to alter their behavior fail does the *qāḍī* arrange for arbitrators, one from his relatives and one from hers, to recommend that the couple be separated or reconciled (although reconciliation is less likely to follow the failure of the reliable man).

Concluding Discussion

In a comparison between the way topics of marriage and divorce are treated in the formative and classical periods, the most obvious contrast is an increase in the number of details covered. Sometimes, as in the question of whether a woman receives maintenance and lodging, only lodging, or neither during her *ʿidda*, the later jurists mainly reiterate earlier positions. Often they simply describe additional possibilities, as in the Ḥanafī addition of another category (*aḥsanuʾl ṭalāq*) to *ṭalāq al-sunna*. But they can also clarify particular issues, some real and some not. For example, there are instances where not all consanguine siblings of two foster-siblings become related to each other within the forbidden degrees; at the same time, it is improbable that two infants will be nursed by an animal instead of a human wet nurse. Classical jurists sometimes also add details that can change earlier positions. For example, on the question of the necessity of a *walī* to conclude a woman's marriage contract, classical authors discuss a number of circumstances that limit a Ḥanafī woman's ability to conclude her own contract and make it unlikely that she would ever do so, and the later Mālikī view is that not even a lowly woman can conclude her own marriage contract, which means that no women can. In one instance I have compared formative and classical discussions of a Qurʾān verse. Qurʾān 65:2 says that two trustworthy witnesses should attest a husband's return to his wife after a non-final divorce. All classical jurists give different, overlapping reasons for why this verse recommends rather than requires witnesses.

On two issues, *kafāʾa* and *khulʿ*, there is a sharp difference between the formative and classical treatments, which reflect practical change. On the question of *kafāʾa*, it is clear that local social conditions had to be taken into account, and jurists no longer discussed only Arabs versus *mawālī*. For the procedure to be followed when a woman initiates a *khulʿ* divorce, all except Ḥanafī jurists incorporated a new figure, the trusted man, into the process.

CHAPTER FIVE

WOMEN'S LIVES

All *fiqh* works have chapters devoted to marriage and divorce and, as we have seen, in essence cover the same topics even if the variety of different details sometimes results in different emphases and over time, in significant change. This is not the case when it comes to women's lives in and outside their homes. Coverage of daily life is more uneven. There are topics not covered at all in some works, and often those that are discussed are scattered in different chapters. Material relevant to women as witnesses, for example, may be in a chapter on judgments and evidence, or in one on witnessing in general, or in the chapter on marriage as part of a discussion on whether and under what circumstances a strange man may see a woman's face. The classical jurists studied in Chapter 4 have more to say about women's lives than the jurists of the formative period, so in this chapter I rely mainly on classical texts to describe women's lives and refer to material from the formative period only when it provides a background helpful for understanding what classical authors have said.

Women at Home

Maintenance

1. The Prophet said: "When a Muslim provides for his family, with regard to the Hereafter, it is counted as his having given alms."[1]
2. Muʿāwiya al-Qushayrī said: "I asked the Messenger of God, 'What does one of us owe his wife?' He replied, 'That you feed her what she eats, clothe her in what she wears, do not beat her face, do not censure her and do not keep apart from her, except in your home.' "[2]
3. ʿĀʾisha said: "Hind bt. ʿUtba said to the Prophet, ʿAbū Sufyān is stingy. He does not give me enough for my son and me, unless

[1] Bukhārī, *Ṣaḥīḥ*, 3:424, *Kitāb al-nafaqāt*, no. 5351.

[2] Abū Dāwūd, *Sunan*, 3:127, *Kitāb al-nikāḥ*, no. 2143. In his commentary Ibn al-Jawziyya says that "except in your home" can mean either that a man should not shun his wife, or, that he should not turn her out of the house.

> I take it secretly.' The Prophet said, 'Take what you and your son need, with fairness.' "[3]

Although the Qurʾān does not explicitely mention maintenance (*nafaqa*), it figured as part of Wāḥidī's explanation for Qurʾān 4:128 (see Chapter 1 above). Wāḥidī said that according to ʿĀʾisha, a woman who wishes to remain in her husband's household and avoid being divorced, can offer to relieve him from providing her with maintenance. In Chapter 3, we saw disagreement about the circumstances in which a widow or a divorcee receives maintenance during her *ʿidda*, as well as disagreement about whether she receives lodging. In discussions about marriage rather than divorce, the notion of maintenance includes both food and clothing, as well as lodging.[4] Once a couple are married, and a wife has been delivered into her husband's care and is available for sexual intercourse, he is expected to maintain her.[5] The first and second traditions above state that a husband owes his wife good treatment. The third says that a wife should be maintained "with fairness (*biʾl-maʿrūf*)," and all discussions of maintenance refer to "with fairness" regardless of whether they actually mention these instructions the Prophet gave Hind bt. ʿUtba.

To "feed her what she eats" and "clothe her in what she wears" are the two basic things a husband must provide to maintain his wife. What she eats and wears are generally agreed to vary depending on the status of the spouses and the time and place in which they live. Some say that the level at which a wife should be supported is based on her husband's status, some say on hers, others on a combination of both of theirs. Different texts emphasize various aspects of domestic maintenance.

For the Ḥanafīs, Qudūrī says that a man must provide his wife with food, clothing and one maid if she is accustomed to having one. For lodging, he says that a wife must be lodged in a separate dwelling that does not include any of her husband's relatives, unless she chooses otherwise. If her husband has a child by another wife, that child cannot be lodged with her. Qudūrī adds that a husband can forbid his wife's parents and any children she may have from a previous marriage from

[3] Bukhārī, *Ṣaḥīḥ*, 3:427, *Kitāb al-nafaqāt*, no. 5364. For Hind bt. ʿUtba, mother of the first Umayyad Caliph, Muʿāwiyya, see *EI*, s.v. For variants on this tradition, see also Ibn Saʿd, *Ṭabaqāt*, s.v. "Hind bint ʿUtba," 8:170–72.

[4] See *EI*, s.v. "Nafaḳa."

[5] However, a wife who has not received her marriage portion has the right to refuse to have intercouse with her husband and at the same time to receive maintenance.

entering her house.[6] Marghīnānī qualifies this last point by saying that some have understood it to mean he can forbid them from actually residing with her, but not from seeing and speaking with her.[7] For the Mālikīs, Ibn Abī Zayd says that a man must maintain his wife regardless of whether she herself is rich or poor, and if he is wealthy he should provide her with servants.[8]

Shīrāzī is specific about food. He says, "A wealthy husband should provide his wife with two *mudd*s of the grain which is eaten in that town; if he is poor, one *mudd*; if he is medium well off, one and a half *mudd*s. But if she would prefer an equivalent, that is lawful in accordance with the prevailing opinion of the school, but it is also said that it is not lawful." He goes on to mention condiments and meat, again in accordance with the customs of the town. Next he moves on to personal accoutrements such as hair oil and henna. Her husband need not provide a woman with money for perfume, doctor's fees or medicines, but he must clothe her, a rich woman more sumptuously than a poor one. He must also provide her with a servant if she is accustomed to having one.[9]

Ibn Qudāma begins his discussion of maintenance by quoting Qur'ān 65:7: *Let him who has abundance spend of that abundance, and he whose provision is measured, let him spend of that which Allah has given him.* He then mentions food, clothing and lodging with several references to the Prophet's instructions to Hind—"Take what you need with fairness"—to suggest the level at which a man should spend for his wife. His description is like Shīrāzī's except that he includes mention of a number of household furnishings (e.g., bed and pillow for sleeping, a place to sit during the day). He too says that a husband need not support more than one maid for his wife. She may want several maids in order to preserve her possessions and her beauty, but her husband does not need to provide them.[10]

If it turns out that a man is unable to maintain his wife, all scholars except the Ḥanafīs say that she can go to the *qāḍī* to seek—and receive—either a divorce or an annulment of her marriage. For the Mālikīs, Ibn ʿAbd al-Barr says that once a couple have had intercourse, if a husband cannot support his wife, the *qāḍī* separates them if she demands it.

---

[6] See Qudūrī, *Mukhtaṣar*, 3:91–98.
[7] See Marghīnānī, *Hidāya*, 2:649.
[8] Ibn Abī Zayd, *Risāla*, 198 (*First Steps*, nos. 151, 155).
[9] See Shīrāzī, *Tanbīh*, 498–99. The "servant" can be either a slave or a free maid.
[10] Ibn Qudāma, *Mughnī*, 9:232–38.

Some say he does so after a time delay of three days, others say a week, others, thirty days, still others, two months, But these times are all incorrect, according to Ibn 'Abd al-Barr, because it is up to the *qāḍī*'s judgment and depends on the wife's needs and patience. He adds that hunger has no patience![11] Such a separation results in a non-final divorce, and if the husband's circumstances improve while the wife is waiting her *'idda*, he can return to her.3[12] Shīrāzī says that a wife is granted the right to choose to have her marriage annulled if her husband cannot support her. Further, she can initially choose to remain married and have her maintenance be an outstanding debt of his and then subsequently choose annulment. If she does, there are two opinions about when the annulment takes place: one, that it is immediate; the other, and according to Shīrāzī the better one, that it becomes valid after three days. He adds that if a husband is either well off or moderately well off, no annulment takes place as long as his debt (i.e., that incurred when the wife supports herself on his credit) does not become large. Also, no annulment takes place if the problem is only that he cannot afford a maid for her. It does take place if he cannot clothe her. If he cannot lodge her, it is permissible that the marriage be annulled, but it is also permissible that it not be.[13] For the Ḥanbalīs, Ibn Qudāma covers much the same ground as Shīrāzī, and adds that a separation effected by the *qāḍī* is tantamount to a non-final divorce. He also says that if a woman decides not to seek a separation from her husband for lack of maintenance, she can, nonetheless, refuse to have intercourse with him. Further, since keeping her in without provisions harms her, her husband cannot forbid her from going out to earn whatever she needs to.[14]

Qudūrī explains the different Ḥanafī view, that a couple are *not* separated when a husband cannot maintain his wife. Rather, the wife is instructed to treat her maintenance as debt against her husband's assets. If, over a period of time, her husband has still failed to provide maintenance for a wife and she demands it, she receives nothing unless the *qāḍī* has mandated maintenance for her, or she had a prior

[11] Ibn 'Abd al-Barr, *al-Kāfī*, 2:560–61.

[12] Ibn 'Abd al-Barr, *al-Kāfī*, 2:560. If the couple have not had intercourse and they are separated by the *qāḍī* because the husband cannot support his wife, that is an instance of divorce before intercourse, and the husband owes his wife half her marriage portion.

[13] Shīrāzī, *Tanbīh*, 501–02.

[14] See Ibn Qudāma, *Mughnī*, 9:243–49.

agreement with her husband on a set sum.[15] Marghīnānī explains this difference by contrasting the Ḥanafī with the Shāfiʿī position. He says that if the *qāḍī* declared that a husband who could not afford to maintain his wife were to be divorced from her, then the husband's right to her would be destroyed, and that is a far greater harm than the fact that her maintenance is merely in arrears.[16]

If a wife is guilty of *nushūz* (recalcitrance), her husband can stop maintaining her. When *nushūz* is used specifically of a wife's behavior, it refers either to the fact that she has gone out of the house without her husband's permission or against his orders, or that she has refused to have sexual intercourse with him. If she goes out without permission, her husband can suspend her maintenance until she returns. He can also suspend it if she refuses to have sexual intercourse with him when it is lawful for her to do so. Ibn ʿAbd al-Barr, for example, says that if a wife is rebellious (*nāshiz*), she receives no maintenance, unless she is pregnant. Once she returns to her husband, maintenance is due from then on. Ibn Qudāma says that her husband can force a wife to perform those ritual ablutions that are required after menstrual periods and childbirth, before a couple resumes sexual intercourse.[17]

Treatment of Wives

1. The Prophet said: "Treat women well! They are created from a curved rib and the curved part is the best. If you try to straighten it, will break, but if you leave it, it will remain curved. Treat Women well!"[18]
2. The Prophet said: "The best of wives is the one who smiles when her husband looks at her, obeys him when he gives her an order and does not contradict him in any matter regarding herself or his property."[19]

---

[15] In their translation of Qudūrī's *Mukhtaṣar*, Bousquet and Bercher note that in Ḥanafī law, maintenance is a pious gift not an obligation incurred as an aspect of the marriage contract itself. For maintenance to become a payable obligation, the *qāḍī* has to intervene either to fix the amount of a wife's maintenance, or to ratify and execute an agreement about it which has previously been concluded between the spouses. See 60, n. 36. See also Meron, *L'Obligation alimentaire* for a full explanation of the evolution of the concept of maintenance in the Ḥanafī school.

[16] Marghīnānī, *Hidāya*, 2:647. He also explains that if the wife takes it upon herself to acquire debt for her husband without a ruling from the *qāḍī*, she herself becomes liable for it, not her husband.

[17] See Qudūrī, *Mukhtaṣar*, 3:92–93; Shīrāzī, *Tanbīh*, 500; Ibn ʿAbd al-Barr, *al-Kāfī*, 2:559; Ibn Qudāma, *Mughnī*, 8:128.

[18] Bukhārī, *ṣaḥīḥ*, 3:383, *Kitāb al-nikāḥ*, no. 5186. See *EI*, s.v. "Hawwā" for the creation of Eve from Adam's rib.

[19] Ibn Ḥanbal, *Musnad*, 2:432.

These two traditions exemplify some of the concerns about marital relations dealt with by different jurists. In the first, men are exhorted to treat their wives well. A man *may* behave in a variety of ways. He *should* treat his wives well. The second points to the absolute obedience a wife owes her husband. All jurists say that a man has complete control over his wife, and that in return for obedient and submissive behavior, she deserves kind treatment, in accordance with Qurʾān 4:19 (*consort with them in kindness*). Two other verses frequently quoted as a basis for relations between husband and wife are Qurʾān 2:228 (*men are a degree above them*) and Qurʾān 4:34 (*men are in charge of women*). If a wife is in any way rebellious, she is guilty of *nushūz* and her husband has the right to discipline her. As we just saw, he can withhold her maintenance, and as we saw in Chapter 1, Qurʾān 4:34 recommends that he do so in progressively severe stages (*admonish*, *banish to beds apart*, *scourge*).[20]

Within this framework, two points receive particular attention. The first is that a man can forbid his wife from leaving the house. It is recommended that he permit her to go out to attend her parents' funerals, but he is not obliged to. Shīrāzī, for example, says, "It is reprehensible for him to forbid her from visiting her father if he falls ill or from attending his burial when he dies." The reason Shīrāzī says is "because forbidding her from that leads to estrangement and incites her to disobedience."[21] The second is that a wife must make herself available for sexual intercourse whenever it is lawful for her to do so. Shīrāzī quotes a tradition in which the Prophet said, "If one of you calls his wife to his bed and she refuses, so he spends the night angry at her, the angels curse her until morning."[22] A husband's kind treatment of his wife means that in addition to maintaining her, he gives her a fair share of his attention.

Division of a Husband's Time

1. Abū Ḥurayra said that the Prophet used to divide [his time] among his wives and be fair, and he would say, "O God, this is my division which

[20] See again Rispler-Chaim, "*Nushūz* between Medieval and Contemporary Islamic Law."

[21] Shīrāzī, *Muhadhdhab*, 2:66. See also *Tanbīh*, 437–38. For funeral practices, see *EI*, s.v. "Djanāza" and Hughes, *Dictionary of Islam*, s.v. "Burial."

[22] Quoted by Shīrāzī, *Muhadhdhab*, 2:66–67. For a similar tradition, see also Muslim, *Ṣaḥīḥ*, 9:258, *Kitāb al-nikāḥ*, no. 1436.

I control. Do not blame me for what You, not I, control," meaning the love of the heart.[23]

2. The Prophet said: "When a man marries a bikr he spends seven nights with her, and when he marries a thayyib he spends three nights with her.[24]

The first tradition above is often quoted to show that a man who is married to more than one wife should treat them equally regardless of how he feels about them. In another, the Prophet says, "Whoever has two wives and prefers one over the other will be lopsided when he is resurrected on the day of judgment."[25] The second tradition above is often quoted to show that a man who has more than one wife should spend extra time with a new one and then resume impartial treatment of them. Variant versions of it connect the question of how a man with more than one wife allocates his time, to the Prophet's marriage with Umm Salama who was widowed when her husband died of wounds received at the Battle of Uḥud. This story is understood in one way by the Mālikīs, Shāfiʿīs and Ḥanbalīs, who take it to mean that a man initially spends extra time with a new bride, and in another, by the Ḥanafīs, who say that a man does not. Both Mālik and Shāfiʿī reported that after their wedding night the Prophet offered to stay with Umm Salama either for seven or for three nights before he resumed rotating among his wives and that she chose three. They understood the tradition to mean that a man initially spends extra time with a new bride.[26] Ibn Ḥanbal agreed with Mālik and Shāfiʿī.[27]

Shaybānī disagreed and says that a man does not differentiate between new brides and their co-wives. His obligation is always to spend an equal amount of time with all of them: "As for a man who marries a second wife, regardless of whether the second wife is a *bikr* or a *thayyib*, Abū Ḥanīfa said he does not spend any more time with her than he does with his first wife."[28] Shaybānī too cited the tradition about the Prophet's marriage to Umm Salama, but he interpreted it

[23] Abū Dāwud, *Sunan*, 3:121, *Kitāb al-nikāḥ*, no. 2134. Abū Dāwud adds that "what You not I, control" means the heart.

[24] Bukhārī, *ṣaḥīh*, 3:391, *Kitāb al-nikāḥ*, no. 5213.

[25] Abū Dāwud, *Sunan*, 3:121, *Kitāb al-nikāḥ*, no. 2133.

[26] Mālik, *Muwaṭṭa'*, 3:134–36; Shāfiʿī, *Kitāb al-umm*, 5:190–92. See also 109–11. Shāfiʿī adds that a man may spend between one and three nights with each wife, but that it is preferable that he not lengthen his rotation beyond three nights.

[27] See Ibn Qudāma, *Mughnī*, 159–61. I do not find this issue in the versions of Ibn Ḥanbal's *Masāʾil* available to me.

[28] Shaybānī, *Kitāb al-ḥujja*, 3:246.

differently. He reported that after their wedding night, the Prophet told Umm Salama he would stay with her seven or three nights, whichever she wished and then rotate, and she chose three. Shaybānī then said, "We adopt this. If he were to spend seven nights with her, he would spend seven with them, and he would not spend more time with her than with them; and if three nights with her, then three with them. This is Abū Ḥanīfa's doctrine and that of the majority of our scholars."[29]

Qudūrī repeats this point of view for the Ḥanafīs: if a man has two wives he treats them equally, regardless of whether one was a *bikr* or a *thayyib* (i.e., when he married each of them). However, he need not treat them equally when it comes to deciding which wife to take with him when he travels. But, Qudūrī adds, it is best that he draw lots to decide which one to take. One wife is free to give a co-wife her day, but she may also change her mind.[30]

Ibn ʿAbd al-Barr repeats the Mālikī position that a man spends seven nights with a new bride who is a *bikr* and three with one who is a *thayyib* and adds further detail. Once a man resumes dividing his time equally among his wives, he should not have intercourse with one wife on a second wife's day, unless the second wife gives her permission. On the other hand, he should not buy a day from one wife so he can spend it with another, and wives should not buy each other's days. Ibn ʿAbd al-Barr adds that there is no harm in a man providing one of his wives more maintenance and better clothing and jewelry than another, as long as he does not deprive the less favored wife of her due. But, he says, it is also related that a man should not do that, because if he does, he is not treating his wives equally.[31]

Shīrāzī repeats Shāfiʿī's position that a man initially spends seven nights with a new wife who is a *bikr* and three with one who is a *thayyib*. Shīrāzī then goes on to point out that although a husband is not obliged to divide his time equally between his wives, if he intends to (as is recommended), he should not single one out, but instead, draw lots to decide which one to start with. In addition, Shīrāzī says that the fact that a wife may be ill, or menstruating, or have just given birth, or

[29] *Muwaṭṭaʾ Shaybānī*, 213. Shaybānī develops this position more fully in *Kitāb al-ḥujja*, 3:246–53 where he argues against the Medinese understanding of the tradition.
[30] Qudūrī, *Mukhtaṣar*, 3:30–31.
[31] Ibn ʿAbd al-Barr, *al-Kāfī*, 2:562–63.

have an occluded vagina has no effect on the amount of time he spends with her.[32] If a man wishes to take a wife on a trip, he should choose one by drawing lots.[33]

Ibn Qudāma agrees with Ibn ʿAbd al-Barr—that after initially spending seven or three nights with a new wife, a man resumes an equal rotation among them. He also says that if a man and one of his wives agree to grant her time with him to a second wife, the second wife is not free to refuse because her husband's right to her company is absolute. Ibn Qudāma mentions Sawda's giving up her day to ʿĀʾisha and notes that a wife can give up a day permanently (the way Sawda did), or merely give up a single day.[34]

The time a man spends with a wife is often correlated with sexual intercourse, but it need not be. Marghīnāni, for example, says that although a man can divide his time equally he cannot be expected to have sexual intercourse on the same schedule, and we just saw that Shīrāzī specifically said that a man spends the same amount of time with each of his wives regardless of whether they are available for intercourse. Shīrāzī adds that a man is not obliged to have intercourse with all his wives, but it is recommended that he treat them equally in this, as in other regards. There was disagreement about the practice of coitus interruptus. It was viewed as a method of birth control which was disliked but might be an economic necessity. At the same time it denied a woman her right to have children.[35] In a tradition on the authority of ʿUmar, he says, "'The Prophet forbade coitus interruptus with a free woman without her permission.'"[36] Ibn ʿAbd al-Barr says that her husband must ask a free wife's permission to practice coitus interruptus, but Shīrāzī says that if a man's wife does not give her husband permission to practice it, there are two opinions. One is that coitus interruptus is not forbidden because her right is to sexual fulfillment, not ejaculation. The other is that it is forbidden, because it interferes with conception which has no harm attached to it. Ibn Qudāma says

[32] However, if a man has both slave and free wives (a possibility we saw in Chapter 2), when he divides his time, he should spend twice as much of it with a free, as with a slave wife.

[33] Shīrāzī, *Tanbīh*, 438.

[34] Ibn Qudāma, *Mughnī*, 8:152–53.

[35] See *EI*, s.v. "ʿAzl." A slave concubine has no right to children. If a man has a slave wife, however, he must consult her owner who would also own any children she might bear.

[36] Ibn Ḥanbal, *Musnad*, 1:31.

that it is reprehensible because it interferes both with conception and with sexual fulfillment.[37]

Custody

> A woman came to the Prophet and said, "O, Messenger of God, [As for] this son of mine, my womb was a vessel for him, my breasts are a milk skin for him and my care of him is all-embracing. But now his father has divorced me and wants to wrest him from me!" The Prophet said, "You have the most right to him as long as you do not remarry."[38]

As we saw in Chapter 1, the Qur'ān states that a husband and his wife may decide that she will nurse her own child, or they may decide to procure a wet nurse (2:233). If a man repudiates his wife while she is nursing their infant, he owes her a nursing fee (65:6).[39] Otherwise, as the tradition above shows, *ḥaḍāna*, child custody or upbringing, becomes an issue of contention when a couple divorce.[40] Two points are raised here: first, a mother has the most right to custody of her infant; second, her right lapses if she remarries. Although the tradition recognizes a mother's love for her infant, *ḥaḍāna* is considered a right of the child's not its parents. Therefore if a mother remarries, she loses custody because it is assumed that in a new marriage she will be occupied with her husband to the detriment of her child. At that point custody is awarded to her mother or grandmother.[41] Once an infant has been weaned, if a mother has custody she retains it while the infant is still a small child. The Prophet's response in the above tradition is always understood to mean that she does retain custody if it is the case that she remarries and her new husband is related to the child within the forbidden degrees. She loses custody if he is a "stranger."[42] A mother who has custody of a child cannot move with it to live too far from the father. If she does so, she loses custody. Ibn ʿAbd al-Barr says the

[37] See Shīrāzī, *Muhadhdhab*, 2:66–8. Ibn Qudāma, 8:122–23. For a woman's right to children and to sexual satisfaction, see Musallam, *Sex and Society in Islam*, Chapter 2, "Contraception and the rights of women."

[38] Abū Dāwud, *Sunan*, 6:265, *Kitāb al-ṭalāq*, no. 2273.

[39] See Shaybānī, *Ḥujja*, 4:75–78 where he says a widow too is owed a fee for nursing hers and her late husband's child.

[40] See *EI*, s.v. "Ḥaḍāna."

[41] Thereafter, there is no longer unanimity among the schools about which women are next in line for a child's custody. The Ḥanafī view is that it moves to a child's maternal aunts, the Mālikī, Shāfiʿī and Ḥanbalī views, to the paternal grandmothers.

[42] A close relative of the child's (e.g., a paternal uncle) is expected to be concerned with its welfare and therefore not jealous of his new wife's attention to it.

distance she can put between herself and the child's father cannot be so far as to make it necessary to shorten prayer when traveling between the two points.[43] A father, on the other hand may wish to resettle elsewhere, and in that case he can demand custody of his child, unless his ex-wife is willing to move to the same locale. A mother who has custody must also be of sound morals, not an adulteress (*fājira*) and not so lowly that she is incapable of caring for the child if she becomes ill.[44] She need not be a Muslim, but if there is any danger that she try to turn the child away from Islam, it is removed from her.

Assuming a mother's custody of an infant and a very young child, there are different views of exactly when a father takes over his children from an ex-wife. For a son, a father intervenes at some point to give him a religious education and train him in professional activity. For a daughter, he arranges a marriage. But he can do these things regardless of whether the child in question lives with him. Qudūrī says that a girl is in her mother's custody until she menstruates; Ibn Abī Zayd, that she remains in her mother's custody until she has married and her marriage has been consummated; Shirāzī, that a girl may choose whom she wishes to live with until she is given in marriage. Ibn Qudāma is more specific about what is at stake. He says the goal of custody is that a child flourish, and he insists that after seven years of age, a girl needs to be in the custody of her father. The reason is that once she has reached seven years she is getting ready to be given in marriage, and her father is the person from whom her hand is sought and who is most knowledgeable about *kafāʾa*. Ibn Qudāma draws a contrast between the upbringing of girls and boys. Regardless of whether a boy lives with his mother or father, he should spend the day with his father who is able thereby to guide his religious and professional education. In contrast, a girl stays home all day wherever she lives, because her training and upbringing in things such as spinning and cooking take place in the home.[45]

---

[43] Ibn ʿAbd al-Barr, *al-Kāfī*, 2:625–26. See *EI*, s.v. "Ṣalāt," no. 4. F. for the shortened "travel prayer."

[44] See Ibn ʿAbd al-Barr, *al-Kāfī*, 2:625 and again *EI*, s.v. "Ḥaḍāna." For the view that a suckling infant imbibes the character of the woman nursing him, see Spectorsky, *Chapters*, 221, §250. For the view, based on Ḥanafī sources, that the character of a wet nurse is not transmitted to a nursing infant through her milk, see, Johansen, "Die sündige gesunde Amme," in *Contingency in a Sacred Law*, 172–88.

[45] Qudūri, *Mukhtaṣar*, 3:101–103; Ibn Abī Zayd, *Risāla*, 198 (*First Steps*, 44, nos. 148–150); Shīrāzī, *Muhadhdhab*, 2:169–72; Ibn Qudāma, *Mughnī* 9:298–310 (much of his discussion is taken up with the order in which various relatives assume custody in the absence of a child's mother, as well as with rules specifically for boys).

Women Outside the Home

The description of women at home makes it clear that as long as they receive maintenance wives are expected to stay home at all times. They should go out only with the permission of their husbands and if they go out without it they are guilty of *nushūz*. However, sometimes a woman should be seen by strangers and sometimes she should leave her home.

ʿAwra

As we saw in Chapter 1, *ʿawra* is the term used to refer to the parts of the bodies of both men and women that modest dress is expected to cover in public. It literally means genitals (male or female) and is also the term used for nudity. More generally, it refers to the parts of the body that should be seen only in the privacy of a person's home. A male or female is nude when the body is uncovered between the navel and the knee. Women may look at the bodies of other women, and men at those of other men, but not between the navel and the knee. Spouses may see all parts of each other's bodies. Men are assumed to be sexually aroused by looking at a woman's body, and since sexual activity must be confined to marriage, they must be prevented from seeing women who are strangers. In this context all of a woman's body save her face and her hands is *ʿawra* and must be concealed from men who are strangers. Qurʾān 24:31 mentions those male relatives within the forbidden degrees in whose presence women need not *draw their veils over their bosoms*. These are men permanently within the forbidden degrees, such as a woman's father, father-in-law, sons, stepsons, brothers and nephews.[46] However, at times, it is either desirable, necessary or unavoidable that a man who is a "stranger" look at a woman. One desirable time is when he wishes to marry her.

1. Al-Mughīra b. Shuʿba asked for a woman's hand, and the Prophet said to him, "Go and look at her. It is best that there be love between the two of you."[47]
2. Muḥammad b. Salama said: "I asked for a woman's hand, then I concealed myself from her so that I could take a look at her [when] she was in a palm grove of hers." Someone said to him, "You, a Companion

[46] The verse includes slaves, old men and children. See again *EQ*, s.v. "Modesty."
[47] Tirmidhī, *Sunan*, 2:275, *Nikāḥ*, no. 1093.

> of the Prophet's, did that!" He replied, "I heard the Prophet say, 'If God puts it into a man's heart that he wishes to ask for a woman's hand, there is no harm in his looking at her.' "[48]

For the Ḥanafīs, Marghīnānī says that a man may look at a woman he wishes to marry, and he quotes the Prophet saying, "Go and look at her. It is best that there be love between the two of you," to prove it.[49] But another strain of opinion remained against it. Ibn ʿAbd al-Barr, for example, reports that Mālik said he could not look at her face. However, Ibn ʿAbd al-Barr continues, it has also been related on Mālik's authority that a man could look at a potential bride if she were clothed. Those scholars who said that this was permitted said he could look at her face and the palms of her hands, because those parts of her are not covered when she prays.[50] Shīrāzī says a man who wishes to marry a woman may see her face and the palms of her hands, but any other aspect of her is *ʿawra*.[51] Ibn Qudāma says that a man can look at a woman he wishes to marry, and he points to the two traditions above, as well as others in a similar vein. However, a man should not be alone with a potential bride. Here Ibn Qudāma quotes the Prophet saying, "Do not let a man be alone with a woman, for the third with them is the devil." There is no disagreement, Ibn Qudāma says, among scholars that it is permissible to look at a woman's face because it is not *ʿawra*. There *is* disagreement about whether he can look at the palms of her hands or at her feet.[52]

Women as Witnesses

The one time when it is both desirable and unavoidable for a woman's face to be seen by strangers and in public is in court when she is either testifying as a witness, or the subject of a case brought against her.[53] The judge and any other parties to a case need to be able to recognize her. Ibn Qudāma points out it is also lawful for a woman's agent engaged in a sale or rental on her behalf to see her face. That way he will be certain of who she is, in case he has a claim against her.[54] If a woman is testifying as a witness, there is disagreement both about when

---

[48] Ibn Māja, *Sunan*, 1:599, *Nikāḥ*, no. 1864.
[49] Marghīnānī, *Hidāya*, 4:1488.
[50] Ibn ʿAbd al-Barr, *al-Kāfī*, 2:519.
[51] Shīrāzī adds that a woman can also look at a man, since what pleases a man about a woman, also pleases a woman about a man. *Muhadhdhab*, 2:34.
[52] Ibn Qudāma, *Mughnī*, 7:453–54.
[53] See *EI*, s.vv. "Shahāda" and "Shāhid."
[54] See Ibn Qudāma, *Mughnī*, 7:459.

women's testimony is acceptable and, when it is, about whether a case can ever be decided if a woman is the sole witness.

1. Zuhrī said: "The *sunna* has been established that women's witnessing is lawful for things to which men are not privy, such as childbirth and women's physical flaws (i.e. leprosy, vaginal occlusion, etc). For the cry of a newborn infant, the witnessing of only one midwife is permitted; in other cases, two women [are required]."[55]
2. ʿAṭāʾ said: "Women's witnessing is permissible in all things which only they are privy to, but fewer than four of them are not permissible."[56]
3. The Prophet was asked, "What is lawful for witnessing in a case of nursing?" He replied, "One man and one woman and one woman."[57]
4. The Prophet was asked, "What is lawful for witnessing in a case of nursing?" He replied, "one man and one woman."[58]

In Chapter 1, we saw that in place of one of the two men required to witness a contract that involves a debt, Qurʾān 2:282 permits two women. Thus there is general agreement that in that particular circumstance, two women equal one man. All jurists dealt with the question of whether in cases where two witnesses are required, two women can always equal one man and all answered that they cannot. There is unanimity, for example, that women cannot be witnesses in cases that involve potential *ḥadd* punishment. There is also unanimity that only women and never men can be witnesses for things men are not privy to, in particular childbirth and questions asked about women's bodies which can be answered only if women examine other women "between the navel and the knee." As the traditions above show, there was disagreement about whether one, two or four women were required in such cases and whether men could also be witnesses to nursing.[59] The above traditions, chosen from Ibn Abī Shayba's and ʿAbd al-Razzāq's *Muṣannaf*s, and Ibn Ḥanbal's *Musnad*, cover most possibilities. In the first, a midwife alone can testify that a newborn infant cried and therefore was born alive.[60] Otherwise when women witness alone, two of

[55] Ibn Abī Shayba, *Muṣannaf*, 5:82, *Kitāb al-buyūʿ waʾl-aqḍiya*, no. 1.
[56] ʿAbd al-Razzāq, *Muṣannaf*, 7:482, no. 13972.
[57] Ibn Ḥanbal, *Musnad*, 2:35.
[58] Ibn Ḥanbal, *Musnad*, 2:109.
[59] For a discussion of the role of women witnesses in a number of post-classical texts, see Fadel, "Two women, One Man: Knowledge, Power, and Gender in Medieval Sunni Legal Thought." For a discussion of women as expert witnesses, see Shaham, "Women as Expert Witnesses."
[60] Even if an infant dies shortly after birth, his brief existence affects the inheritance portions of his relatives.

them substitute for two men. In the second, the fact that in Qurʾān 2:282 two women can substitute for one man is taken to mean that for information only women are privy to, there must be four of them. In the third, two women equal one man, and in the fourth, one woman alone is an adequate stand in for one man.

In the formative period, Shaybānī said that in addition to cases involving *ḥadd* punishment, women could not witness cases involving retaliation. In all other cases they could witness along with men. Shaybānī reported that Abū Ḥanīfa said that Ibrāhīm al-Nakhaʿī used to permit women to witness the first cry of a newborn. Shaybānī expressed his agreement with that view, as long as they are trustworthy Muslims. Abū Ḥanīfa disagreed and said that it was not acceptable for women alone to witness the first cry of a newborn, rather it must be witnessed by two men, or one man and two women. However, Shaybānī said that both he and Abū Ḥanīfa agreed that for childbirth, a woman's witnessing is accepted, as long as she is a trustworthy Muslim woman.[61]

Mālik disagreed and considered the first cry of the newborn a condition of childbirth and therefore something that only women witness. However, he insisted on two women. At no time, according to Mālik, can there be one woman as a witness for anything, regardless of whether she is trustworthy. There must always be at least two.[62] Shāfiʿī agreed with Mālik and presented logical reasoning for this number. Women, he explained, can witness in two cases. One is that they can witness property obligations between men, but however many women there are, there must also be one man. The other is that they can witnesses in matters concerning the parts of women's bodies that must not be revealed to men. In these instances, they can witness on their own. However, if women witness on their own, there must be at least four of them. This, he explained, is analogous to God's ruling that two women replace one man.[63] Ibn Ḥanbal was willing to accept the testimony of one woman that she nursed a husband and wife, but only if she is trustworthy and also takes an oath that she nursed both of them, which suggests that like Mālik, he really preferred that there be two women to witness women's things. However, he said that if a woman claims that she is currently a wet nurse for a particular infant, that can be checked.[64]

[61] *Āthār Shaybānī*, 141–42, nos. 646, 647.
[62] See Saḥnūn, *Mudawwana*, 2:411–12 and 5:158.
[63] Shāfiʿī, *Kitāb al-umm*, 7:47–48.
[64] Presumably by two women; see Spectorsky, *Chapters*, 60, §1:169–70, §89.

In the classical period, the Ḥanafīs continue to have the most inclusive or possibly lenient view of women's witnessing. Qudūrī says that four men are required as witnesses for *zinā* (unlawful intercourse) and two men for other cases involving *ḥadd* punishments and retaliation. For all other cases such as those concerning marriage, divorce, agency or bequests, regardless of whether property is involved, two women equal one man.[65] For matters men are not privy to such as childbirth, virginity or women's physical flaws, one woman alone suffices. He notes that nursing is not included in the category of matters that men are not privy to, and therefore must be witnessed by two men or one man and two women.[66]

Ibn ʿAbd al-Barr disagrees and following Mālik's opinion says that one woman alone is never adequate; when women are allowed to witness, there must always be two. In the case of childbirth, if one of the women witnesses is also the midwife, she can act as the second of two witnesses as long as she is trustworthy. Ibn ʿAbd al-Barr goes on to say that only women can witness the cry of the newborn, although among the Medinese there are those who say it must be witnessed by men. He continues, "Our practice is that childbirth as well as the cry of the newborn can be witnessed only by women. Regardless of whether men or women witness the cry of the newborn, there must be more than one witness."[67] Ibn ʿAbd al-Barr disagrees with Qudūrī about areas in which women are not accepted as witnesses; his list is much longer. He says, for example, they cannot witness in cases of marriage divorce, agency, bequests, return after non-final divorce, manumission, kinship or affiliation by *walāʾ*.[68] Like Ibn ʿAbd al-Barr, Shīrāzī says that one woman alone is never an adequate witness. Otherwise, following Shāfiʿī he adheres strictly to the equation that two women equal one man. Therefore, in matters that men are not privy to, there must be four women witnesses.[69] Among the Ḥanbalīs, Khiraqī agrees with Qudūrī that one woman alone can witness those things that men are not privy

[65] For agency, see *EI*, s.v. "Wakāla." For bequests, see *EI*, s.v. "Waṣiyya."

[66] Qudūrī, *Mukhtaṣar*, 4:36 and 55–6. It is permissible for a woman's close male relatives to see her nursing.

[67] Ibn ʿAbd al-Barr, *al-Kāfī*, 2:906–7.

[68] For the full list, see *al-Kāfī*, 2:906. Ibn Abī Zayd makes the point that two women plus the oath of one of the parties to a dispute can sometimes equal one male witness plus an oath, but it is up to the *qāḍī* to decide on a case by case basis whether to accept two women plus an oath. See Ibn Abī Zayd, *Risāla*, 262 (*First Steps*, 60, no. 196).

[69] Shīrāzī, *Tanbīh*, 604.

to such as childbirth, menstruation, the end of a woman's *'idda* and questions that can be answered only by examining another woman's body (e.g., leprosy, virginity). Unlike Qudūri, he includes nursing. Ibn Qudāma adds to Khiraqī's statement that the testimony of one midwife is acceptable and that, in general, whenever women can witness without men, one woman alone suffices.[70]

Women on the Ḥajj

1. 'Ā'isha said: "O Messenger of God, shouldn't we [women] participate with you in *jihād*? and he replied, 'No, your *jihād* is the pilgrimage, sinlessly performed. That is your *jihād*.' "[71]
2. A man asked the Prophet, "What clothing should we wear for the *iḥrām*?" He replied, "Do not wear shirts, trousers, turbans, skullcaps, or leather boots, unless a man has no sandals. In that case, let him cut down the boots below the ankle. Also, he should not wear clothing dyed with saffron or *wars*. A woman should not wear a *niqāb* or gloves."[72]

The pilgrimage is a *farḍ 'ayn*. Therefore, just as a man is obliged to, a woman who has the wherewithal must also perform the pilgrimage once in her lifetime. This means that she must leave her home and her husband should not forbid her from doing so. In the first tradition above the Prophet stresses this obligation for women by informing 'Ā'isha that it replaces *jihād* for them. Given its obligatory character, all jurists assume that women will be performing the pilgrimage rituals along with men.

The second tradition points to the fact that while women do not don special clothing for the pilgrimage the way men do, they must not veil their faces or wear gloves. It is also representative of the fact that their presence on the pilgrimage is remarked upon separately when they are expected to be different from men, in this case in dress, but also in other cases when their presence in some way affects men. Shaybānī, for

---

[70] Khiraqī, *Mukhtaṣar*, 228; Ibn Qudāma, *Mughnī*, 12:15–17.

[71] Ibn Ḥanbal, *Musnad*, 6:71. For "sinlessly performed," see Lane, s.v. *b-r-r, mabrūr*. For one variant of this tradition, see Bukhārī, *Ṣaḥīḥ*, 2:325, *Kitāb al-jihād*, no. 2875. For other variants, see Wensinck, *Concordance*, s.v. "*jihād*."

[72] Bukhārī, *Ṣaḥīḥ*, 1:476, *Kitāb al-ḥajj*, no. 1542. See also Ibn Ḥanbal, *Musnad*, 2:119 for the same tradition. For appropriate dress during the pilgrimage, see *EI*, s.v. "Iḥrām." *Wars* is a plant from Yemen which provides a saffron-like dye. See Lane, *Lexicon*, *w, r, s* and also Stillman, *Arab Dress*, 23. A *niqāb* is a face veil with two openings for the wearer's eyes. See Dozy, *Dictionnaire détaille des noms des vêtements*, 424–26.

example, included a tradition in his *Āthār* which says that a man in a state of *iḥrām* who kisses his wife lustfully while on the *ḥajj* can complete his pilgrimage once he has atoned for such a lapse by sacrificing a sheep.[73]

It is expected that a woman will make the pilgrimage accompanied by a close male relative (her husband or a man too closely related to her for marriage), but Mālik and Shāfiʿī both pointed to the importance of her pilgrimage outweighing the necessity of her being accompanied by a male relative. Mālik said, "A woman who has never performed the pilgrimage who has no close male relative, or who has one who cannot go with her, should not forego an obligatory duty to God, but instead make the pilgrimage as part of a group of women." Shāfiʿī agreed and pointed out that if a woman has the financial and physical ability to make the pilgrimage, she must do so.[74] But Ibn Ḥanbal said that if a close male relative was not available to accompany a woman on her pilgrimage, she was not obliged to undertake the trip to Mecca.[75]

Above we saw that discussions of *ʿawra* tend to exclude a woman's face and palms from the rest of her body which must be concealed in public, but the second tradition above suggests that a woman expects to cover both hands and face in public. The classical jurists discuss this as a problem for women on the pilgrimage. Qudūrī says that a woman who is uncomfortable revealing her face may draw her head covering in front of it to hide it from the men surrounding her who are strangers. Ibn ʿAbd al-Barr mentions specifically that she may cover her face with her head covering by letting it down over her face, but she must not secure it with a pin. Shīrāzī says that if she wishes to be shielded from people, she can draw a veil across her face, but it should not touch her skin. Ibn Qudāma says that a woman who is dressed for the pilgrimage cannot cover her face just as a man cannot cover his head. Like Qudūrī he says she can draw her head covering over her face if she needs to conceal it from throngs of men who may be passing near her.[76]

---

[73] See Shaybānī, *Āthār*, 71, no. 349.

[74] Mālik, *Muwaṭṭaʾ*, 2:401. See also Shāfiʿī, *Kitāb al-umm*, 2:117–20 for a longer discussion of the problems associated with a woman going undertaking a pilgrimage on her own.

[75] Ibn Ḥanbal, *Masāʾil Abī Dāwūd*, 106.

[76] Qudūrī, *Mukhtaṣar*, 1:195; Ibn ʿAbd al-Barr, *al-Kāfī*, 1:388; Shīrāzī, *Tanbīh*, 220. Shīrāzī says here that there are two opinions on whether a woman can wear gloves; the best is that it is not allowed. Ibn Qudāma, *Mughnī*, 3:305.

As for aspects of a woman's pilgrimage besides her dress, classical jurists mention a variety of details. For example, in his discussion of the fact that everyone who is able should make the pilgrimage, Ibn Abī Zayd notes that although a woman wears normal clothing, she otherwise behaves as a man does on the pilgrimage.[77] Shīrāzī points to the fact that the ability to make the pilgrimage implies that a person has adequate provisions, adequate transport, a safe route and, for a woman, someone to accompany her with whom she feels personally safe.[78] Qudūri, Marghīnānī and Ibn Qudāma discuss a woman's behavior as she performs some of the pilgrimage rites. Qudūrī says that a woman's behavior differs from that of a man in that she does not raise her voice for the *talbiya*, she does not quicken her pace for the *ṭawāf*, and she does not run but walks between Ṣafā and Marwa.[79] Marghīnānī comments on these restrictions by pointing out that her voice can cause discord (*fitna*), that breaking out of a walk would disturb the concealment of her *ʿawra* and that the reason she wears sewn clothing is to protect her *ʿawra*.[80] Marghīnānī also says that a woman does not touch the Black Stone if the area around it is crowded, because she must not be in contact with men. She can touch it if the area around it is empty.[81] Ibn Qudāma says that it is preferable for a woman to perform the *ṭawāf* at night. At that time darkness provides a cover for her and there are many fewer people, so she can approach the Kaʿba and touch the Black Stone.[82]

Women and Ḥadd *Punishment*

As we saw in Chapter 1, both woman and men are subject to the *ḥadd* punishments, that is those mentioned in the Qurʾān for unlawful intercourse, false accusation of unlawful intercourse, drinking wine, theft and highway robbery. These crimes are regarded as rights of God (*ḥuqūq Allāh*) rather than rights of men (*ḥuqūq al-ʿibād*) which means,

---

[77] Ibn Abī Zayd, *Risāla*, 148.

[78] Shīrāzī, *Tanbīh*, 220.

[79] Qudūrī, *Mukhtaṣar*, 1:195. See also Shīrāzī, *Tanbīh*, 237. A description of the pilgrimage that remains useful is found in von Grunebaum, *Muhammadan Festivals*.

[80] Men's pilgrimage clothing consists of seamless garments. See *EI*, s.v. "Iḥrām."

[81] Marghīnānī, *Hidāya*, 1:381–82. Marghīnānī introduces this point with the word "*qālū*," Literally "they say," but it can also be translated "it is said." The editors note in their introduction that Marghīnānī uses "*qālū*" to indicate disagreement on a particular point.

[82] Ibn Qudāma, *Mughnī*, 3:311.

among other things, that the punishment is fixed, and it is required for the general good rather than to redress a wrong done to a particular person or persons.[83] Theoretically, a woman can commit all five of these crimes, but most attention is paid to her when the requirements for proving adultery or fornication and meting out punishment for these crimes are discussed.

The *ḥadd* punishment for illegal intercourse specified in Qur'ān 24:2 is one hundred lashes. However, in accordance with the *sunna* of the Prophet, the penalties for fornication and adultery are distinguished, resulting in two penalties for illegal intercourse. The fornicator is flogged one hundred lashes and the adulterer is stoned to death if he is *muḥṣan* (feminine, *muḥṣana*). Someone who is *muḥṣān* possesses the quality of *iḥṣān*, moral respectability, which a free Muslim acquires by consummating a valid marriage.[84] The Ḥanafīs and Ḥanbalīs say that the quality is acquired only by marriage with a free Muslim, the Mālikīs and Shāfiʿīs, that consummation in a marriage with a slave and, in the case of a man, marriage with a Jewish or Christian woman, also confers this quality on the free Muslim spouse.

1. ʿUbayd Allāh b. ʿUmar said he heard Abū Hurayra and Zayd b. Khālid say, "A man came to the Prophet and said, 'O Messenger of Allāh, I implore you by Allāh to pass judgment on me in accordance with the Book of Allāh.' His adversary who was better at *fiqh* than he was said, 'Yes, pass judgment between us and allow me to speak.' The Prophet said, 'Speak!' He said, 'My son was hired by this man and then he fornicated with his wife. I was told that my son deserved to be stoned to death, so I ransomed him for one hundred sheep and a slave. Then I asked the people of knowledge [the scholars], and they informed me that my son deserved one hundred lashes and banishment for one year and that the woman deserved to be stoned to death.' The Prophet answered, 'By the One Who holds my soul in His hand, I shall certainly judge between you in accordance with the Book of Allāh. As for the slave and the sheep, they must be returned to you. Your son deserves one hundred lashes and banishment for one year. Go, Unays, to this man's wife. If she confesses, stone her to death.' Then Unays went to the woman and she confessed, so the Prophet ordered that she be stoned."[85]

[83] "Since the objective of *ḥadd* penalties is to protect public interest, they are labelled as claims of God (*ḥuqūq Allāh*) and not claims of men, which apply to the interests of private persons." Peters, *Crime and Punishment in Islamic Law*, 54.

[84] For this definition, see Schacht, *Introduction*, 125. Schacht explains that a second meaning of the term is a free Muslim who has never committed unlawful intercourse and therefore can only be slandered if accused. See also *EI*, s.v. "Muḥṣan."

[85] Bukhari, 4:256–57, nos. 2267 and 2268.

2. The Prophet said: "Avert *ḥadd* punishments from Muslims to the extent that you are able to."[86]

The first tradition separates the penalties for married and unmarried offenders. The second points to the fact that in all potential cases of *ḥadd* punishment, including that for *zinā*, an effort is made to avert the punishment if at all possible. One of the ways this is possible is by the existence of uncertainty (*shubha*). For example, a couple who believe they are legally married are not punished for having had intercourse if it turns out that for some reason their marriage is invalid, but they were unaware of this fact.[87] They may be too closely related to marry without knowing it, or a defect in their original marriage contract could turn up. For a woman, she may believe that her *ʿidda* has ended, or she may claim that she was raped, or attacked while she was sleeping and therefore does not know who her attacker was. Illegal intercourse is proven by confession (as in the first tradition above) or by the testimony of the four eye-witnesses demanded in Qurʾān 24:13. The witnesses must be men, there must be four of them, they must be trustworthy and there cannot be discrepancies in their testimony. Further, they must actually witness penetration.[88] If they do not meet these standards, they are guilty of slander (*qadhf*) and are punished with eighty lashes.

Within this general framework, we can look at some of the points different jurists made particularly about women. Shaybānī included a tradition in his *Āthār* in which he says that if a married couple have had intercourse, the woman who is proved to have had unlawful intercourse is *muḥsana* and therefore is stoned. If a woman is unmarried, or married but not yet had intercourse with her husband, and she has fornicated, she receives one hundred lashes. In another tradition, if an unmarried couple have illicit intercourse, they are both lashed and then banished.[89] Mālik said that a woman who is raped does not receive a *ḥadd* punishment, and her attacker owes her a fair marriage portion.[90] But if a pregnant woman claims she was raped or married at the time she was was impregnated, she is not believed unless she provides

[86] Tirmidhi, *Sunan*, 2:438–39, *Kitāb abwāb al-ḥudūd*, no. 1447.
[87] For a fuller discussion of *shubha*, in addition to *EI*, s.v. "Shubha," see Peters, *Crime and Punishment*, 21–23. See also Schacht, *Introduction*, 178–79.
[88] As Ibn Abī Zayd puts it, "like a kohl stick entering a kohl jar." *Risāla*, 252–53.
[89] Shaybānī, *Āthār*, 134, nos. 613, 614.
[90] Mālik, *Muwaṭṭaʾ*, 4:12–13, *Kitāb al-aqḍiya*, no. 1481.

evidence. If she cannot, she receives a *ḥadd* punishment.[91] Like Mālik, Shāfiʿī said that a woman who is raped does not receive a *ḥadd* punishment. He also pointed out that the punishment is averted from a woman who had thought her husband was dead, waited an *ʿidda* in good faith and then remarried and had intercourse.[92] Ibn Ḥanbal pointed to the fact that if stoning is to take place because of a confession, the *qāḍī* throws the first stone.[93]

The classical jurists provide more detail, much of it relevant to the second tradition above in which the Prophet urges that the *ḥadd* punishments be avoided if possible. Qudūrī, for example, explains that every attempt must be made to disprove a claim of unlawful intercourse. If four witnesses testify against a couple, they are asked who the couple are, when and where the unlawful act took place and exactly what occurred. If they respond satisfactorily, the *qāḍī* conducts both a public and a secret investigation of their trustworthiness, and only if he finds that all four are credible witnesses does he act on their testimony. As for confession, Qudūrī continues, once the person (male or female) has confessed four times, the *qāḍī* asks her what constitutes unlawful intercourse, with whom it was committed and where it took place. Only if all questions are answered satisfactorily is the *ḥadd* punishment implemented. Qudūrī also says that if adultery has been proven by witnesses, they throw the first stones. If they are unwilling to do so, stoning does not take place.[94] Ibn ʿAbd al-Barr describes the procedure for establishing the trustworthiness of the four witnesses. Like Qudūrī, he says that it requires in turn witnesses to their trustworthiness. He also says that a woman who is pregnant is not punished until she has delivered her infant, and if she is nursing, she is not punished until the infant has been weaned.[95] Shīrāzī describes the actual conditions for flogging a woman. She cannot be pregnant or nursing. A man is flogged standing, but a woman should be sitting and another woman should

[91] Ibid., 4:150, *Kitāb al-ḥudūd*, no. 1609.

[92] Shāfiʿī, *Kitāb al-umm*, 6:155. This is an example of the application of the notion of *shubha*. In this case, the woman in question knew what the law was but was mistaken about the facts of her case.

[93] Ibn Ḥanbal, *Masāʾil Abī Dāwūd*, 225–26.

[94] Qudūrī, *Mukhtaṣar*, 3:181–83.

[95] Ibn ʿAbd al-Barr, *al-Kāfī*, 2:1071–1073. He specifically says that a woman's husband cannot be one of the witnesses to her adultery. If he is, the other three receive the punishment for *qadhf*, and the husband must either institute *liʿān* proceedings against his wife, or he too receives the punishment for *qadhf*. In Shaybānī's *Athār* no. 613 says that in fact a husband can in fact be one of the witnesses to his wife's adultery.

make sure she is covered by her clothing. He says that if the adulterer has confessed, it is preferable that the ruling authority (or the *qāḍī* in his stead) throw the first stone. If witnesses testified to the crime, they must throw the first stones.[96] Khiraqī notes that if a man (but presumably also a woman) is being stoned on the basis of a confession and recants, the stoning must be stopped.[97]

Discussion

The material in this and previous chapters shows that women are expected to marry and carry on their lives as wives. Therefore, in general, descriptions of a woman inside her home are essentially extensions of topics relevant to marriage and divorce. A woman's husband is expected to maintain her at the level she is accustomed to and if he is her equal in status, as he is expected to be, he has the wherewithal to do so. If he heeds the exhortations in the Qur'ān and the *sunna*, he will treat a wife kindly; and if he has more than one wife, he will divide his time and attention among them fairly. If a woman has been divorced, she has a right to custody of her young children, although she may lose it if her next husband is not a related to her children, or if she and her former husband move too far away from each other.

She may go out with her husband's permission, but as a rule a woman remains in her home. On two occasions she is expected to leave it. One is when she is needed as a witness. Regardless of how different jurists interpret the question of when and whether two women equal one man, if a case involves matters only women are privy to, their testimony is required. The other is when she makes the pilgrimage to Mecca, a religious duty for all Muslims. A third occasion when she would be outside her home and exposed to public view would arise if she were to incurs a *ḥadd* punishment, but in fact, the discussion of *ḥadd* punishments for women largely focuses on cases of adultery or fornication and the procedural hedges around the proof of the crime and the application of the punishment.

Although they are not necessarily referred to directly in these particular texts, several of the Prophet's wives figure in traditions that form part of the understanding of the material we have just gone over,

[96] It is assumed that they will be unwilling to stone someone they have falsely accused. Shīrāzī, *Tanbīh*, 562–63.

[97] Khiraqī, *Mukhtaṣar*, 191.

traditions that would be familiar to scholars or students reading or listening to any of the eight jurists of the classical period whose works I have used in this and the previous chapter. As we saw in Chapter 1, ʿĀʾisha is associated with the revelation of Qurʾān 4:11–20 and particularly with 4:13 in which four witnesses are required for a valid accusation of adultery or fornication. Sawda figures in the occasion of revelation for Qurʾān 4:128 (*If a woman feareth ill treatment from her husband,*) where she is depicted giving up her share of the Prophet's time to prevent him from divorcing her, and Umm Salama is associated with the ruling that a husband spends three nights in a row with a new wife if she is a *thayyib* or seven nights with her if she is a *bikr* and thereafter resumes sharing his time equally among them.

In the areas of women's lives covered here, the patriarchal framework within which they are expected to live is depicted vividly. Obviously the opportunities men are given to misuse their power is enormous. However, in each of these areas the limitations on men's behavior and the protection of women's interests are as much a part of the discussion as the extent of a man's authority over his wife and daughters.

CONCLUSION

I began this study by observing that early Muslim jurists answered the question, what should a woman do, by assuming that she would marry. The previous chapters have filled out the details of how they envisioned a woman's life. The typical bride or wife or divorcée in these discussions is an upper class woman, or at least one who is prosperous enough for money and possessions to play a significant role in an appropriate marriage portion or adequate maintenance for her. She lives in an extended patriarchal family in an urban environment. She and her family have access to a *qāḍī* who is expected to be versed in the law. If a woman is lowly, or she or her husband are among the common people, these facts are noted as exceptional. If she lives in a remote area and the local *qāḍī* is not a scholar, that too is noted as exceptional.

In addition to being married and having a role as a wife and mother, some women certainly also had responsibilities or activities outside their homes. When we looked at women as witnesses in Chapter 5, we saw that some of them were midwives, and in a variety of sources which we have not used here they are shown in a number of other professions.[1] Further, a number of women were outstanding *ḥadīth* scholars and transmitters.[2] However, since *fiqh* works are devoted to understanding the Qurʾān, they are particularly concerned with women in their homes.

The Qurʾān outlines rules and regulations for the proper conduct of the Muslim community. Accordingly, it has provisions for a woman's marriage, for her divorce and for her appropriate behavior. In the 21st century, Qurʾān 4:34 (*admonish...banish...scourge*) receives much attention, but a fuller picture of the way women should be treated requires that equal attention be given to the many verses that urge believers to behave honorably. Such attention is in fact reflected in the

---

[1] For professional women in the Mamluke period, see Rapoport, *Marriage, Money and Divorce*, Chapter 2, "Working women, single women and the rise of the female *ribāṭ*."

[2] See Ṣiddiqī, *Ḥadīth Literature*, Appendix I: Women in *ḥadīth* scholarship.

discussions of the jurists. Women are subject to the oversight of a father or guardian. But a father arranging a marriage for his daughter and a guardian arranging one for his ward are expected to do so in her best interests. Her best interests include consulting her about her future groom and then giving her in marriage to a man who is her equal in status and who is able to maintain her in a manner befitting that status. Once a woman is married, has received her marriage portion and has taken up residence in her husband's house, she owes him absolute obedience. In return, he owes her considerate and kind treatment. In a tradition that sums up the significance placed on the moral rectitude expected of a husband, the Prophet said: "Any man who promised a woman her marriage portion while God knew he did not mean to give it to her has seduced her away from God and falsely made her private parts lawful to himself. Therefore, God will find him an adulterer on the Day of Judgment."[3]

A question often asked about the content of *fiqh* works—the collections of responses, the handbooks, the commentaries—is what they describe. The answer is that they record what the jurists were thinking about, which was both the issues they discuss and the process of developing the law. To consider the issues themselves raises another question, which is whether any of these discussions have a bearing on real life. The answer is yes and no. In Chapter 4 where I examined what classical jurists had to say about *kafāʾa* we saw that they incorporated social change into their thinking. In Chapter 5, in the discussion of what a wife should do if her husband is not maintaining her, Ibn ʿAbd al-Barr's statement that "Hunger has no patience" introduced a note of universal reality into his description of the way a *qāḍī* should handle a woman's complaint that she has been left without provisions, and it may reflect his actual experience as a *qāḍī*. The connection between *fiqh* and reality is also shown in sources not examined here. This is particularly true of collections *fatwā*s issued by *muftī*s then and since who have invoked the history of the way a particular problem had been handled by different jurists to respond to questions about cases being heard in *qaḍī* courts.[4]

[3] Ibn Ḥanbal, *Musnad*, 4:332.

[4] See Masud, Messick and Powers, eds., *Islamic Legal Interpretation* for some examples of the way *muftī*s call upon the history of a particular legal problem to formulate their answers. See also Powers, *Law, Society and Culture in the Maghrib* for a recent study of *fatwā*s issued in the 7th/14th and 8th/15th centuries in Morocco.

With regard to the process of developing the law, in 1906 in their introduction to their translation of Ibn Abī Zayd's *Risāla*, Russell and Suhrawardy wrote, "The student who masters the concise rules here laid down, will, on his further advance into the intricacies of Arab jurisprudence, find that in each of them he possesses the key to some great controversy which has been waged among the jurists." This is *ikhtilāf* both within and among the schools. I have described much of it here, and gone into detail on a variety of subjects. For as the jurists thought about these subjects, they were attempting to extend the reach of the law to all aspects of communal life; in addition, they were engaged in the equally important activity of rethinking them and thereby engaging with the past in an ongoing effort to understand the Qur'ān. It is this activity, as much as the often conflicting content of their opinions, that we refer to when we speak of Islamic law.

WORKS CITED

EI = *Encyclopaedia of Islam*, New Edition.
EQ = *Encyclopaedia of the Qur'ān*
GAS = Sezgin, *Geschichte des Arabischen Schrifttums*

Arabic Sources

ʿAbd al-Razzāq b. Ḥammām al-Ḥimyarī. *al-Muṣannaf*. Edited by Ḥabīb al-Raḥmān al-Aʿẓamī. 11 vols. Beirut, 1983.

Abū Dāwūd, Sulaymān b. al-Ashʿath al-Sijistānī. *Sunan*. In Ibn Qayyim al-Jawziyya, *ʿAwn al-maʿbūd fī sharḥ sunan Abī Dāwūd*. 14 vols. in 7. Beirut, 1990.

Abū Yūsuf. *Kitāb al-āthār*. Commentary by Shaikh Abu'l-Wafā'. Hyderabad, 1355 A.H.

al-Bukhārī, Abū ʿAbd Allāh Muḥammad b. Isma'īl. *al-Jāmiʿ al-ṣahīh*. 4 vols. Cairo, 1400 A.H.

Ibn Abī Shayba, ʿAbd Allāh b. Muḥammad. *al-Musannaf fi'l-aḥādīth wa'l-āthār*. Edited by Saʿīd al-Laḥām. 9 vols. Beirut, 1989.

Ibn ʿAbd al-Barr, Yūsif b. ʿAbd Allāh. *al-Kāfī fi'l fiqh*. 2 vols. Riyad, 1980.

Ibn Ḥanbal, Aḥmad. *Masā'il al-Imām Aḥmad b. Ḥanbal*. Edited by Muḥammad Bahja al-Baytār. Cairo, 1934.

——. *Masā'il al-Imām Aḥmad b. Ḥanbal*. Edited by Zuhayr Shāwīsh. Beirut, 1981.

——. *Masā'il al-Imām Aḥmad b. Ḥanbal*. 2 vols. Edited by Zuhayr Shāwīsh. Beirut, 1974–79.

——. *Musnad*. 6 vols. Cairo, 1895. Reprint. Beirut, 1985.

Ibn Juzayy al-Gharnātī, Muḥammad b. Aḥmad. *Qawānīn al-aḥkām al-sharʿiyya wa masā'il al-furūʿ al-fiqhiyya*. Beirut, 1968.

Ibn Māja, Muḥammad b. Yazīd. *Sunan*. 2 vols. Edited by Muḥammad Fu'ād ʿAbdu'l-Bāqī. Cairo, 1952–53.

Ibn Qudāma, Muwaffaq al-Dīn. *al-Mughnī*. 12 vols. Edited by Shaikh Rashīd Riḍā. Cairo, 1929 (reprinted Beirut, 1983).

Ibn Saʿd, Muḥammad. *Kitāb al-ṭabaqāt al-kabīr*. 9 vols. Edited by Eduard Sachau. Leiden, 1905–40.

Jasṣāṣ, Aḥmad b. ʿAlī. *Aḥkām al-Qur'ān*. 3 vols. Beirut, 1978.

Kasānī, ʿAlā' al-Dīn Abū Bakr b. Masʿūd. *Badā'iʿ al-ṣanā'iʿ fī tartīb al-sharā'iʿ*. 7 vols. Beirut, 1974.

Khatīb al-Baghdādī, Abū Bakr Aḥmad b. ʿAlī. *Tārīkh Baghdad*. 14 vols. Cairo, 1931.

al-Khiraqī, Abu'l-Qāsim. *Mukhtaṣar*. Damascus, 1964.

Mālik b. Anas. *Muwaṭṭa' Yaḥyā b. Yaḥyā*. 4 vols. Commentary by Muḥammad al-Zurqānī. Cairo, 1379/1959.

Marghīnānī, Burhān al-Dīn ʿAlī b. Abī Bakr. *al-Hidāya, sharḥ bidāyat al-mubtadi'*. Edited and annotated by Muḥamad Muḥamad Tāmir and Ḥāfiẓ ʿĀshir Ḥāfiẓ. 4 vols. Cairo, 2000.

Muslim b. al-Ḥajjāj. *Saḥīḥ*. In *Sharḥ ṣaḥīḥ Muslim li'l-Nawawī, Muḥyī al-Din Abī Zakariyya Yaḥyā b. Sharaf*. 19 vols. in 10. Beirut, 1987.

al-Nasā'ī, Aḥmad b. Shu'aib. *Sunan.* 6 vols. Commentary by Jalāl al-Dīn al-Suyūṭī. Beirut, n.d.
Qudūrī, Aḥmad b. Muḥammad, *Mukhtaṣar.* In 'Abd al-Ghānī al-Ghanīmī al-Maydānī, *al-Lubāb fī sharḥ al-kitāb.* 4 vols. in 2. Beirut, 1991.
Saḥnūn b. Sa'īd al-Tanūkhī. *al-Mudawwana al-kubrā.* 16 vols. Cairo. Reprinted in 6 vols., Baghdad, n.d.
Sarakhsī, Muḥammad b. Aḥmad Abū Sahl. *al-Mabsūṭ.* 30 vols. in 15. Reprint of edition published in Cairo, 1906–12. Beirut, 1993.
al-Shāfi'ī, Muḥammad b. Idrīs. Kitāb al-umm *with* Mukhtaṣar al-Muzanī. 8 vols. in 6. Beirut, n.d.
Shīrāzī, Abū Iṣḥāq Ibrāhīm b. 'Alī. *al-Muhadhdhab fī fiqh al-Imām al-Shāfi'ī.* 2 vols. Cairo, n.d.
——. *al-Tanbīh fī fiqh al-Imām l-Shāfi'ī.* Beirut, 1997.
Shaybānī, Muḥammad b. al-Ḥasan. *al-Āthār.* Karachi, 1998 or 1999.
——. *Kitāb al-Ḥujja 'alā ahl al-Madīna.* 4 vols. Beirut, 1983.
——. *al-Jāmi' al-ṣaghīr.* Commentary by 'Abdalhai al-Luknawi. Karachi, 1987.
——. *Muwaṭṭa' Shaybānī.* Commentary by 'Abdalhai al-Luknawi. Kasan, 1909.
Ṭabarī, Abū Ja'far Muḥammad. *Jāmi' al-bayān 'an ta'wil al-Qur'ān.* Edited by Aḥmad Shākir. 15 vols. Cairo, 1960.
——. *Jāmi' al-bayān 'an ta'wil al-Qur'ān.* 12 vols. Beirut, 1986–87.
Tirmidhī, Muḥammad b. 'Īsā. *Sunan.* 5 vols. Medina, 1965–67.
al-Wāḥidī al-Nīshābūrī, Abū'l-Ḥasan 'Alī b. Aḥmad. *Asbāb al-nuzūl.* Cairo, 1968.

Secondary Works and Translations

Bearman, Peri, Rudolph Peters, and Frank E. Vogel, eds. *The Islamic School of Law: Evolution, Devolution, and Progress.* Harvard Series in Islamic Law. Cambridge, MA, 2005.
Bell, Richard. *A Commentary on the Qur'ān.* 2 vols. Journal of Semitic Studies Monograph, no. 14. Manchester, 1991.
Berkey, Jonathan P. *The Formation of Islam: Religion and Society in the Near East, 600–1800.* Themes in Islamic History. Cambridge; New York, 2003.
Bousquet, G.-H., ed. and trans. *Kitâb et-tanbîh; ou, Le livre de l'admonition touchant la loi musulmane selon le rite de l'Imâm ech-Chafé'î.* By Abū Isḥāq Ibrāhīm ibn 'Alī al-Shīrāzī. Bibliothèque de la Faculté de droit de l'Université d'Alger. Algiers, 1949–52.
Bousquet, G.-H., and Léon Bercher, eds. and trans. *Le statut personnel en droit musulman hanéfite.* Texte et traduction annotée du Muhtasar. By Aḥmad ibn Muḥammad Qudūrī. Institut des hautes études de Tunis. Bibliothèque juridique et économique. Paris, 1953.
Bravmann, M. M. *The Spiritual Background of Early Islam: Studies in Ancient Arab Concepts.* Leiden, 1972.
Brockopp, Jonathan E. *Early Maliki Law: Ibn 'Abd al-Hakam and His Major Compendium of Jurisprudence.* Studies in Islamic Law and Society, vol. 14. Leiden, 2000.
Brunschvig, Robert. "Métiers vils en Islam." *Studia Islamica*, no. 16 (1962 1962): 41–60.
Burton, John. "The Exegesis of Q. 2:106 and the Islamic Theories of *Naskh: mā nansakh min āya aw nansahā na'ti bi khairin minhā aw mithlihā.*" *Bulletin of the School of Oriental and African Studies, University of London* 48, no. 3 (1985): 452–59.
——. *An Introduction to the Ḥadīth.* Islamic Surveys. Edinburgh, 1994.
——. "Law and Exegesis: The Penalty for Adultery in Islam." In *Approaches to the Qur'an*, edited by G.R. Hawting and Abdul-Kader A. Shareef. Routledge/SOAS

Series on Contemporary Politics and Culture in the Middle East, 269–84. London; New York, 1993.
——. "The Meaning of *Iḥsān*." *Journal of Semitic Studies* 19 (1974): 47–75.
——. "Rewriting the Timetable of Early Islam." Review of *Studies in Early Muslim Jurisprudence* by Norman Calder. *Journal of the American Oriental Society* 115, no. 3 (1995): 453–62.
——. *The Sources of Islamic Law: Islamic Theories of Abrogation*. Edinburgh, 1990.
Buskens, Léon. "A Medieval Islamic Law? Some Thoughts on the Periodization of the History of Islamic Law." In *O Ye Gentlemen: Arabic Studies on Science and Literary Culture in Honour of Remke Kruk*, edited by Arnoud Vrolijk and Jan P. Hogendijk. Islamic Philosophy, Theology, and Science, vol. 74, 469–84. Leiden; Boston, MA, 2007.
Calder, Norman. "Law." In *History of Islamic Philosophy*, edited by Seyyed Hossein Nasr and Oliver Leaman. Routledge History of World Philosophies, vol. 1. London; New York, 1996.
——. *Studies in Early Muslim Jurisprudence*. Oxford, 1993.
Chehata, Chafik T. *Études de droit musulman*. Travaux et recherches de la Faculté de droit et des sciences économiques de Paris. Série "Afrique," no. 7. Paris, 1971.
Coulson, N. J. *Succession in the Muslim Family*. Cambridge, 1971.
Crone, Patricia. *Roman, Provincial, and Islamic Law: The Origins of the Islamic Patronate*. Cambridge Studies in Islamic Civilization. Cambridge, 1987.
Denny, Frederick Mathewson. *An Introduction to Islam*. New York, 1994.
Doumato, Eleanor A. "Hearing Other Voices: Christian Women and the Coming of Islam." *International Journal of Middle East Studies* 23, no. 2 (1991): 177–99.
The Encyclopaedia of Islam. New Edition. Edited by H. A. R Gibb et al. Leiden, 1960 [i.e. 1954]-2009.
Encyclopaedia of the Qur'ān. 6 vols. Jane Dammen McAuliffe, gen. ed. Leiden, 2001–6.
Esposito, John L. *Islam: The Straight Path*. New York, 1991.
Esposito, John L., and Natana J. DeLong-Bas. *Women in Muslim Family Law*. Contemporary Issues in the Middle East. Syracuse, N.Y., 2001.
Fadel, Mohammad. "Two Women, One Man: Knowledge, Power and Gender in Medieval Sunni Legal Thought." *International Journal of Middle East Studies* 29 (1997): 185–204.
Fierro, Maribel. "Ill-Treated Women Seeking Divorce: The Qur'anic Two Arbiters and Judicial Practice Among the Malikis in al-Andalus and North Africa." In *Dispensing Justice in Islam: Qadis and Their Judgements*, edited by Muhammad Khalid Masud, Rudolph Peters, and David S. Powers. Studies in Islamic Law and Society, 323–48. Leiden; Boston, 2006.
Friedmann, Yohanan. *Tolerance and Coercion in Islam: Interfaith Relations in the Muslim Tradition*. Cambridge Studies in Islamic Civilization. New York, 2003.
Gleave, Robert. "Shiʿite Exegesis and the Interpretation of Qur'ān 4:24." In *University Lectures in Islamic Studies*, vol. 2, series ed. Alan Jones, 79–122. London, 1997.
Goldziher, Ignaz. *Muslim Studies*. Edited by S. M. Stern. Translated by S. M. Stern and C. R. Barber. London, 1971.
——. "Über Geheimehen bei den Arabern." *Globus* 68 (1895): 32–33 (Repr. *Gesammelte Schriften*, 3:395–6).
Gribetz, Arthur. *Strange Bedfellows:* Mutʿat al-Nisāʾ *and* Mutʿat al-Ḥajj: *A Study Based on Sunnī and Shīʿī Sources of* Tafsīr, Ḥadīth. Islamkundliche Untersuchungen, vol. 180. Berlin, 1994.
Grunebaum, Gustave E. von. *Muhammadan Festivals*. New York, 1951.
Guillaume, Alfred. *The Life of Muhammad: A Translation of Ibn Isḥāq's* Sīrat Rasūl Allāh. Lahore, 1967.

Hallaq, Wael B. *Authority, Continuity and Change in Islamic Law*. Cambridge; New York, 2001.

—— "On Dating Mālik's *Muwaṭṭa*." *UCLA Journal of Islamic and Near Eastern Law* 1, no. 1 (2001–2): 47–65.

Hamilton, Charles, trans. *The Hedaya: A Translation of Marghīnānī's* al-Hidāya. Lahore, 1957.

Hawting, G. R. "An Ascetic Vow and an Unseemly Oath?: *Īlā'* and *Ẓihār* in Muslim Law." *Bulletin of the School of Oriental and African Studies, University of London* 57, no. 1 (1994): 113–25.

——. "The Role of Qur'ān and *Ḥadīth* in the Legal Controversy About the Rights of a Divorced Woman During Her 'Waiting Period' (*'idda*)." *Bulletin of the School of Oriental and African Studies* 52 (1989): 430–45.

Heffening, Willi. "Zum Aufbau der islamischen Rechtswerke." In *Studien zur Geschichte und Kultur des Nahen und Fernen Ostens: Paul Kahle zum 60. Geburtstag*, edited by Willi Heffening and Willibald Kirfel. Leiden, 1935.

Hodgson, Marshall G.S. *The Venture of Islam: Conscience and History in a World Civilization*. Chicago, 1974.

Houdas, O. V., and W. Marçais, eds. and trans. *El-Bokhâri. Les traditions islamiques traduites de l'arabe*. Translation of *Jāmi' al-ṣaḥīḥ*. By Muḥammad ibn Ismā'īl Bukhārī. Publications de l'École des langues orientales vivantes, IV ser. Paris, 1903–14.

Howard, I. K. A. "*Mut'a* Marriage Reconsidered in the Context of the Formal Procedures for Islamic Marriage." *Journal of Semitic Studies* 20 (1975): 82–92.

Humphreys, R. Stephen. *Islamic History: A Framework for Inquiry*. Rev. ed. Princeton, 1991.

Idris, H.R. "Deux juristes Kairouanais de l'époque zīrīde: Ibn Abī Zayd et al-Qābisī." *Annales de l'Institut d'études orientales (Algiers)* (1954), 121–98.

Jeffrey, Arthur. *Materials for the History of the Text of the Qur'ān*. Leiden, 1937.

Johansen, Baber. "Casuistry: Between Legal Concept and Social Praxis." *Islamic Law and Society* 2 (1995): 135–56.

——. *Contingency in a Sacred Law: Legal and Ethical Norms in the Muslim* Fiqh. Studies in Islamic Law and Society, vol. 7. Leiden; Boston, 1999.

Kamali, Mohammad Hashim. *Principles of Islamic Jurisprudence*. 3rd rev. and enl. ed. Cambridge, UK, 2003.

Khadduri, Majid, and Herbert J. Liebesny. *Origin and Development of Islamic Law*. Vol. I of *Law in the Middle East*. Washington, 1955.

Lane, Edward William. *Arabic-English Lexicon*. 8 parts. Edited by Stanley Lane-Poole. Beirut (reprint), 1980.

Laoust, Henri, trans. *Le précis de droit d'Ibn Qudāma, jurisconsulte musulman d'école hanbalite*. Translation of *Al-'umdah fi aḥkām al-fiqh*. By Muwaffaq al-Dīn 'Abd Allāh ibn Aḥmad Ibn Qudāmah. Beirut, 1950.

——. "Le Hanbalisme sous le califat de Baghdad." *Révue des études islamiques* 27 (1959): 67–128.

Lowry, Joseph E. *Early Islamic Legal Theory: The* Risāla *of Muhammad Ibn Idrīs al-Shāfi'ī*. Studies in Islamic Law and Society, vol. 30. Leiden; Boston, 2007.

Lucas, Scott C. "Divorce, *Hadith*-Scholar Style: From al-Darimi to al-Tirmidhi." *Journal of Islamic Studies* 19 (2008): 325–68.

Makdisi, George. "*Ṣuḥba* et *riyāsa* dans l'enseignement médiéval." In *Recherches d'islamologie: recueil d'articles offerts à Georges C. Anawati et Louis Gardet par leurs collèques et amis*. Bibliothèque Philosophique de Louvain. Louvain, 1977.

Masud, Muhammad Khalid, Brinkley Messick, and David S. Powers, eds. *Islamic Legal Interpretation: Muftis and Their Fatwas*. Harvard Studies in Islamic Law. Cambridge, MA., 1996.

Melchert, Christopher. *Ahmad Ibn Hanbal*. Makers of the Muslim World. Oxford, 2006.

——. *The Formation of the Sunni Schools of Law, 9th–10th Centuries C.E.* Studies in Islamic Law and Society, vol. 4. Leiden; New York, 1997.

——. "The Meaning of *Qāla 'l-Shāfi'ī* in Ninth Century Sources." In *Abbasid Studies: Occasional Papers of the School of 'Abbasid Studies, Cambridge, 6–10 July 2002*, edited by James Montgomery. Orientalia Lovaniensia Analecta. Leuven; Dudley, MA, 2004.

——. "Traditionist-Jurisprudents and the Framing of Islamic Law." *Islamic Law and Society* 8, no. 3 (2001): 383–406.

Meron, Ya'akov. *L'obligation alimentaire entre époux en droit musulman hanéfite.* Bibliothèque de droit privé. Paris, 1971.

Motzki, Harald. "*Wa'l-muḥṣināt mina n-nisā'i illā mā malakat aimānukum* (Koran 4:24) und die koranische Sexualethik." *Der Islam* 63, no. 2 (1986): 192–218.

Muranyi, Miklos. "Die frühe Rechtsliteratur zwischen Quellenanalyse und Fiktion." Review of *Studies in Early Muslim Jurisprudence* by N. Calder. *Islamic Law and Society* 4, no. 2 (1997): 224–41.

Musallam, B. F. *Sex and Society in Islam.* Cambridge, 1983.

Peters, Rudolph. *Crime and Punishment in Islamic Law: Theory and Practice from the Sixteenth to the Twenty-First Century.* Themes in Islamic Law. Cambridge, UK; New York, 2005.

Powers, David S. *Law, Society, and Culture in the Maghrib, 1300–1500.* Cambridge Studies in Islamic Civilization. Cambridge; New York, 2002.

Powers, Paul R. *Intent in Islamic Law: Motive and Meaning in Medieval Sunnī* Fiqh. Studies in Islamic Law and Society, vol. 25. Leiden; Boston, 2006.

Rapoport, Yossef. *Marriage, Money and Divorce in Medieval Islamic Society.* Cambridge Studies in Islamic Civilisation. Cambridge; New York, 2005.

——. "Matrimonial Gifts in Early Islamic Egypt." *Islamic Law and Society* 7, no. 1 (2000): 1–36.

Rescher, Oskar. *Vocabulaire du recueil de Bokhârî.* Stuttgart, 1922.

Rispler-Chaim, Vardit. *Disability in Islamic Law.* International Library of Ethics, Law, and the New Medicine, vol. 32. Dordrecht, The Netherlands, 2007.

——. "Nušūz Between Medieval and Contemporary Islamic Law: The Human Rights Aspect." *Arabica* 39, no. 3 (1992): 315–27.

Russell, Alexander David, and Abdullah al-Ma'mūn Suhrawardy, eds. and trans. *First Steps in Muslim Jurisprudence: Consisting of Excerpts from* Bākūrat-al-Sa'd *of Ibn Abī Zayd.* With Arabic text, English translation, notes and a short historical and bibliographical introduction. London, 1906.

Russell, Alexander David, and Abdullah Suhrawardy. *A Manual of the Law of Marriage from the* Mukhtaṣar *of Sīdī Khalīl.* Lahore, 1979.

Schacht, Joseph. "Adultery as an Impediment to Marriage." *Revue internationale des droits de l'antiquité* 2ième series 1 (1952): 105–23.

——. *An Introduction to Islamic Law.* Oxford, 1964.

——. "On Shāfi'ī's Life and Personality." In *Studia Orientalia Ioanni Pedersen Septuagenario A.D. VII Id. Nov. Anno MCMLIII.* Hauniae, 1953.

——. *The Origins of Muhammadan Jurisprudence.* Oxford, 1950.

——. "Sur la transmission de la doctrine dans les écoles juridiques de l'Islam." *Annales de l'Institut d'études orientales (Algiers)* 10 (1952): 399–419.

Sezgin, Fuat. *Geschichte des Arabischen Schrifttums.* Vol. I. Leiden, 1967.

Shaham, Ron. "Women as Expert Witnesses in Pre-Modern Islamic Courts." In *Law, Custom, and Statute in the Muslim World: Studies in Honor of Aharon Layish*, edited by Ron Shaham. Studies in Islamic Law and Society. Leiden; Boston, 2007.

Ṣiddīqī, Muḥammad Zubayr. *Ḥadīth Literature: Its Origin, Development and Special Features.* 2nd ed. Edited and revised by Abdal Hakim Murad. Cambridge, 1993.

Spectorsky, Susan A., ed. and trans. *Chapters on Marriage and Divorce: Responses of Ibn Ḥanbal and Ibn Rāhwayh.* With introduction and notes. Austin, 1993.

Stern, Gertrude H. *Marriage in Early Islam*. London, 1939.
Stewart, Devin J. *Islamic Legal Orthodoxy: Twelve Shiite Responses to the Sunni Legal System*. Salt Lake City, 1998.
Stillman, Yedida Kalfon. *Arab Dress: A Short History: From the Dawn of Islam to Modern Times*. Rev. 2nd ed. Edited by Norman A. Stillman. Themes in Islamic Studies, vol. 2. Leiden; Boston, 2003.
Stowasser, Barbara Freyer. "The Status of Women in Early Islam." In *Muslim Women*, edited by Freda Hussain, 11–43. London, 1984.
——. *Women in the Qur'an, Traditions, and Interpretation*. New York, 1994.
Toledano, Henry. *Judicial Practice and Family Law in Morocco: The Chapter on Marriage from Sijilmasi's* al-ʿAmal al-Mutlaq. Near and Middle East Monographs. Boulder, CO, 1981.
Tyan, Émile. *Histoire de l'organisation judiciaire en pays d'Islam*. 2nd edition, rev. and corr. Leiden, 1960.
Watt, W. M. *Muhammad at Medina*. Oxford, 1977.
Weiss, Bernard G. *The Spirit of Islamic Law*. The Spirit of the Laws. Athens, 1998.
Wensinck, A. J. *Concordance et indices de la tradition musulmane*. Leiden, 1936–88.
——. *A Handbook of Early Muhammadan Tradition*. Leiden, 1960.
Yanagihashi, Hiroyuki. "The Doctrinal Development of *Maraḍ al-Mawt* in the Formative Period of Islamic Law." *Islamic Law and Society* 5 (1998): 326–58.
Ziadeh, Farhat J. "Equality (*Kafāʾah*) in the Muslim Law of Marriage." *The American Journal of Comparative Law* 6, no. 4 (1957): 503–17.

INDEX OF QUR'ĀN VERSES

2:106 52n110
2:177 43
2:222 33
2:223 31
2:226–27 37, 136
2:228 21, 31, 32, 34, 52, 53, 58, 109, 125, 184
2:229 24, 39, 40
2:229–30 124–27, 172, 175
2:232 35, 150
2:233 41, 188
2:234 43, 114
2:235 35, 43n77
2:236 25, 31, 82
2:237 25, 31, 82, 88
2:187 31
2:229 34–35, 39–40, 124–27, 172, 175
2:230 35
2:231 35n47
2:232 35, 150
2:235 35
2:282 51, 192–93
3:36–37 46
4:3 21, 25–27, 29, 43, 52, 57, 96
4:4 25, 27, 29–30, 34, 82
4:6 26, 43
4:11–12 43–44
4:11–20 202
4:15 52
4:19 27, 52–52, 184
4:20 30, 34, 82
4:22 28, 153
4:22–24 72
4:23 28–29, 72
4:24 29–30, 82, 93–94
4:25 27, 52n111, 96
4:34 21, 31–32, 52–53, 57, 59, 174–75, 184, 203
4:35 39, 127–28, 176
4:128 32, 174, 180, 202
4:176 43
5:5 25, 27, 30, 82
5:38 51
6:137 41
17:23 40
17:31 41
17:32 51, 51n109
20:12 39n61
24:2 52, 198
24:4 38, 52
24:6–9 38–39, 128–31
24:11–12 47–48, 202
24:13 199
24:30 50
24:31 50, 190
24:32 27n22
24:33 30
25:68 52n109
30:21 31
31:33 40
33:4 37n53
33:4–5 41–42
33:6 44
33:28–29 37, 48, 122, 141
33:30–33 44–45, 52n113
33:36–37 46–47
33:40 42
33:53 45, 47, 50
33:59 45, 50–51
46:15 41n69
49:13 77, 101, 166, 168
58:2–4 36–37, 135
65:1 34, 34n46, 36, 113, 140, 162
65:2 35, 116, 159, 161, 177
65:4 34–35, 114
65:6 36, 112, 113, 141, 162, 188
65:7 181
66:1–5 49–50

INDEX OF NAMES

ʿAbd Allāh b. ʿUmar b. al-Khaṭṭāb (d. 73/693), Companion, son of the Caliph ʿUmar, 5, 10, 83, 87, 94, 96, 106–107, 114–15, 126, 140
ʿAbd Allāh b. ʿAbbās (d. 68/687–88), Companion, Qurʾān commentator, 5, 37–39, 42, 55, 57, 71, 80, 92, 96, 97n159, 107–8, 114, 122, 125–27, 136–37, 141, 172
ʿAbd al-Raḥmān b. ʿAwf (d. 31 or 32/651 or 652), Companion, 119
ʿAbd al-Razzāq, b. Ḥammām al-Ḥimyārī (d. 211/827), traditionist, 8, 12, 63, 66n13, 67n14, 69n22, 71n35, 72n37, 73nn41, 44, 75n53, 78nn73, 76, 84n100, 85n105, 86n108, 87n113, 89n117, 92n135, 93n138, 100, 105n1, 111nn27, 30, 113n41, 118n63, 120n74, 122n8, 125n89, 127nn100–101, 129n107, 134n134, 135n140, 136nn142–43, 147, 192
Abū Dāwūd Sulaymān b. al-Ashʿath al-Sijistānī (d. 275/888), jurist, traditionist, 8n21, 15n50, 63, 68n18, 125, 147n17, 165nn72, 74, 168, 171n93, 179n2, 196n75, 200n93
Abū Ḥanīfa (d. 150/767), eponymous founder of the Ḥanafī *madhhab*, 9–10n28, 12, 17, 61–62, 67, 69–71n30, 74n47, 75, 77–78n68, 80, 83, 85–88, 91, 97–98, 101, 106–11n29, 112n34, 114, 116, 119–21, 123–24, 126, 129–31, 133, 136n144, 137–41, 144n4, 146, 147n16, 148–50, 155, 158, 166–67, 172, 176, 185–86, 193
Abū Hurayra (d. 58/678), Companion, 165, 184, 198
Abū Thawr (d. 240/854), jurist, 155
Abū Yūsuf, Yaʿqūb b. Ibrāhīm (d. 182/798), jurist, founder of Ḥanafī *madhhab* with Abū Ḥanīfa and Shaybānī, 10–12, 15n51, 17, 61, 83, 87n111, 94, 95n147, 97n158, 106, 108, 112, 114n45, 116nn53–54, 129, 130nn111–12, 131, 138n151, 139n157, 146, 148–49, 158, 166–67
ʿĀʾisha bt. Abī Bakr (d. 58/678), wife of the Prophet, 8, 10, 26, 32, 37, 38n56, 44n82, 46–48n95, 52, 54–55, 64–65, 72–74, 98, 101, 109, 110n23, 121n78, 123–24n86, 141, 150, 155, 171, 179–80, 187, 195, 202
ʿAlī b. Abī Ṭālib (d. 40/661), Companion and cousin of the Prophet, Caliph, 5, 22n2, 82–83, 97, 123, 127n101, 129, 132, 136, 145nn8–9
Anas b. Mālik (d. 91–3/709–11), Companion, 5, 9, 33
al-Aswad b. Yazīd (d. 74–5/693–4), Successor, 137, 140
ʿAṭāʾ b. Abī Rabāḥ (d. 114/732), Successor, 66, 92, 95, 108, 111, 113–14, 127, 137, 192

al-Bukhārī, Muḥammad b. Ismāʿīl (d. 256/870), traditionist, 8, 38n59, 63, 121n78, 147n17, 148n21, 165n72, 179n1, 180n3, 183n18, 185n24, 195nn71–72

al-Ḍaḥḥāk b. Muzāḥim (d. 105/723), Successor, Qurʾān commentator, 109, 125

Fāṭima bt. Qays, contemporary of the Prophet, 78, 83, 111–13n40, 158, 162–64

Ḥabība bt. Sahl, contemporary of the Prophet, 126n93, 171–72
Ḥafṣa bt. ʿUmar (d. 45/665), wife of the Prophet, 48, 98
al-Ḥakam b. ʿUtayba (d. 117/735), Successor, 115, 123, 138
Ḥammād b. Abī Sulaymān (d. 120/738), Successor, 10, 100, 110, 138
Ḥasan al-Baṣrī (d. 110/728), Successor, 69, 75, 82, 92, 96, 111, 113, 127, 139
Hind bt. ʿUtba, contemporary of the Prophet, 179–81

Ibn ʿAbd al-Barr, Yūsuf b. ʿAbd Allāh (d. 463/1070), Mālikī jurist, 144–46,

149–50n28, 157, 160, 163–64, 168, 170, 173, 174nn100–101, 181–83n17, 186–88, 189nn43–44, 191, 194, 196, 200, 204
Ibn Abī Laylā (d. 148/765), judge
Ibn Abī Shayba, ʿAbd Allāh b. Muḥammad (d. 235/849), traditionist, 8, 63, 64nn8–9, 66n12, 67n14, 68–69n23, 70n28, 71n36, 72n40, 73n42, 75n55, 78n74, 82n89, 83n95, 84n100, 85n104, 89n119, 90nn125–26, 93n137, 95n151, 106n5, 108n17, 109, 111n31, 115n51, 116n55, 118n61, 120n73, 122n82, 125n91, 133n125, 136n141, 137nn148–50, 138n155, 147, 192
Ibn Abī Zayd al-Qayrawānī (d. 389/998), Mālikī jurist, 144, 145n6, 146, 149, 152–54, 155n43, 157, 159, 173, 181, 189, 194n68, 197, 199n88, 205
Ibn Ḥanbal, Aḥmad b. Muḥammad (d. 241/855), eponymous founder of the Ḥanbalī *madhhab*, 7, 9, 11–12n39, 13n42, 15n50, 18, 61, 63, 64n8, 68, 70–71, 74–75, 77–78n69, 80–84n100, 85n102, 86–88, 90, 92, 95, 97–101, 107–8, 110–11, 113, 115–16, 118–21, 122n79, 124, 127–28, 131, 133–35, 137–41, 145, 147, 153–54, 156, 158–59, 161–63, 165nn74, 76, 166, 168–69, 172, 176, 183n19, 185, 187n36, 192–93, 195nn71–72, 196, 200, 204n3
Ibn Māja, Muḥammad b. Yazīd (d. 273/887), traditionist, 8n21, 63, 148n19, 153n38, 158n51, 159n56, 165nn72, 76, 171n92, 191n48
Ibn Masʿūd, ʿAbd Allāh (d. 32/652), Companion, 10, 93–94, 110, 122–23, 136, 138, 140, 156, 169
Ibn Qāsim al-ʿUtaqi (d. 191/806), Mālikī jurist
Ibn Qudāma, Muwaffaq al-Dīn (d. 620/1223), Ḥanbalī jurist, Qudāma 134n133, 145–46n12, 148, 150, 151n29, 153, 156–57, 159, 161–64n71, 168–71, 175–76n105, 181–83n17, 185n27, 187, 188n37, 189, 191, 195–97n82
Ibn Wahb (d. 197/812), Mālikī jurist, 62, 71
Ibrāhīm al-Nakhaʿī (96/715), Successor, 10, 69n22, 78, 108, 110, 116, 122, 193
ʿImrān b. al-Ḥusayn (d. 52/672), Successor, 159

Jābir b. ʿAbd Allāh (d. 78/697), Companion, 31, 114
Jābir b. Zayd (d. c. 100/718), Successor, 90

Khansāʾ bt. Khudhām, contemporary of the Prophet, 66, 71, 98, 148
al-Khiraqī, Abuʾl-Qāsim (d. 334/945), Ḥanbalī jurist, 145–46n13, 148, 150, 152–53n40, 156, 159, 161, 163, 175, 194–95n70, 201

Mālik b. Anas (d. 179/795), eponymous founder of the Mālikī *madhhab*, 5, 9–13n43, 18, 33, 61–63, 66n13, 67–71n34, 73–75n51, 77, 79–81, 83–84n101, 86–89n121, 92, 95–96n156, 98–102, 107–8, 110–17, 119–21n76, 123–24n85, 126–28n102, 130–31n119, 133–41, 149, 154–55, 158–60, 162–63n70, 166, 168, 170, 172, 174n101, 176, 185, 191, 193–94, 196, 199–200
al-Marghīnānī, Burhān al-Dīn (d. 593/1197), Ḥanafī jurist, 144, 146, 149, 151n29, 155, 157–58n53, 160, 162, 163n68, 166–67n80, 169, 181, 183, 187, 191, 197
Masrūq b. al-Ajdaʿ (d. 63/682), Successor, 122
Muʿādh b. Jabal (d. 18/639), Companion, 15, 105
al-Mughīra b. Shuʿba (d. 48 or 51/669 or 671), Companion, 190
Muḥammad, the Prophet (d. 9/632), 4–8, 9n25, 10–11, 13–16, 17n59, 22, 24, 28n23, 31–33n40, 34n46, 35n48, 37–39n62, 42, 44–50, 52, 61, 63–68n18, 71–74, 78–79, 81–84n101, 86–87, 89–90, 92–95, 98, 100–103, 105–7, 111–14, 116, 121nn77–78, 122–26, 130, 132–34, 137–38, 140–41, 146, 148, 150–51, 153–58, 162–68, 171, 179–81, 183–88, 190–92, 195, 198–202, 204
Mujāhid b. Jabr (d. 104/727), Successor, 55, 137
Muslim b. al-Ḥajjāj (d. 261/875), traditionist, 184n22

Nāfiʿ b. ʿUmar (d. 117/735), Successor, 10, 82
al-Nasāʾī, Aḥmad b. Shuʿayb (d. 303/915), traditionist, 121n78

al-Qāsim b. Muḥammad (d. 106/725), Successor, 62, 67–69, 77, 80, 86, 107, 138n152, 145
Qatāda b. Diʿāma (d. 117or 18/735 or 36), Successor, 55, 85, 120, 136
al-Qudūrī, Abu'l-Ḥuṣayn (d. 428/1037), Ḥanafī jurist, 144, 146, 148, 149n22, 151–53n39, 155, 158, 160, 162, 164, 166, 169, 172–73, 180, 181n6, 182, 183n15, 186, 189, 194, 196–97n79, 200

Sahl b. Saʿd al-Sāʿidī (d. 88 or 91/707 or 710), Companion, 130
Saḥnūn b. Saʿīd al-Tanūkhī (d. 240/854), Mālikī jurist, 62, 67n14, 69n23, 70n28, 71n34, 73n42, 77, 80, 81n87, 84n99, 86n107, 87nn109–10, 113, 88nn114–15, 99n161, 107n10, 115n50, 117n58, 119n67, 121n76, 128n103, 133n127, 137n145, 138n153, 139n158, 144, 193n62
Saʿīd b. al-Musayyab (d. 94/712), Successor, 37, 72, 83, 88n115, 89, 96, 115, 121, 125, 129, 134, 137
Sālim b. ʿAbd Allāh b. ʿUmar b. al-Khaṭṭāb (d. 106/725), Successor, 67–68, 106
Sawda bt. Zamʿa (d. 54/673–74), wife of the Prophet, 32–33, 187, 202
Shaʿbī, Abū ʿAmr ʿĀmir (d. 110/728), Successor, 82, 85, 89, 108, 111, 127, 136n143, 137, 158, 162
Shāfiʿī, Muḥammad b. Idrīs (d. 204/820), jurist, eponymous founder of the Shāfiʿī *madhhab*, 2, 9, 11–13n43, 15–16n54, 18, 61–63, 66n13, 67–71n34, 74–77n64, 80–81n88, 83–84n101, 86–90n122, 92, 95–103n170, 107–13n37, 114n45, 115–17n59, 120–22n79, 124, 126, 127n98, 128, 130n116, 131, 133–35n138, 137–41, 145–46, 148, 150, 152–55n47, 157–59, 162, 166–67, 171–72, 174, 176, 183, 185–86, 188n41, 193–94, 196, 200
Shaybānī, Muḥammad b. al-Ḥasan (189/805), jurist, founder of Ḥanafī *madhhab* with Abū Ḥanīfa and Abū Yūsuf, 10–13, 17, 61–63, 67, 69–71n33, 74, 75n52, 77–80n80, 83, 85–88n116, 90–91, 92n131, 93n137, 94, 95nn146–47, 97–99, 101–2, 107, 108nn16, 19, 109n20, 110–11n29, 112n34, 114, 116–17n57, 119–21n75, 123–24, 126, 130, 133, 135n138, 136–41, 144, 146, 148–50, 151n29, 155, 158–59, 166–67, 172, 185–86n29, 188n39, 193, 195, 196n73, 199, 200n95
Shīrāzī, Abū Isḥāq Ibrāhīm b. ʿAlī (d. 476/1083), Shāfiʿī jurist, 145–46, 150, 152–53n39, 155–57, 159–60, 161n61, 163–64, 167, 169, 174–75n103, 181–82n13, 183n17, 184, 186–87n33, 188n37, 189n45, 191, 194, 196–97n79, 200, 201n96
Shuʿba b. Ḥajjāj (d. 160/776), traditionist, 115, 123, 190
Shurayḥ (first century of Islam), judge, 111, 119n66, 132
Sufyān b. ʿUyayna (198/813), jurist, traditionist, 58, 109
Sufyān al-Thawrī (d. 161/772), jurist, 85, 129, 132
Sulaymān b. Yasār (d. 107/725), Successor, 35n48, 110, 121, 137, 138n152

Ṭabarī, Abū Jaʿfar Muḥammad (d. 310/922), Qur'ān commentator, jurist, 23, 25n14, 27, 28n23, 31n34, 32, 33nn40–41, 35, 39–40n63, 42, 46, 50–51n104, 53, 54nn115–16, 55–59n130, 125, 127, 145
Ṭāwūs b. Qaysān (d. 106/724), Successor, 78, 106, 108, 125, 134–35
Tirmidhī, Muḥammad b. ʿĪsā (d. 279/892), 8, 154n41, 165n73, 190n47, 199n86

ʿUbayd b. ʿUmayr (74/642), Companion, 75
ʿUbayy b. Kaʿb (d. 22/642), Companion, 93, 118–19
ʿUmar b. al-Khaṭṭāb (d. 23/644), Caliph of Medina, 5, 10, 34n46, 70–71, 75–76, 78–80, 82–83, 91–92, 94–95, 106–7, 110, 112, 113n40, 118–19n66, 121n77, 122–23, 132, 153, 162, 163n68, 168, 187
Umm Salama (d. 59/678–9), wife of the Prophet, 116, 165, 185–86, 202
ʿUrwa b. al-Zubayr (d. 94/712), Successor, 73, 109, 118–20
ʿUthmān b. ʿAffān (35/656), Caliph of Medina, 5, 118–21

al-Wāḥidī, Abu'l-Ḥasan ʿAlī b. Aḥmad (d. 468/1076), Qurʾān scholar, 22–23, 26–28n23, 29n29, 30–33n44, 34n46, 35n48, 37–38n57, 39n60, 42–43, 44n80, 45, 48–49n97, 54n116, 55n118, 57, 76n61, 130n113, 141, 180

Yaḥyā b. Saʿīd b. Qays al-Anṣārī (d. 144/761), Successor, 82, 109,
Yaḥyā b. Yaḥyā al-Laythī (d. 234/848), jurist, 62, 67n16, 74, 173, 174n101

Zayd b. Ḥāritha (d. 8/629), Companion, 42–43, 46–48
Zaynab bt. Jaḥsh (d. 20/640–41), wife of the Prophet, 42–43, 46–47
al-Zuhrī, Ibn Shihāb (d. 124/742), Successor, 10, 73, 78, 90–91, 93, 112, 116, 123, 129–30, 133–34, 138n152, 192

SUBJECT INDEX

Ablutions, 183
Abrogation, 23, 52, 52n, 93–4, 110
Abstinence, from sexual intercourse, 37, 136
Adoption, 41, 42–3, 46n, 47, 73, 87
Adultery (*zinā*), 35, 51, 75; accusation of, 38, 47, 51–52, 128, 130, 202; punishment for, 52, 65, 75, 78–79, 100, 194, 198–99, 200–202
Agnate, 28, 43n79, 66, 69–70n27, 169
ʿĀlim (plural, *ʿulamāʾ*). *See* Scholars
Allāh, 5, 10–11n34, 30–31, 34n46, 37n54, 39–41, 48–49, 64n8, 67–68, 74n50, 95n150, 105–6, 114–15, 117n58, 122, 126n97, 131, 138–39n158, 145, 197, 198n83
Analogy (*qiyās*), 15–16, 18, 146, 147n16
Annulment, 181–82. *See also Khulʿ*
Anṣār, 31–32
Aqrāʾ. *See Qurʾ*
Arbitration, 39–40, 127, 173–75. *See also Khulʿ*
Asbāb al-nuzūl, 22–3, 49n98
Aṣḥāb al-ḥadīth, 15. *See also* Traditionists
Aṣḥāb al-raʾy, 15
Āthār, definition of, 17n59
ʿAwra (*also ʿawrāt*), 50, 190
ʿAyb. *See* Flaw
Ayyim (a woman who has been married), 63–64, 67, 68nn17, 21. *See also Thayyib*

Bidʿa, 107, 158
Bikr (virgin), 63–69n22, 102, 120n69, 185–86, 202
Birth control, 187
Bride, 1n1, 25–26, 30, 31n34, 65, 67n14, 70, 78, 80, 81n86, 82, 84–85, 89n120, 92, 98–99, 154–55, 161n63, 166–70n91, 185–86, 191, 203
Brother, as a sister's guardian, 69, 70; as a foster brother, 28, 49, 72, 152, 190. *See also* Foster relationship

Children, 24, 26n15, 32, 34, 40–43, 99n161, 180, 187; custody of, 99, 188–89, 201
Choice, *See Takhyīr*
Clothing, appropriate, 45, 50, 115–16, 186, 190, 195–97, 201
Companions of the Prophet, 4–11, 13, 15, 22, 31, 33, 37, 39, 47, 63, 81, 94, 124, 163
Coitus interruptus, 187–88
Conditions in a marriage contract, 89, 120
Consanguinity, 28, 72, 108, 151–52, 157
Consensus. *See Ijmāʿ*
Contract of marriage, 1, 4, 17, 27, 29n27, 31n34, 59, 61–103, 105–6, 108, 126n95, 148–51, 154–57, 161, 164–66, 168, 173, 177, 183, 192, 199
Cry of a newborn, 192–94
Cupping, 165, 168
Custody, 99, 138, 162, 188–89, 201

Death, 4, 10–11, 27–8, 43, 44, 52, 61, 66, 70, 85–86, 87n113, 99, 109, 110, 115, 118, 120n72, 130n114, 145, 152, 198, 200
Definite divorce, 93–94, 106, 122–23, 126, 129–30, 132–34, 140–41, 172–73
Delirium, 121
Disability, 64, 90, 91n128
Disagreement (*ikhtilāf*), 12–14, 17–19, 59, 61–63, 75, 87–88, 96–98, 101, 107, 114, 119, 121, 123, 127, 129, 131–32, 135–36, 139, 158, 160n60, 171, 180, 187, 191–92, 197n81, 205
Disapproved of (*makrūh*). *See* Reprehensible
Divorce, 105–41. *See also* Definite divorce, *Īlāʾ*, *Khulʿ*, *Liʿān*, *Takhyīr*, Repudiation, Triple divorce, *Ẓihār*

Elephantasis, 90–92
Equality. *See Kafāʾa*
Evidence, 2, 9, 50, 57, 155, 179, 200
Expiation of an oath, 134–36

Family 2n2, 4–5, 7, 22, 24, 26n17, 37, 42n72, 47, 68n18, 83–84, 97, 114, 118n64, 127, 133–34, 167, 169, 174n100, 179, 203
Faqīh, 2, 5
Farḍ. *See* Obligatory
Fāsiq, 166–67
Faskh, 91n130, 125
Fasting, 8, 31, 81n88, 88, 134–36
Father of a potential bride or wife, 1n1, 25–26, 28, 30, 32, 41–42, 64–70, 74n50, 76–78, 81, 93, 95n150, 97–99n161, 102, 125, 131, 135, 148, 152–53, 170, 184, 188–90, 204
Fatwā, 107, 174, 204
Fiqh, 2, 8–12, 17
Flogging, 51n108, 200
Forbidden. *See Ḥarām*
Forbidden degrees. *See* Foster relationship
Fornication, 51n108, 52nn109–10, 65, 75, 81, 92, 96, 152, 198, 201–2
Foster relationship (*raḍāʿ*), 18n62, 28–29, 66, 71–75, 101, 108, 151–52, 157, 177, 190. *See also* Brother, Sister, Uncle
Founders, of Sunni *madhhabs*, 3, 6–7, 9–10, 12–14, 16–18, 143, 146–47, 153, 164, 171
Furūʿ, 2–3, 16–18n63, 146, 161

Groom, 1, 25, 63, 67–68, 76, 84, 98, 100, 155, 161n63, 166, 204
Guardian (*walī*), 1, 21, 25–28, 30–31, 35, 52, 54, 56, 59, 63–71, 77–81, 91–93, 97–98, 148–151, 154–57, 161, 166–67, 177, 204

Ḥaḍāna. *See* Custody
Ḥadd, 1, 14n45, 51, 65, 78, 79n77, 100, 117, 120n74, 121, 128n106, 131, 192–94, 197–201
Ḥadīth, 6–7, 8n24, 9, 15–16, 18, 22, 23n7, 29n29, 38n57, 39, 85n102, 94n144, 101, 113, 123, 130, 144, 147n18, 203
Ḥajj, 8, 11, 88, 115, 144–45, 195–97, 201
Ḥākim, 156, 175n102
Ḥarām (forbidden), qualification of act, 14; divorce, 107, 133; marriage, 27–29, 54, 71–75; *mutʿa* marriage, 92–95. *See also* Adoption, *Ḥadd*
Ḥasab wa-nasab, 70, 76–77, 97, 165, 169
Heirs, 43–44
Ḥijāb, 45, 47, 50, 73. *See also* Veiling
Household, 25n14, 30n30, 32, 48, 54, 59, 69n22, 73, 83, 97, 122, 180–81
Hunger, 151, 182, 204
Ḥuqūq Allāh, *ḥuqūq al-ʿibād*, 197–98
Husband, 1, 18, 21, 25–28, 31–32n39, 34–40, 43–44, 52–53, 58–59, 64–66, 69, 72, 76–77, 81–82, 84n100, 85–93, 94n144, 95, 97–98, 100, 105–6, 108–17n59, 118–34, 136–38, 141, 148–49, 152, 154, 158–64, 166–67, 171–77, 180–88n39, 193, 195–96, 199–204
Hypocrites, 45

ʿIbādāt, 8, 12
ʿIdda (waiting period of a woman after end of marriage), 1, 33–36, 43, 46, 58, 87, 88n116, 93–94n144, 105–20, 122, 124, 126, 130, 136, 139–41, 152, 158–60, 162–64, 172n97, 173, 177, 180, 182, 195, 199–200
Idiocy, 120
Iḥrām, 88, 195–96, 197n80
Iḥṣān, 29n28, 128n106, 198-99
Ijmāʿ (consensus), definition of, 16; 50, 99, 146, 156
Ijtihād. *See* Opinion
Ijtimāʿ, 127–28
Ikhtilāf. *See* Disagreement
Īlāʾ, 36–37, 135–37, 141, 143, 160n59
Illness, 33, 90, 118–21
Imāmī Shīʿīs, *mutʿa* marriage and, 93–94
Imbecile, 90
Impotence, 92
Infancy, 72, 74, 151
Infanticide, 41
Inheritance, 8, 43nn78–79, 44, 59, 69, 87, 93–94n144, 109, 114, 118n64, 120n69, 192n60
Insanity, 90–91, 120
Intentions, 95, 117, 123, 132–34, 139n157, 140, 141
Intercourse, 25, 29–35, 37, 51, 55, 57–58, 64–65, 72, 75, 79, 85–88, 90–92, 94n144, 100, 106–9, 113, 117, 119–20, 128n106, 133–40, 152–55, 157–60, 173n99, 180–84, 186–87, 194, 197–200
Intoxication, 120
Isnād, 7–9, 16, 18, 74n48, 120n71, 124n86, 147, 153
Istidlāl (rationale), 103
Istithnāʾ, 139

Jāhiliyya, 33, 55, 58
Jihād, 14n44, 59, 195
Judge, 18, 156, 191. *See also Qāḍī*
Jurists, 2–6, 11–16, 18, 61, 63, 66–67, 69, 86, 88, 94, 96–99, 101–2, 106–7, 109, 114, 116–17, 120n72, 122–23, 128n104, 129, 134–35, 140–41, 143–44, 146–48, 151–55, 158–59, 161–62, 164, 166–67, 174n101, 175, 177–79, 184, 192, 195–97, 199–205

Ka'ba, 11, 197
Kafā'a, 70, 75–77, 98, 101, 164–171, 178, 189, 204
Khaliyya, bariyya, bā'in divorces, 132–34. *See also* Definite divorce
Khaybar, battle of, 93n137, 94–95n147
Khul', 39, 52, 124–28, 127, 140–41, 164, 171–76, 178

Li'ān, 38–39, 59, 128–31, 141, 200n95

Mabsūṭ, definition of, 18–19
Maintenance (*nafaqa*), 32, 36, 77, 93, 109, 111–15, 130, 141, 162–64, 167, 177, 180–84, 186, 190, 203
Marriage portion, 1n1, 17, 25–28, 30, 31n34, 34, 38n57, 39, 43, 54, 57, 63, 65, 67, 70, 75, 77, 82–88, 89n120, 90–93, 96, 99–102, 108, 117n59, 119, 125–26n95, 138, 140–41, 152–54, 164, 166–73, 176–77, 180n5, 182n12, 199, 203–4
Masā'il, definition of, 12
Mawlā (plural *mawālī*), 10, 42n71, 75–78, 165–66, 168, 170, 17
Mecca, 5, 11, 24, 44, 56, 75n54, 93–94, 196, 201
Menstruation. *See Qur'*
Minor. *See Ṣaghīr*
Mother, 28–29, 36, 37n54, 41, 43–44, 47 68, 72–74, 78, 99, 129, 135–36, 152, 157, 169–70, 180n3, 188–89n45, 203
Mu'āmalāt, 8, 12
Mubāḥ, definition of, 14
Muftī(s), 143, 204
Muḥṣān (fem. *muḥsana*). *See Iḥsān*
Mukhtaṣar, definition of, 18–19
Mūlī. See Īlā'
Muṣannaf, definition of, 7–8
Musnad, definition of, 7
Mustaḥabb. See Recommended
Mut'a (marriage), 93–94
Mut'a (divorce gift), 31, 67, 82, 87

Nafaqa. See Maintenance
Nāshiz, See Nushūz
Naṣṣ, 16
Nephew, 69, 190
Newborn, 192–94
Niece, 28, 44, 73
Niqāb, 195
Niyya, 132
Nursing, 41, 101, 113, 188, 192, 194–95, 200. *See also* Foster relationship, Wet nurse
Nushūz (rebellion, refractoriness), 40, 57, 58, 128, 172, 174–75, 183–84n20, 190

Oaths, 36, 49, 134, 136, 139n158
Obligatory (*farḍ*, *wājib*), 14, 195–96
Opinion (*ra'y*), 15; and *ijtihād*, 15, 156; and *qiyās*, 15; and *ikhtilāf*, 17–19. *See also Aṣḥāb al-ra'y*
Orphans, 21, 25–27, 43, 53–57, 69

Parents, 28n24, 40–41, 48, 77, 180, 184, 188
Paternity, 1, 34, 38, 128–30
Patriarchy, 24, 59, 97, 202–3
Pilgrimage. *See Ḥajj*
Polygamy, 21, 56–57

Qadhf (slander), 51–52, 128, 130, 199, 200n95
Qāḍī, 5–6, 10, 15, 40, 64n8, 65, 70, 77–78n68, 97–99, 128–31n117, 137, 143, 145, 149, 160n59, 173–77, 181–83n16, 194n68, 200–201, 203–4. *See also* Judge
Qiyās. See Analogy
Qualifications of acts, 14, 59, 102
Qur' (plural, *qurū'* or *aqrā'*. 1. Menstrual period; 2. the interval between two periods), 109–10.
Qur'ān, 1, 4–7, 11–12, 14–16, 21–59, 61, 63, 67n14, 72–76, 80n80, 82, 84–85, 88–89, 93–94n144, 97, 100–102, 108–9, 111–14, 116, 121n77, 122, 124–25, 127–28, 130, 135–37n149, 140–41, 146–47, 150, 153, 159–62, 168, 172, 174–77, 180–81, 184, 188, 190, 192–93, 197–99, 201, 202–3, 205
Quraysh, 42, 54, 77–78, 166–67, 171

Raḍāʿ. *See* Foster relationship
Rajʿa (return after non-final divorce), 1, 35–37, 58–59, 105–106, 109, 111–12, 115–18, 122, 124, 132–33, 139, 159–61
Ramaḍān, 31, 88
Rank. *See Kafāʾa*
Ransoming. *See Khulʿ*
Rape, 199–200
Raʾy, 11, 15–16. *See also* Opinion
Recommended (*mandūb* or *mustaḥabb*), definition of 14; 59, 102, 160–64, 164, 184
Refractoriness. *See Nushūz*
Remarriage, 28, 33, 35, 56, 87, 109, 119, 126n95, 173n99, 200
Reprehensible (*makrūh*), definition of, 14; 59, 68, 80, 95–96, 100, 102, 107, 126, 172, 175, 184, 187, 188
Repudiation, 105, 158–60, 175n103
Respectability. *See Iḥsān*
Rukhṣa (dispensation), 73, 101n167

Ṣaghīr (minor), 17, 26n15, 40n64, 41n68, 59n131, 61, 63, 64, 66, 69, 77, 85, 87n110, 88n114, 90n123, 107n9, 117n57, 121n78, 123n84, 130n112, 144, 149n23
Scholars (*ulamāʾ*), 3, 5–7, 12–14, 17–19, 22, 50, 62–63, 94, 107, 127, 138, 140, 143–47, 151, 157, 161, 164, 168, 171, 173, 181, 186, 191, 198, 202–3
School of law (*madhhab*), 2–3, 6–9, 17–19, 143–48, 153–205 passim. *See also* Founders
Sharīʿa, 2, 3n7, 18n61, 146n14
Shighār, 86–87
Shīʿī, 6, 11, 93
Shubha, definition of, 79n77; 117, 153, 199, 200n92
Siblings, 28, 72, 152, 170, 177
Sin, 29, 32, 35, 39, 41, 43, 46, 56n121, 96, 125
Sister, 28–29, 43, 49, 88n116, 152, 169–70
Slander, 38–39, 47, 128, 129, 130–31, 141, 155, 199
Slaves, 2, 25, 27, 29–30, 36–7, 45, 48–9, 52n111, 54, 56, 57n125, 71–2, 75, 87, 89n121, 91, 93n140, 94n144, 95–8, 105, 126, 131, 138, 150, 154, 165n75, 167n75, 181n9, 187nn32, 35, 190n46, 198
Son, 5, 28, 29, 34n46, 41–42, 46, 49, 69, 73, 74n50, 75, 112n3
Spouse(s), 35, 40, 52, 54n115, 64, 82–83, 85, 91, 94–96, 98, 111n29, 120, 127, 130–31, 172n96, 174–77, 180, 183n15, 190, 198
Stoning, 52, 79, 95, 101n166, 198–201
Stranger (not a relative), 108, 118, 120, 131, 188, 190–91, 196
Successors, 4–16, 55–56, 63, 67, 69, 75n54, 100, 137, 163
Suckling, 28–29, 41, 72, 74, 101–2, 151, 189n44
Suitor, 54, 80, 109, 129, 133, 141
Sulṭān, 64–65, 70–71, 79
Sunna, 4–8, 11, 13, 15–16, 34n46, 63, 68, 102–3, 106–7, 130–31, 140, 146, 158–59, 164, 177, 192, 198, 201
Sunnī, 2, 3n7, 6–9, 10n27, 12–13, 17, 47, 67, 93, 94, 146, 192n59
Sūra, 22n4, 23, 25, 37, 44–45, 48

Tafsīr, Chapter One pasim
Tafwīḍ, 87, 168
Taḥlīl, 95, 106
Takhyīr, 37, 48, 52, 122–24, 141
Ṭalāq See Divorce
Tamlīk, 122–24, 141
Ṭawāf, 197
Taʿzīr (discretionary punishment), 117
Testimony. *See* Witnesses
Thayyib, 63, 65–66, 69, 93, 120n69, 148–49, 185–86, 202. *See also Bikr*
Traditionists, 6, 9n26, 12, 15n53, 16, 63, 141, 147n18
Traditions, discussion of, 7–9
Triple divorce, 18, 95, 106–113n40, 115–16, 118–26, 130–34, 139–41, 158–59, 162–64, 173–75
Trustworthiness, 51n103, 55, 78, 80, 103, 154–57, 159–61, 166n79, 173–77, 193–94, 199, 200

Uḥud, battle of, 44, 57, 66, 102, 103n169, 185
Ulamāʾ. *See* Scholars
Unborn child, responsibility for, 34, 131
Uncle, 44, 72–73, 188n42
Upbringing. *See* Children
Uṣūl (legal theory), 2–3, 14, 16–18, 145–46, 161

Veiling, 45, 49, 50, 51n102, 72, 190

Wājib. See Obligatory
Walā' (clientage), 194. *See also Mawlā*
Walī. See Guardian
Walīma (wedding banquet), 81
Weaning, 41, 74n47
Weaving, 165–68
Wedding, 47, 81–82, 185–86
Wet nurse, 28–29, 41, 72–73, 151, 177, 188, 193
Widow, 27–28, 43–44, 47, 52, 57, 65–66, 87, 94, 109, 113–16n53, 118, 180, 185, 188n39
Wife, 1, 2, 8, 10, 18, 21, 25–27, 30–34, 36–40, 42, 43–50, 52n113, 53–59, 64, 66n12, 71–73, 76–77, 79, 82–93n140, 94n144, 95n148, 96–97, 100–101, 105–11, 115–20, 122–41, 152, 154, 158–61, 163–68, 171–77, 179–89, 190, 193, 196, 198, 200n95, 201–4
Witnesses, 1, 26, 35, 38, 47, 50–52, 63, 71, 93, 99–100, 116–18, 154–57, 159–61, 164, 166n79, 177; of a marriage contract, 78–82; of adultery, 38–39, 47, 52, 199–203; women as, 51, 80, 155–56, 179, 191–95

Ẓihār, 36, 37n54, 134–37, 141
Zinā, See Adultery